Jesuit Missions in Coastal and South India (1543–1773)

Brill Research Perspectives in Jesuit Studies

Editor

Robert A. Maryks (*Adam Mickiewicz University, Poznań*)

Editorial Board

Ariane Boltanski (*Université Rennes 2*)
Carlos Eire (*Yale University*)
Alison Fleming (*Winston-Salem State University*)
Paul Grendler (*University of Toronto*, emeritus)
Stephen Schloesser, s.j. (*Loyola University Chicago*)

The *Brill Research Perspectives in Jesuit Studies* series invites leading scholars in Jesuit studies to reflect on their fields of expertise. It complements the related Brill publications: the *Journal of Jesuit Studies*, the *Jesuit Studies* book series, and the *Jesuit Historiography Online*.

Volumes published in this Brill Research Perspectives title are listed at *brill.com/rpjss*

Jesuit Missions in Coastal and South India (1543–1773)

Between Mission and Empire

By

Ines G. Županov

BRILL

LEIDEN | BOSTON

Library of Congress Control Number: 2025932376

Typeface for the Latin, Greek, and Cyrillic scripts: "Brill". See and download: brill.com/brill-typeface.

ISSN 2589-7446
ISBN 978-90-04-72702-1 (paperback)
ISBN 978-90-04-72739-7 (e-book)
DOI 10.1163/9789004727397

This book is printed on acid-free paper and produced in a sustainable manner.

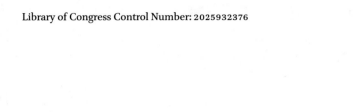

Contents

Acknowledgments VII
List of Figures VIII
Abbreviations IX
Notes on Translation and Transliteration X
1 Introduction 1
2 Historiography 3
3 Under the Portuguese Padroado 12
3.1 *Papal Bulls and the Portuguese Padroado* 15
3.2 *The Church and the State in Portuguese Asia* 17
3.3 *Goa: the Mission Hub* 19
3.4 *Rituals and Religious Art: Estheticizing Religious Propaganda* 27
3.5 *Indigenization of Christianity and the Inquisition* 31
4 Missionary Frontiers 36
4.1 *Portuguese "Reform" and Division of the Syrian Christians of Kerala* 37
4.2 *Parava Christians: a Case of "Communal" Conversion* 42
4.3 *The Madurai Mission: Jesuit Controversial Social and Religious Experiments (1606–1660s)* 49
4.4 *Marava Country: Mass Conversion to Martyrdom* 58
4.5 *Tamil "Fringe" Christianity* 61
4.6 *Mysore Mission* 63
5 French Jesuit Mission 66
5.1 *The Malabar Rites Controversy* 70
6 Knowledge 77
6.1 *Linguistic Enterprise* 77
6.2 *"Ethnographic" Production* 88
6.3 *Natural History* 94
7 Suppression and Return 102
Bibliography 105
Index 129

Acknowledgments

This book was commissioned by Robert Aleksander Maryks, and he is the reason the book exists. It was written in a short time between two other books as a challenge to prove to myself that I could write a properly historical and useful work of synthesis on the topic. I am grateful to colleagues and friends who accompanied me during the decades of research in Jesuit history or contributed directly or indirectly to ideas and sources used in the book. Most of them are quoted in the book: Paolo Aranha, Anand Amaladass, Gauvin Alexander Bailey, Zoltán Biedermann, Charlotte de Castelnau, Alexandre Coello de la Rosa, Francis X. Clooney, Gérard Colas, Jorge Flores, Simon Ditchfield, Rômulo da Silva Ehalt, Pierre-Antoine Fabre, Ronnie Po-chia Hsia, Paula Findlen, Sumit Guha, Ebba Koch, Heike Liebau, Anthoni Muthu Mahimai Dass, Pius Malekandathil, Giuseppe Marcocci, João Vicente Melo, Cristina Muru, Maria Cristina Osswald, Sabina Pavone, István Perczel, Dhruv Raina, Joan-Pau Rubiés, Camilla Russell, Ulrike Strasser, Alan Strathern, Will Sweetman, *Hélène* Vu-Thanh, Margherita Trento, Ângela Barreto Xavier. I was privileged to have met Fathers Josef Wicki (1904–93) and Edmund Lamalle (1900–89) when I started my research at the Archivum Romanum Societatis Iesu. Their encouragement was important. Easy access to Jesuit historical sources in Rome and France, and the generosity of the Jesuit librarians and archivists, is one of the reasons for my lasting interest in Jesuit history. Malcolm and Vesna Hardy provided logistics and friendship during my research in Rome and London. My sincere thanks go to Jérôme Petit and the Bibliothèque Nationale de France for making the reproduction of images and maps available and free for scholars. Tim Page was a dream editor. My *saheli* support group in "permanent exile"—Olga Grlić, Gordana de la Roncière, Marta Nakić, Tamara Smokvina, Marie Fourcade, Tea Marion—cannot be thanked enough.

The book and everything else make sense because of Christophe and Ante.

Figures

1 Francis Xavier, *Copie dunne lettre missive envoiee des Indes, par monsieur maistre Francois Xavier, frere treschier en Jhesuchrist, de la societe du nom de Jhesus, a son prevost monsieur Egnace de Layola, & tous ses freres estudians aux lettres a Romme, Pavie, Portugal, Valence, Coulogne, & a Paris. Item deux aultres epistres faictes et envoiées par ledict seigneur maistre Francois Xavier a son prevost & freres treschiers en Jhesuchrist de la societe du nom de Jhesus, lunne de la cité de Goa, & lautre de Tatucurim*, 1546, Bibliothèque nationale de France, département Réserve des livres rares, RES P-O2K-493 (2), https://gallica.bnf.fr/ark:/12148/bpt6k54535853# 4

2 Vestiges of the Hospital of the Poor, Goa 22

3 The church of Bom Jesus and sacristy, Goa 30

4 "Carte des missions des P.P. de la Compagnie de Jésua dans le Maduré et les royaumes circonvoisins, 1600–1799," Bibliothèque nationale de France, https://gallica.bnf.fr/ark:/12148/btv1b84466697d 49

5 A Jesuit eating in Madurai. Aquarelle. Source: manuscript confusingly mislabeled *Usages du Royaume de Siam: Cartes, plans et vues en 1688* [peinture], 1688–1700, Bibliothèque nationale de France, https://gallica.bnf.fr/ark:/12148/btv1b55007288r/f87.item 52

6 A Jesuit penitent in Madurai. Aquarelle. Source: manuscript confusingly mislabeled *Usages du Royaume de Siam: Cartes, plans et vues en 1688* [peinture], 1688–1700, Bibliothèque nationale de France,https://gallica.bnf.fr/ark:/12148/btv1b55007288r/f87.item 59

7 Map entitled "Carte des missions des pères de Compagnie de Jésus dans les Indes orientales," before 1719, Source: manuscript confusingly mislabeled *Usages du Royaume de Siam: Cartes, plans et vues en 1688* [peinture], 1688–1700, Bibliothèque nationale de France, BNf, Pet. fol. Od 55, view 87, https://gallica.bnf.fr/ark:/12148/btv1b55007288r/f87.%20%20Ms 67

8 Drawing of the church for the nobles and the pariahs within the same exterior walls, and the missionary residence. *Disegno della Chiesa de' Nobili, e Parreas, entro lo stesso recinto di muro esteriore, e della casa del missionario*. Source: anonymous [Broglia Antonio Brandolini], *Risposta alle Accuse date al praticato sin'ora* [...] *parte seconda* (Cologne, 1729), 600–1 75

9 Jay Prakash, Jantar Mantar (Astronomical Observatory), Jaipur, India 98

10 Joseph Tiefenthaler and Abraham Hyacinthe Anquetil-Duperron's 1784 map of the Ganges and Ghaghara (Karnali) river system, public domain, https://upload.wikimedia.org/wikipedia/commons/d/db/1784_Tiefenthaler_Map_of_the_Ganges_and_Ghaghara_Rivers%2C_India_-_Geographicus_-_Ganges-teifentaller-1784.jpg 101

Abbreviations

AHSI	*Archivum Historicum Societatis Iesu*
ARSI	Archivum Romanum Societatis Iesu
DI	*Documenta Indica*
LEC	*Lettres édifiantes et curieuses*
MEP	Missions étrangères de Paris

Notes on Translation and Transliteration

All translations from Latin, French, Portuguese, Italian, German, and Tamil are mine unless indicated otherwise. For toponyms used in the Jesuit letters, I maintain the original spelling and add the name commonly used today in local and anglicized versions. To some, I added current Tamil transliteration if easily identifiable. Concerning the names of the people, I use the name in the source and add Tamil and/or anglicized variations. For example, there are different ways to spell the name of the French enclave on the Coromandel coast: Pondicherry (English version), Pondichéry or Pontichéry (French version), and the recently accepted Puducherry. I use Puducherry except in direct quotations. Some other Indian place names have been officially changed from their anglicized versions, such as Cochin into Kochi, Quilon into Kollam, Cannanore into Kannur, and Calicut into Kozhikode. I use the recent version but leave other versions in direct quotations. The same rule is applied to other names of the towns in India. Tamil words are mostly transliterated according to the Madras Tamil Lexicon, but some well-known anglicized versions are also included. Konkani, Marathi, Kannada, Hindi, and Malayalam are quoted according to the sources and histories I used. The adjective and noun "Hindu" is used as a shortcut for people and practices—distinguished from Muslim and Christian—that were not yet defined as Hindu by the historical actors but had a variety of names (or no names) in Jesuit sources: gentile, *gentio*, *da terra*, and so on.

Jesuit Missions in Coastal and South India (1543–1773)

Between Mission and Empire

Ines G. Županov
CNRS (CESAH/EHESS), Paris, France
zupanov@gmail.com

Abstract

Jesuit missions in coastal and South India were among the first foundations of the Society of Jesus in the world. They represented models of apostolic action imitated, debated and reformulated in other geographical locations worldwide. This book traces the history of the Jesuit missionary beginning and end in the early modern period, and how they navigated, between European colonial maneuvers, and local conversion to Christianity through proselytizing and accommodation. Jesuit missionary efforts were pragmatically divided between disciplining Portuguese and later on French colonial communities, and attracting converts living among regional polities under Muslim and Hindu rulers.

Keywords

accommodation – Portuguese empire – French – Francis Xavier – mission – martyrdom – Roberto Nobili – Goa – Puducherry – Madurai – languages – sciences – translation – conversion

1 Introduction

In the first decade of the seventeenth century, a Jesuit historian in Goa, Sebastião Gonçalves (1555?–1619), casting a historical glance over the beginning of the Christianization of Asia, unwittingly wove together three important historiographical topics: Portuguese regal messianism, a close relation between temporal and spiritual conquest, and the importance of the Iberian kingdom and the Society of Jesus in all religious matters concerning the Catholic expansion:

 | DOI:10.1163/9789004727397_002

> Let me point out what happened at the time when King Dom Manoel sent Vasco da Gama to discover India in the year 1497, in the same year Blessed Father Francis was born in Navarra because it was understood that God had predestined him to bring the Gospel and sow the seeds of faith in those vast regions after the route had been opened and the field was established using the Portuguese fleets; and that is why he created it, when he moved the heart of the king of Portugal to commit to an enterprise that many of the natives considered ill-advised and the strangers considered [...] insane, but the good king used it to expand the faith of Christ Our Lord, as Dom Afonso had revealed.[1]

Except for the date of Francis Xavier's (1506–52) birth—1506, not 1497—which Gonçalves tweaked to fit his providential chronology for the Society of Jesus, the three "historiographical" propositions, stripped of their hagiographic trappings, are worthy of further comment and generally hold ground.[2] They are, however, only part of the whole story, which was amplified and meandered around the world until the Society's suppression in 1773.

This book focuses on the Jesuit presence in coastal and South India from Xavier's arrival in Goa in 1543 until the suppression of the Society of Jesus in 1773, when the remaining Jesuits were deported to Portugal in chains. In a different scenario, the French Jesuits in Puducherry—a French colonial settlement on the Coromandel Coast—who were not part of the Portuguese Padroado real ("royal patronage of missions") and arrived at the very end of the seventeenth century, were to remain in India and assimilated into the local ecclesiastical structure with their former rivals, the priests of the Missions étrangères de Paris (hereafter MEP).

The scene of the encounter in South Asia between the Jesuit missionaries and various local religions and religious specialists, some of whom were Christian but not Catholic, created an enormous playground and laboratory for the reformulation of social relations, cultural meanings, political alignments, and personal psychological predispositions. The book will track the transformation of Christianity from its basic medieval and humanist, albeit Eurocentric premises, into a global/world religion, highlighting in the process

1 Sebastião Gonçalves, *Primeira parte da história dos religiosos da Companhia de Jesus e do que fizeram com a divina graça na conversão dos infieis a nossa sancta fee catholica nos reynos e provincias da India Oriental* [1614], ed. Josef Wicki, S.J., 3 vols. (Coimbra: Atlântida, 1967), 1:46.

2 Georg Schurhammer, S.J., "Jugendprobleme des hl. Franz Xaver," *Studia missionalia* 2 (1946): 83–86.

a series of essential questions of identity, nationality/ethnicity, politics, and morality that the Jesuits commented on and were called to mediate or resolve.

The cross-cultural and transcontinental religious encounters, the hallmark of Jesuit apostolic objectives, are studied in this book both in diachronic and geographical order to underscore the similarities, particularities, and contingencies of different historical phenomena and mission locations. Starting with Portuguese colonial expansion, before and after the Jesuit arrival, under whose royal patronage religious conquest was set in motion, the storyline leads to specific geographical locations in South Asia—where Catholicism either temporarily or permanently gained ground. Readers should be aware that for certain geographical regions, the historiography is ample, and the archives are published and available, such as in the case of sixteenth-century Goa, while for others, such as the Mysore mission and, in general, the Padroado missions in the seventeenth century, the sources still need to be excavated from the Archivum Romanum Societatis Iesu (ARSI) and various other scattered Jesuit regional and local archives. Therefore, not all stories will be told with the equal attention they deserve. The reader should expect highlights rather than an all-encompassing, synthetic history of the Jesuits in coastal and South India.

Laying out the development and contours of historiography is the first step in understanding history.

2 Historiography

The historiography of the Jesuit missions is already a vast discursive field invented and carefully curated by the actors who pledged to convert non-Christians and wrote about it in real time. The Jesuits wrote their order's history as they built it up through their enthusiastic apostolic deeds. Xavier's famous *Copie dunne lettre missive envoiee des Indes* (A copy of a letter sent from the Indies [1545]) represents the first Jesuit historiographical effort at printing primary sources (see fig. 1).[3]

Jesuit historiography, therefore, proleptically starts with the present—with actors writing about themselves—pointing to the fact that Jesuit history had

3 *Copie dunne lettre missive envoiee des Indes, par monsieur maistre Francois Xavier* [...] (Paris, 1545). http://gallica.bnf.fr/ark:/12148/bpt6k54535853/f1.image (accessed September 2, 2024). For the full list of the early Jesuit letters, see John Correia-Afonso, *Jesuit Letters and Indian History: A Study of the Nature and Development of the Jesuit Letters from India (1542–1773) and Their Value for Indian Historiography* (Bombay: Indian Historical Research Institute, St. Xavier's College, 1955).

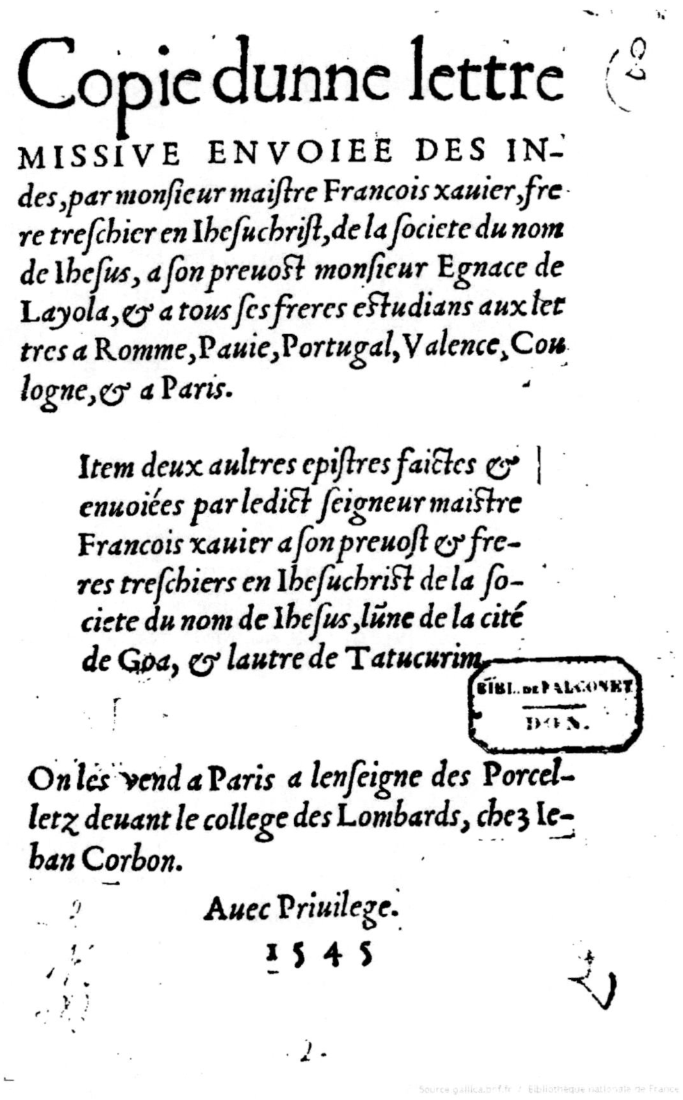

Copie dunne lettre
MISSIVE ENVOIEE DES INdes, par monſieur maiſtre Francois xauier, frere treſchier en Ihesuchriſt, de la ſociete du nom de Ihesus, a ſon preuoſt monſieur Egnace de Layola, & a tous ſes freres eſtudians aux lettres a Romme, Pauie, Portugal, Valence, Coulogne, & a Paris.

Item deux aultres epiſtres faictes & enuoiées par ledict ſeigneur maiſtre Francois xauier a ſon preuoſt & freres treſchiers en Ihesuchriſt de la ſociete du nom de Ihesus, lūne de la cité de Goa, & lautre de Tatucurim.

On les vend a Paris a lenſeigne des Porceletz deuant le college des Lombards, chez Iehan Corbon.

Auec Priuilege.
1545

FIGURE 1 Francis Xavier, *Copie dunne lettre missive envoiee des Indes, par monsieur maistre Francois Xavier, frere treschier en Jhesuchrist, de la societe du nom de Jhesus, a son prevost monsieur Egnace de Layola, & tous ses freres estudians aux lettres a Romme, Pavie, Portugal, Valence, Coulogne, & a Paris. Item deux aultres epistres faictes et envoiées par ledict seigneur maistre Francois Xavier a son prevost & freres treschiers en Jhesuchrist de la societe du nom de Jhesus, lunne de la cité de Goa, & lautre de Tatucurim*, 1546, Bibliothèque nationale de France, département Réserve des livres rares, RES P-O2K-493 (2), https://gallica.bnf.fr/ark:/12148/bpt6k54535853#

been simultaneously *in the making* and already *in use* as a template for action. The distinction between "us" and "others," reporting for internal and external audiences, colored the style and genre of Jesuit writing and historical texts. The pervasively edifying and exhortative mode aimed at the integration of an ever-growing and diversifying membership within the Society of Jesus and consequently at establishing efficient conflict-solving strategies, but it was also a way to "inflame" the general readership for the cause of the Catholic missions. Another particularity of the early Jesuit historiographical gestures that remain its most important feature even today is that the order's historiography is written in many different languages and has been supported by many different patrons. Letters from the missionaries in India, working exclusively under the Portuguese Padroado, appeared in print in the sixteenth century, often simultaneously in Italian, Portuguese, Spanish, German, French, and Latin. Even those edited and translated remain precious documents, since not all original autographs are extant.[4]

According to Robert Streit, the first history, or a short digest of historical events in the Asian missions, was written by Manuel da Costa (1540–d. after 1572) in 1568 and sent to Rome, where Giovanni Pietro Maffei (1533–1603) translated it to Latin and published it in Dillingen in 1571 under the title *Rerum a Societate Iesu in Oriente gestarum ad annum usque à Deipara Virgine MDLXVIII, commentarius Emanuelis Acostae Lusitani, recognitus, & Latinitate donatus* (Of the deeds done by the Society of Jesus in the Orient until the year 1568 after the Virgin birth, a revised commentary of Manuel da Costa, and translated to Latin).[5] It was, however, Alessandro Valignano's (1539–1606) *Historia del principio y progresso de la Compañía de Jesús en las Indias Orientales* (History of the beginning and progress of the Society of Jesus in the East Indies [1542–64]), first published in the twentieth century, that provided material for Maffei's *Historiarum Indicarum libri XVI* (Indian histories, book 16 [1588]).[6] Similarly, Gonçalves, who resided in Goa, provided the information and facts to the metropolitan historians; subsequently, his manuscripts remained unpublished until the twentieth century. Gonçalves's *Primeira parte da história dos religiosos da Companhía de Jesus* (The first part of the history of the religious of the Society of Jesus) was an essential source to draw from to prepare Xavier's

4 The early published letters are listed in Correia-Afonso, *Jesuit Letters and Indian History*, 176–86.

5 See Correia-Afonso, *Jesuit Letters and Indian History*, 114, and Robert Streit, *Bibliotheca missionum* (Münster: Achener Missionsdrukerei A.-G., 1929), 4:249.

6 Giovanni Pietro Maffei, *Historiarum indicarum libri XVI* (Florence: Apud Philippum Iunctam, 1588).

beatification and canonization process in Rome.[7] The manuscript was sent from Goa in 1614 accompanied by the relic of the future saint's right arm, today encased in a silver reliquary and placed on the right-hand side altar in the Chiesa del Gesù in Rome.[8] Another long-unpublished history by a missionary in India is *História do Malavar* (History of Malabar) by Diogo Gonçalves (1561–1640). The manuscript, which Josef Wicki (1904–93) dates to around 1615, is not a narrative history of the Society of Jesus but a combination of geography and ethnography of Kerala.[9] A social-cultural history *avant la lettre*.

However, when the process of Xavier's canonization gained momentum, the *vitae* (lives) of Xavier were published and were widely read: Orazio Torsellini's (1545–99) *De vita Francisci Xaverii* (Of the life of Francis Xavier [1596]), often reprinted and translated into Italian and French; and João de Lucena's *Historia da vida do padre Francisco de Xavier* (History of the life of the father Francis Xavier [1600]), translated by a Jesuit Lodovico Mansoni (1547–1610) and published in Italian in 1613 in the printing press of Bartolomeo Zannetti (?–1621).[10]

Fernão Guerreiro's *Relaçam annual das cousas que fizeram os padres da Companhia de Jesus* (Yearly account of the things done by the fathers of the Society of Jesus) published in five parts, is a comprehensive history of the Portuguese Jesuit assistancy at the turn of the seventeenth century.[11] Based on Jesuit correspondence, particularly annual reports from the missions, the books were organized chronologically, with entries combining biographical, ethnographical, and geographical descriptions. On an almost capillary level, his accounts infiltrated all subsequent "national" or regional histories of the early Jesuit missions from Brazil to Japan. A synthetic, translated version of the same chapters in French appeared in Pierre du Jarric's (1566–1617) *Histoire des*

7 Gonçalves, *Primeira parte da história*.

8 Ines G. Županov, *Missionary Tropics: The Catholic Frontier in India (16th–17th Centuries)* (Ann Arbor: University of Michigan Press, 2005), 81.

9 Diogo Gonçalves, *História do Malavar*, ed. Josef Wicki (Münster: Aschendorffische Verlagsbuchhandlung, 1955).

10 Orazio Torsellino or Torsellini (Horatius Tursellinus), *De vita Francisci Xaverii libri VI* (Rome: Ex typographia Aloysii Zannetti, 1596); João da Lucena, *Historia da vida do padre Francisco de Xavier* (Lisbon: Pedro Crasbeck, 1600); Lucena, *Vita del B. P. Francesco Xavier* [...]: *Composta* [...] *in lingua portughese, et trasportata nell'italiana dal p. Lodovico Mansoni* (Rome: Bartolomeo Zannetti, 1613).

11 Fernão Guerreiro's *Relaçam annual das cousas que fizeram os padres da Companhia de Jesus, nas partes da India Oriental, & em alguas outras da conquista deste reyno* (Lisbon: Pedro Crasbeeck, 1611), published in five parts. Modern edition: *Relacão anual das coisas que fizeram os padres da Companhia de Jesus nas sua missões*, ed. Artur Viegas, 3 vols. (Coimbra: Imprensa da Universidade, 1930, 1931, 1942).

choses plus mémorables (History of the most remarkable things).[12] Du Jarric, whose ardent desire was to be sent overseas as a missionary, compensated for his sedentary career in Bordeaux by becoming a historian. In this book, he exhorts the king of France, Henry IV (1553–1610, r.1589–1610), to imitate Portuguese royal endeavors and support Catholic missions.

Moreover, du Jarric claimed in his "Advertissment au lecteur" (Notice to the reader; vol. 1, unpaginated) to have been in direct touch with missionaries such as Alberto Laertio or Laerzio (1557–1630), who had been posted to India and commented on the historical works already published in Europe. A mission's history gains authenticity if it frequently quotes missionary letters and opinions *in situ*. Laerzio, however, was not just a proofreader of Jesuit historiographical production but a player in one of the most game-changing Jesuit suspense dramas of the early decades of the seventeenth century, since he was a superior and staunch supporter of the method of accommodation in the Madurai mission, heralded by Roberto Nobili (1577–1656).

The printing press accelerated the process of turning recent events into a fixed past, controlled by the Jesuit imprimatur. It also opened the door to anti-Jesuit appropriation. Nonetheless, in the early modern period, Jesuits were actors in and writers of their own and other people's histories. They were both local and global heroes for their Catholic audience. Their identity was also multiple and appropriated in historiography by different geographical locations and institutions. Xavier is as much a Spanish as an Indian and Japanese saint.

Written by Jesuits from the sixteenth to the eighteenth centuries, Jesuit historiography resembles a single composite body of cross-references, borrowings, and multiple translations. Though "national" styles and inclinations are discernable, it is densely factual and apologetic. The Italian view of Daniello Bartoli (1608–85) can be compared with the influential Goan Jesuit account expressing the Portuguese view in *Oriente conquistado* (The Orient conquered)

---

12 Pierre du Jarric, *Histoire des choses plus memorables advenues tant ez Indes Orientales, que autres païs de la descouverte des Portugais*, 3 vols. (Bordeaux: Simon Millanges, 1610–14). British historians in the twentieth century used his work extensively to piece together the history of the Mughals. See C.H. [Charles Herbert] Payne, ed. and trans., *Akbar and the Jesuits: An Account of the Jesuit Missions to the Court of Akbar by Father Pierre Du Jarric, S.J.* (New York: Harper & Brothers, 1926). Payne also published Jesuit letters from the Mughal court during Jahangir's reign, translated from Guerreiro's text: *Jahangir and the Jesuits with an Account of the Travels of Benedict Goes and the Mission to Pegu* (London: George Routledge & Sons, 1930).

by Francisco de Sousa (1628–1713).[13] Jesuit historians, the first in Rome and the second in Goa, narrate the first half-century of the Jesuit presence in India with barely disguised national agendas within a universalizing framework. The *oeuvre* of another Jesuit historian, and Portuguese patriot, Fernão de Queirós (1617–88), remained unpublished in the seventeenth century, except for the *História da vida do veneravel irmaõ Pedro de Basto* (History of the life of the venerable brother Pedro de Basto [1689]).[14] Queirós was a prolific writer with a long Jesuit career in India (fifty-three years), but many of his manuscripts were lost in the 1664 fire that engulfed the Goan College of St. Paul.[15] Many Jesuit literary and historical works were lost in similar disasters and subsequent archival neglect. Queirós's major history, *Conquista temporal e espiritual de Ceylão* (The temporal and spiritual conquest of Ceylon), written toward the end of his life, remained in manuscript and was only published in the twentieth century because his political project of the reconquest of Sri Lanka was judged obsolete and unfeasible by the Estado da Índia.[16]

From the late seventeenth and early eighteenth centuries, Jesuit historical sources, some of which were self-consciously crafted as historical writings from South Asia, took a national and defensive turn. With the arrival of the French Jesuits, sent by the French king and defying the Portuguese Padroado system, the letters written from the two missions in Tamil Nadu—an already famous Madurai mission under the Padroado, and the Mission du Carnate (Carnatic mission), a French mission on the east coast of India, today in Tamil Nadu, Andhra Pradesh, and Telangana—were immediately published

---

13 Francisco de Sousa, *Oriente conquistado a Jesus Christo pelos padres da Companhia de Jesus da província de Goa*, 2 vols. (Lisbon: Valentim da Costa Deslandes, 1710).

14 Fernão de Queirós, *Historia da vida do veneravel irmaõ Pedro de Basto coadjutor temporal da Companhia de Jesus, e da variedade de sucessos que Deos ilhe manifestou* (Lisbon: Miguel Deslandes, 1689). On this fascinating temporal coadjutor and fount of spirituality and providential energy, Pedro (Machado) de Basto (arrived in India in 1586–1645), see Zoltán Biedermann, "'Was it a vision or a waking dream?' Exploring the Oneiric World of a Seventeenth-Century Jesuit Visionary in Portuguese India," in *From the Supernatural to the Uncanny*, ed. Stephen M. Hart and Zoltán Biedermann (Cambridge: Cambridge Scholars Publishing, 2017), 43–70.

15 He managed to save only one manuscript, that of the life of Pedro de Basto. Fernão de Queiroz, *The Temporal and Spiritual Conquest of Ceylon*, trans. and ed. S.G. Perera, 3 vols. (New Delhi: Asian Educational Services, 1992 [Colombo, 1930]), 1:6*. The original Portuguese text has also been published: Fernão de Queirós, *Conquista temporal e espiritual de Ceylão*, ed. Paul E. Pieris (Colombo: H. C. Cottle, 1916). On Queirós, see Alan Strathern, *Kingship and Conversion in Sixteenth-Century Sri Lanka: Portuguese Imperialism in a Buddhist Land* (Cambridge: Cambridge University Press, 2008).

16 Queirós's *Conquista temporal* remains the most important single source for over 150 years of Sri Lankan history.

in a famous collection entitled *Lettres édifiantes et curieuses* (Edifying and curious letters).[17] While the publication of the *Cartas* in the early years of the Society of Jesus had been haphazard, the letters in the French collection were a self-conscious effort at promoting the new French missions. The letters were not simply reproduced but retailored by the editors in Paris.[18] Some of the volumes were subsequently published in German by the Jesuit Joseph Stöcklein (1676–1733) in his collection *Der Neue Welt-Bott. Mit allerhand Nachrichten dern Missionariorum Soc. Iesu* (The new world messenger: With all kinds of news from the missionaries of the Society of Jesus).[19] According to Ulrike Strasser, this German edition promoted a German colonial fantasy that imaginatively substituted and barely concealed the absence of German colonial possessions overseas.[20] On the other hand, a famous English translation by John Lockman (1698–1771) was a downright hostile Protestant appropriation by the English, who equally coveted the regions described by the Jesuits politically. As a way of introduction and dedication to Arthur Onslow, Esq. (1691–1768), speaker of the House of Commons, Lockman defined Jesuits as "a body of Men whose literary Productions will be as acceptable to you, as the Tenets and Practices ascribed to them must be distasteful."[21]

The publication of the *LEC* was a veritable *machine de guerre* of the French Jesuits against Protestant and some Catholic rivals. While residing in Puducherry, the Jesuits avoided angering the Portuguese ecclesiastical Padroado in India but were involved in permanent quarrels with the French Capuchins and the MEP, their direct ecclesiastical and missionary rivals. Attacks on Jesuits by their compatriots and Jesuit responses to theologians in Rome became essential sources for understanding and studying the Malabar rites controversy.[22] As the Sacra Congregatio de Propaganda Fide (hereafter Propaganda Fide) strived to replace the Padroado in the missionary field in

17 A collection of missionary letters published in Paris in thirty-four volumes between 1702 and 1776 (*LEC* hereafter).

18 There were four editors at different periods. The most important was Jean-Baptiste Du Halde (1674–1743) between 1709 and 1743.

19 He published in forty volumes between 1726 and 1761. On Stocklein's editorial choices, see Renate Dürr and Ulrike Strasser, "Wissensgenerierung als emotionale Praktik: Ethnographisches Schreiben und emotionalisiertes Lesen in Joseph Stöckleins, S.J. Neuem Welt-Bott," *Historische Anthropologie* 28 (2020): 354–78.

20 Ulrike Strasser, *Missionary Men in the Early Modern World: German Jesuits and Pacific Journeys* (Amsterdam: Amsterdam University Press, 2020), 37.

21 John Lockman, *Travels of the Jesuits*, 2 vols. (London, John Noon, 1743), facsimile edition (New Delhi: Asian Educational Services, 1995), 1:i.

22 Ines G. Županov and Pierre Antoine Fabre, eds., *The Rites Controversies in the Early Modern World* (Leiden: Brill, 2018).

Asia, the Jesuits found themselves in a difficult position. They cooperated and resisted Roman efforts at centralizing missionary activities, inspired mainly by Jesuit strategies and "modernized" by the more extensive use of the printing press.

Another front opened by the *LEC* was to shut down reports from various and increasingly famous travelers in India, French libertines, and Protestants coming from rival European countries such as Britain, the Netherlands, and the Holy Roman Empire. Thus, the *LEC* became an ongoing "history" of the French Jesuit mission in eighteenth-century India, since Jesuit historical writing was not in fashion in the way that had previously been the case during the Iberian and Roman sixteenth and seventeenth centuries. The reason was probably that historical writing had been appropriated by secular institutions and political powers that looked at the Jesuit intelligentsia with increasing suspicion.

The French Society of Jesus fought against ever more vocal and articulate enemies at home, some of whom were educated in Jesuit colleges and came to be associated with the Enlightenment.[23] The epistolary form became a preferred means of expression when many certainties were shaken and self-apologetic histories were mistrusted. The missionaries in India, desirous of winning over the French literary public, produced erudite and descriptive texts and letters in which distant people and their history were portrayed as frozen in ancient times or as people tricked into forgetting their Christian origins. Jesuit speculations about historical connections between Brahmans and Jews and other conjectures were incorporated into some of the most influential Enlightenment projects, such as *Cérémonies et coutumes* (Ceremonies and customs).[24] Through their exceptional enlightened erudition, until the end of the century, the Jesuits in the Carnatic mission to the north and west of the Madurai mission, worked to counter the ideas of the *esprits forts* (freethinkers) in Europe and applied what Michel de Certeau (1925–86) called the hermeneutics of

23 See Sylvia Murr's (1947–2002) articles and books, in particular Sylvia Murr, *L'Inde philosophique entre Bossuet et Voltaire: L'Indologie du père Coeurdoux*, vol. 2 (Paris: EFEO, 1987). Carolina Armenteros, "The Enlightened Conservatism of the Malabar Missions: Gaston-Laurent Coeurdoux (1691–1779) and the Making of an Anthropological Classic," *Journal of Jesuit Studies* 6, no. 3 (2019): 439–66; Manonmani Restif-Filliozat, "The Jesuit Contribution to the Geographical Knowledge of India in the Eighteenth Century," *Journal of Jesuit Studies* 6, no. 1 (2019): 71–84.

24 *Cérémonies et coutumes religieuses de tous les peuples du monde representées par des figures dessinées de la main de Bernard Picard: Avec une explication historique, & quelques dissertations curieuses*, 7 vols. (Amsterdam: J. F. Bernard, 1723–37).

the other, consisting of plunging into the culture and language of those whom one wants to convert.[25]

As the opposition to the Society of Jesus grew, everything the Jesuits wrote from the missions was taken against them in the Protestant historiography. Moreover, from the early years of the eighteenth century, a rival Christian mission in India, that of the German Pietists from Halle in Tranquebar, a Danish enclave on the Coromandel Coast, started producing, partly in imitation of the Jesuits, their missionary historiography.[26] The sharpest tongue among the Protestant historians of the early eighteenth century was a former Catholic, Mathurin Vessière de la Croze (1661–1736), who wrote *Histoire du Christianisme des Indes* (History of Christianity in the Indies), a history in which Portuguese and French Jesuits appear side by side with other Portuguese ecclesiastical actors.[27] La Croze established a very long history of Christianity in India, preserved by the St. Thomas Christians in Kerala, while the Jesuits and the Portuguese were portrayed as those who perverted and corrupted the pristine message and the ancient community that resembled a Protestant sect.[28]

Until the eighteenth century, Jesuit historiography—written exclusively by Jesuit authors—and the history of the Society of Jesus—histories about the Jesuits—were interchangeable. As Jesuit and European interest in other people's pasts grew, and although diachrony was often collapsed into ethnography, the Society of Jesus became increasingly objectified and historicized by different, including non-partisan, historiographical opinions.

---

25 Michel de Certeau, *The Writing of History* (New York: Columbia University Press, 1988), 209–43. For a larger question of translation, see Michael Wintroub, "Translations: Words, Things, Going Native, and Staying True," *American Historical Review* 120, no. 4 (October 2015): 1195–217.

26 Danish-Halle missionary letters and reports from Tranquebar were published from 1708 onward as *Halleshe Berichte*, and some of them were translated into English and published in *Propagation of the Gospel in the East*, which started being published by the Society for the Propagation of Christian Knowledge in 1709, as well as in various other histories. See *Propagation of the Gospel in the East: Being an Account of the Success of Two Danish Missionaries, Lately Sent to the East-Indies for the Conversion of the Heathens in Malabar* (London: J. Downing, 1709). See Heike Liebau, "Controlled Transparency: The *Hallesche Berichte* and *Neue Hallesche Berichte* between 1710 and 1848," in *Reporting Christian Missions in the Eighteenth Century: Communication, Culture of Knowledge and Regular Publication in a Cross-confessional Perspective*, ed. Markus Friedrich and Alexander Schunka (Wiesbaden: Harrassowitz Verlag, 2017), 133–48.

27 Mathurin Veyssière de la Croze, *Histoire du Christianisme des Indes* (La Haye: Chez Frères Vaillant, & N. Prevost, 1724).

28 St. Thomas Christians are also known as Syrian (Suriyāni) Christians, Māppiḷḷa Christians, or Nazranies.

In the following pages, Jesuit historiography and Jesuit history are disentangled and combined with other sources to understand the broader context of missionary action in South Asia. In addition to recent, contemporary historiography, Jesuit and non-Jesuit, my analysis is also based on ethnographies of the regions that were Christianized during the early modern period and inspired by the comparative framework provided by the historiography of the global world.

3 Under the Portuguese Padroado

Weakness or authoritarianism are evoked as explanations for regal messianism in early modern Europe. The Portuguese crown was not solitary in dreaming of the *Quinto império* (the fifth and last terrestrial empire) conceived as a Christian utopia, a new beginning under the banner of the dynasty of Avis:

> The idea of the *Quinto imperio*, a tradition popular in the medieval schools, received a mystical sense when the humanistic studies renewed the Hellenic theory of the *Monarchia universal*. In the historical breviaries used in medieval schools, history was divided into Monarchies; and until the thirteenth-century human past, according to the prophesies of Daniel related to the four political monsters, had been dogmatically divided into the four Monarchies of Assyria, Persia, Greece, and Rome.[29]

The fifth one was to come as a Christian utopia. From the fifteenth century, the direction of its fulfillment was increasingly perceived as pointing toward the south and later to the East. With Henry the Navigator, duke of Viseu (1394–1460), and, more importantly, according to his early chronicler Gomes Eanes de Zurara (*c.*1410–*c.*1474), the progressive expansion along the West African coast, conceived in 1442, was—besides gold and slave hunting—nothing less than a way to reach Prester John, the long-lost mythical Christian king of the East, inhabiting, in European minds, the country called Ethiopia, and enrolling him for the final annihilation of Islam and the reconquest of Jerusalem.[30] Ethiopian

---

29 Teófilo Braga, *História da universidade de Coimbra nas suas relações com a instrucção publica Portuguesa* (Lisbon: Na typ. do Academia real das sciencias, 1892), 1:274.

30 It is not without importance that Zurara's *Crónica dos feitos notáveis que se passaram na conquista da Guiné por Mandado do Infante d. Henrique* (Lisbon: Academia portuguesa da história, 1978) received its final touch in the year of the fall of Constantinople (1453). Luís Filipe Barreto, *Descobrimentos e Renascimento, formas de ser e pensar nos séculos XV e XVI*, 2nd ed. (Lisbon: Imprensa Nacional/Casa da Moeda, 1983).

Christians were looking simultaneously for allies against the menace of jihad by their Muslim neighbors in Egypt. However, when the two Christian nations finally established closer contact in the mid-sixteenth century, their mutual admiration and desire for union petered out.[31]

What Zurara was not even able to imagine was that at the very moment of his writing, Islam, or more precisely, Arab and Persian traders, had already brought into being, without the important work of proselytism, a whole federation of Muslim states and communities in Africa and Asia.[32] As they sailed along the East African coast, the first Portuguese expeditions, that of Vasco da Gama (1469–1524) in 1498 and of his successor Pedro Álvares Cabral (1467–1520) in 1500, discovered to their surprise and dismay that the major commercial centers such as Sofala, Mozambique, Kilwa, Mombasa, Malindi, and Mogadishu were administered by Muslim governors.[33] Moreover, even in India—despite Gama's initial mistake in thinking that he had found traces of the lost Christians of the legend—the maritime commerce in Kozhikode, Kochi, Kannur, Kollam, and many other places was solidly in the hands of Islamicized communities, indigenous and foreign.[34] Portuguese crusading zeal against infidels was thus nurtured in the Indian Ocean in combination with the Estado da Índia's mercantile desire to capture and monopolize the spice trade to Europe. Royal interest in trade culminated during the reign of Dom Manuel (1469–1521, r.1495–1521), sarcastically nicknamed "the Grocer King" (*le roi épicier*) by King Francis I of France (1494–1547, r.1515–47).[35]

---

31 Alain Milhou, "Découvertes et christianisation lointaine," in *Histoire du Christianisme: De la réforme à la Réformation (1450–1530)*, ed. Jean-Marie Mayeur et al. (Paris: Desclée, 1994), 521–616. The first Europeans to establish contact with Ethiopian Christians were two Dominicans, Guillaume Adam (?–1341) and Raymond Etienne (dates unknown), around 1313–16. Ethiopia emerged from mythical overlay only in 1527 after a Portuguese expedition described by Francisco Alvares, *Verdadeira informação sobre a terra do Preste João das Indias* [1540], 2 vols. (Lisbon: Alfa, 1989). For the Jesuit mission in Ethiopia, see Leonardo Cohen, "Patience, Suffering, and Tolerance: The Experience of Defeat and Exile among the Jesuits of Ethiopia (1632–59)," *Journal of Jesuit Studies* 9, no. 1 (2022): 76–94.

32 Milhou, "Découvertes et christianisation lointaine," 528. See also Philippe Beaujard, "L'Afrique de l'Est et les réseaux d'échanges océaniques entre les Ier et XVe siècles," *Afriques* [online] 6 (2015), https://journals.openedition.org/afriques/1996 (accessed September 19, 2024); Michael N. Pearson, *Port Cities and Intruders: The Swahili Coast, India, and Portugal in the Early Modern Era* (Baltimore: Johns Hopkins University Press, 1998).

33 Consuelo Varela and Guy Martinière, eds., *L'état du monde en 1492* (Paris: La découverte, 1992), 154.

34 Pius Malekandathil, *Portuguese Cochin and the Maritime Trade of India, 1500–1663* (New Delhi: Manohar, 2001).

35 Sanjay Subrahmanyam, *The Portuguese Empire in Asia, 1500–1700: A Political and Economic History* (London: Longman, 1993), 47. See also Luís Filipe F.R. Thomáz, "Le Portugal et

Although medieval theologians, Thomas Aquinas (1224/25–74) being the most prominent, and Raymond Llull (1232–1316), a Majorcan Franciscan living at the close of the thirteenth century, the most recent, had elaborated the distinction between those who had heard the "glad tidings" but rejected it, such as Jews and Muslims, and those who did not, such as Gentiles, reserving a harsh treatment exclusively to the former, the early Portuguese actions in the Indian Ocean followed the pattern of behavior already rehearsed during their violent conquest of Moroccan *presídios*.[36] Thus Afonso de Albuquerque (1453–1515), whom Luís Vaz de Camões (*c.*1524–1579/80) calls "o Terrível" (the Terrible) for his act of vengeance after the second siege of Goa (1510), personally admitted to massacring all the Muslims except "well built and white" women, whom he planned to baptize and marry off to Portuguese settlers.[37] The confusion of religious and political goals was neither new nor a passing affair, and even if, in the decades and centuries to come, the distinction between them became paradoxically both less obvious and more refined, the fundamental contradictions remained intact.[38]

In addition to the inherited spirit of the Reconquista, Dom Manuel's messianism should not be neglected. His unusual biography, as told by his courtiers Duarte Galvão (1446–1517) and Duarte Pacheco Pereira (1560–1633), is replete with unusual twists and turns that led him to the throne despite initially

l'Afrique au XVe siècle: Les débuts de l'expansion," *Arquivos do Centro Cultural Português* 26 (1989): 61–256.

36 Armand Llinarès, *Raymond Lulle, philosophe de l'action* (Paris: Presse Universitaire de France, 1963), 278–81. After 1517, the authority on the subject of the natural right of the "pagans" is Cardinal Cajetan (1469–1543), followed by Francisco de Vitoria (1483–1546), Bartolomé de la Casas (1484–1566), Domingo de Soto (1494–1560), and Francisco Suárez (1548–1617). See Anthony Pagden, *The Fall of Natural Man: The American Indian and the Origins of Comparative Anthropology* (Cambridge: Cambridge University Press, 1983). On the school of Salamanca and its role in the emergence of colonial normative regimes, see Thomas Duve, José Luis Egío, and Christiane Birr, eds., *The School of Salamanca: A Case of Global Knowledge Production* (Leiden: Brill, 2021). On Llull, see Noel Blanco Mourelle, "Every Knowable Thing: The Art of Ramon Llull and the Construction of Knowledge" (PhD diss., Columbia University, New York, 2017).

37 Michel Chandeigne, "Albuquerque, le conquérant," in *Goa 1510–1685: L'Inde portugaise, apostolique et commerciale*, ed. Michel Chandeigne (Paris: Ed. Autrement, 1996), 19–39; Geneviève Bouchon, *Albuquerque: Le lion des mers d'Asie* (Paris: Editions Desjonquères, 1992), 188–89; Afonso de Albuquerque, *Cartas*, ed. Raymundo Antonio de Bulhão Pato and Henrique Lopes de Mendonça (Lisbon: Typ. da Academia real das sciencias de Lisboa, 1884), 1:26–29.

38 On mutations of "religious" and political" in early modern Europe, see Michel de Certeau, "La formalité des pratiques: Du système religieux à l'éthique des Lumières (XVIIe–XVIIIe s.)," in *L'écriture de l'histoire* (Paris: Gallimard, 1975), 152–214.

better-placed contenders.[39] Messianism and empire-building were natural allies, while Portuguese royal mercantilism was the pillar of this enterprise, which finally never entirely succeeded for reasons larger than one king's life.[40]

Had providence fulfilled Dom Manuel's dreams, the Christianization of Asia, one might suppose, would have worked itself out naturally with the help of Prester John's Christians. However, proselytizing missionary activity before John III's (1502–57, r.1521–57) reign never took off. Nevertheless, precisely simultaneously, the stage was set for the second-largest missionary leap in the history of the church. The Society of Jesus became the vehicle of Catholic and Portuguese spiritual aspirations and, in the process, both won and lost. However, before the Jesuits arrived, some institutions that made it possible were already in place.

3.1 *Papal Bulls and the Portuguese Padroado*

Between the Great Schism (1378–1417) and Martin Luther (1483–1546), Christian unity was the most urgent problem of the Western church. The remedies prescribed were peaceful reconciliation with Eastern Christianity, a search for the lost Christian tribes in Africa and Asia to reclaim the ever-receding spiritual and geographical territory lost to Islam, and the reconquest of Jerusalem.

In a series of bulls, the popes tried to stimulate, more often than not only *post factum*, Portuguese efforts at circumnavigating the West African coast in search of Prester John and oriental Christians.[41] One example of a medieval, crusading bull is the one granted by Martin V (1369–1431, r.1417–31) in 1418 (*Rex regum*) on the occasion of the Portuguese capture of Ceuta three years earlier, while the bull *Romanus pontifex* of 1455 issued by Nicholas V (1397–1455, r.1447–55) presents a new type of bull acknowledging Portuguese political and territorial sovereignty in Africa.[42]

Finally, the partition of sovereignty and jurisdiction between Portugal and Spain over the new conquests encompassing just about all the known

39 Luís Filipe F.R. Thomáz, "L'idée impériale manueline," in *La découverte, le Portugal et l'Europe*, ed. Jean Aubin (Paris: Centre culturel Calouste Gulbenkian, 1990), 35–103 and "Factions, Interests, and Messianism: The Politics of Portuguese Expansion in the East, 1500–1521," *Indian Economic and Social History Review* 28, no. 1 (1991): 97–109.

40 For the cosmographer Duarte Pacheco Pereira (*c.*1460–1533), Dom Manuel was already "César Manuel." Duarte Pacheco Pereira, *Esmeraldo de situ orbis* (Lisbon: Academia Portuguesa de História, 1988), 199–201.

41 Charles-Martial de Witte, "Les bulles pontificales et l'expansion portugaise au XVe siècle," *Revue d'histoire ecclésiastique* (Louvain) 48 (1953): 683–718; 49 (1954): 438–61; 51 (1956): 413–53; 53 (1958): 5–46, 443–71.

42 Milhou, "Découvertes et christianisation lointaine," 560.

territories beyond Europe came to be defined first in the Treaty of Tordesillas (1494), confirmed by Julius II's (1443–1513, r.1503–13) papal bull of 1506, and then in the Treaty of Saragossa in 1529.[43]

Portugal's territorial and political sovereignty over its overseas conquests, sanctioned by the pope, also implied patronage (*padroado*) of the missions and churches within its geographical boundaries. Often interpreted as a sign of the Roman pontiff's weakness in his relations with the Iberian nation-states, the 1456 bull *Inter cetera*, foundational for the Portuguese Padroado, points to another line along which national royal and state centralization took place: by gradually appropriating the privileges and benefices, as well as considerable riches, of the medieval military-religious orders—the Orders of Christ, of Aviz, and Santiago—inheritors of the disbanded Templars.[44] As Dom Manuel ascended to the throne in 1495, the mastership of the Order of Christ was united to the crown, and the Padroado da Ordem de Christo became the Padroado Real, an institution confirmed and sanctioned in 1534 by Paul III (1468–1549, r.1534–49) in the bull *Aequum reputamus*.[45]

With the power to appoint archbishops and bishops and distribute ecclesiastical benefices at their will, usually to family members and to deserving protégés, combined with royal mercantilism, Dom Manuel and later John III tried—without fully succeeding—to centralize and control all aspects of Portugal's overseas expansion. Many royal privileges and prerogatives were implicit in the Padroado system, such as siphoning church revenues and tithes and creating a network of dependents from among the appointed benefice holders and prospective candidates. However, there were also significant and costly obligations involved in creating missions, new bishoprics, convents, and sanctuaries.[46]

---

43 Alonso García-Gallo, "Las bullas de Alejandro VI y el ordenamiento jurídico de la expansión portuguesa y castellana en Africa e Indias," in *Los orígines españoles de las instituciones americanas: Estudios de derecho indiano* (Madrid: R. Academia de Jurisprudencia y Legislación, 1987), 461–830.

44 Henry the Navigator became the administrator of the Order of Christ in 1419, and it was to the office of the grand master of the order that Calixte III (1378–1458, r.1455–58) in 1456 bestowed both spiritual and ecclesiastical jurisdiction over Africans and Indians. Incidentally, the revenues attached to the title enabled this famous Portuguese *infante* to finance his expeditions of discovery.

45 Fortunato de Almeida, *História da igreja em Portugal*, 2nd ed. (Porto: Livraria Civilização, 1968), 2:7–46, 219–21.

46 Levy Maria Jordão and João Augusto da Graça Barreto, eds., *Bullarium patronatus Portugalliae regum in ecclesiis Africae, Asiae atque Oceaniae*, 5 vols. (Lisbon: Ex Typographia nationali, 1868–79).

3.2 *The Church and the State in Portuguese Asia*

Portuguese ecclesiastical institutions overseas reinforced by the Estado da Índia should not be equated with missionary activity despite circumstantial convergence. They were often at odds, especially from the second part of the sixteenth century, when the transnational Society of Jesus "invented," captured, and monopolized the missionary field in Asia.[47] However, let us start from the beginning.

The Portuguese colonial experience in the Atlantic Ocean and Africa in the fifteenth century, based on the management of a discontinuous series of *presídios* and fortified *feitorias*, provided the model of ecclesiastical organization and Christianization that was imported to Goa, where the first efforts at conversion took place as early as 1510, and from there to all other Portuguese enclaves in Asia. For the Portuguese population, primarily soldiers and *casados* (married men), parishes were established together with *irmandades*, religious confraternities, to provide adequate support, a sense of community, and a national and religious identity that was seen as endangered by the vicissitudes of expatriate life. Immense maritime spaces fostering individual freedom opened the way to personal, commercial, and religious experiments. From *degredados*, banned and left on their own along the African and Indian coast, to *lançados*, who penetrated inland in search of riches and fortune, and the *casados*, that is, settlers and private merchants often married to local and Asian women, the authorities perceived the male Portuguese population, ecclesiastical and secular, as being in constant danger of slipping into apostasy and espousing the "pagan" or "infidel" customs and manners of the surrounding non-Christian regions.[48]

Another effect of the early Padroado institution combined with pre-Tridentine ecclesiastical laxism was that it allowed the expatriate church authorities to behave like other colonial actors by profiting from the slave

47 John W. O'Malley, S.J., *The First Jesuits* (London: Harvard University Press, 1993).

48 Charles R. Boxer, *Race Relations in the Portuguese Colonial Empire* (Oxford: Oxford University Press, 1963); Geneviève Bouchon, "Premières expériences d'une société coloniale: Goa au XVIe siècle," in *Inde découverte, Inde retrouvée 1498–1630: Études d'histoire Indo-Portugaise* (Lisbon: Commission Nationale pour les Commémorations des Découvertes Portugaises, Centre Culturel Calouste Gulbenkian, 1999), 291–301; Michel N. Pearson, *The Portuguese in India* (Cambridge: Cambridge University Press, 1987); Teotónio R. de Souza, *Medieval Goa: A Socio-economic History* (New Delhi: Concept Publishing, 1979); Maria Augusta Lima Cruz, "Exiles and Renegades in Early Sixteenth-Century Portuguese India," *Indian Economic and Social History Review* 23, no. 3 (1986): 263–88. For a different, updated view, see Ângela Barreto Xavier, *Religion and Empire in Portuguese India: Conversion, Resistance, and the Making of Goa* (Albany, NY: SUNY Press, 2022). Timothy J. Coates, *Degredados e órfãs: Colonizacão dirigida pela coroa no império português, 1550–1755* (Lisbon: Comissão nacional para as comemoracões dos descobrimentos portugueses, 1998).

and spice trade and even taking local concubines. If one is to believe the sixteenth- and, especially, the seventeenth-century Jesuit writers, the secular clergy, in particular, were also theologically unprepared for efficient proselytism. After the effort to evangelize Congo had failed by the end of the fifteenth and early decades of the sixteenth century, marred by the lucrative slave trade and general lack of missionary method, and after a disappointment with "lost" Ethiopian Christians, whose utter poverty and geographical location meant they were of minor strategic importance for the building of a commercial and political network, the hopes of finding local "Christian" collaborators turned partly to the kingdom of the Monomotapa in Africa, believed to be rolling in gold, and partly to the St. Thomas Christians on India's Malabar Coast, who were in charge of the lucrative spice trade.[49] Monomotapa became famous in Portuguese missionary history before it faded into oblivion as the location of the martyr death of a Jesuit, Gonçalo de Sylveira (1525–61), while the St. Thomas Christians were something of a disappointment in the long run,[50] as they wavered between accepting and resisting the Roman church's efforts at imposing Western liturgical standards on them. They opened a long debate with the Jesuits and other European theologians on the nature of Christianity with its variants and, by extension, other religious practices in India.[51] The distinction between the religious and the political resurfaced as one of the major issues to be disentangled by European theologians and missionaries before new missionary methods were effectively implemented. At that point, the institution of the Portuguese Padroado received its first surreptitious pushbacks from the center that had brought it into being, from Rome and the Roman curia itself.

---

49 Philip Caraman, *The Lost Empire: The Story of the Jesuits in Ethiopia* (London: Sidgwick & Jackson, 1985); Jessica Wright and Leon Grek, trans., and Wendy Laura Belcher, ed., *The Jesuits in Ethiopia (1609–1641): Latin Letters in Translation*, introduced by Leonardo Cohen (Wiesbaden: Harrassowitz Verlag, 2017); Jerónimo Lobo, *The* Itinerario *of Jerónimo Lobo*, trans. Donald M. Lockhart from the Portuguese text, ed. M. Gonçalves da da Costa, with an introduction and notes by Charles Fraser Beckingham (London: Hakluyt Society, 1984). Pedro Páez, *Pedro Páez's* History of Ethiopia, *1622*, trans. Christopher J. Tribe, ed. Isabel Boavida, Hervé Pennec, and Manuel João Ramos (London: Ashgate for the Hakluyt Society, 2011); Leonardo Cohen, *The Missionary Strategies of the Jesuits in Ethiopia, 1555–1632* (Wiesbaden: Harrassowitz Verlag, 2009).

50 Gai Roufe, "The Reasons for a Murder: Local Cultural Conceptualizations of the Martyrdom of Gonçalo da Silveira in 1561," *Cahiers d'études africaines* 219 (2015): 467–87.

51 S.I.G. Mudenge, *A Political History of Munhumutapa, c.1400–1902* (Harare: Zimbabwe Publishing House, 1988); Susan Visvanathan, *The Christians of Kerala* (Madras: Oxford University Press, 1993); Leslie W. Brown, *The Indian Christians of St. Thomas* (Cambridge: Cambridge University Press, 1982).

However, let us sail back to the "Golden Goa," the "Rome of the Orient," and the hub of missionary activity in the East.

3.3 *Goa: the Mission Hub*

All Portuguese naval expeditions in the Indian Ocean were accompanied by one or more official chaplains: members of religious orders or secular priests. Taking care of the sailors' or soldiers' spiritual needs, especially at the point of imminent death in shipwreck or battle, they were also the first to plant crosses (*padrões*) and bless them on the "virgin" land of discovery. A Dominican friar did the same in Goa after Albuquerque's conquest in 1510. The next step in religious implantation was the foundation of churches and chapels, usually built literally on or out of the debris of mosques and Hindu temples. More prominent and sumptuous religious edifices were erected in the years to come, and official papal recognition followed through grants of ecclesiastical benefices.

Thus, the Church of St. Catherine in Goa—a mud and palm leaf construction built by Albuquerque shortly after 1510 and replaced three years later by a stone building—became the cathedral of the first Asian diocese in 1534, comprising a vast territory from the Cape of Good Hope to China. Before March 1539, when the first bishop of Goa, Dom Frei João Afonso de Albuquerque (d.1553, r.1537–1553), a Franciscan Recollect, inaugurated the diocese and celebrated the first Mass, small parties of his co-religionists and some diocesan priests were already beginning the work of conversion in Goa, Kochi, Kannur, and among the Parava communities on the Fishery Coast and in Mylapore on the Coromandel Coast, following very closely the Portuguese commercial and political network. In their letters to Lisbon, some contemporary witnesses complained about the scandalous behavior of the young clerics who had obtained their ecclesiastical appointments in India through family connections and acted more like traders than priests.[52]

The contemporary Portuguese dilemma concerning the overseas empire contrasting free trade (*grande soltura*) and the royal monopoly found an echo or simple parallelism among religious specialists. The problem of overlapping jurisdictions of the royal Padroado and the papacy steadily grew, making the question of the center of ecclesiastical authority always open and disputable. The scramble for the "spiritual conquest" of Asia inaugurated a series of intra-religious hostilities and confusions at the local level. The uneasy relationship between regular and diocesan clergy started in this period. A group of eight Franciscans who arrived in Goa in 1517 and claimed to have converted

52 António de Silva Rego, ed., *Documentação para a história das missões do Padroado Portugês do Oriente, India* (Lisbon: Agência Geral das Colónias, 1947), 1:78, 343.

some eight hundred Hindus quickly complained that the secular fathers hampered their proselytizing efforts at every point.[53] In addition, despite a call for the creation of a new Christian Goa, a kind of utopian dream starting with Albuquerque's marriage arrangements for the Portuguese settlers and Christianization of their native spouses, the drive at proselytism was mitigated by practical constraints such as the fact that Hindu and Muslim merchants brought business into the city and facilitated diplomatic and commercial ties with the kingdom of Bijapur in the Deccan hinterland. Nevertheless, the conversion of the Ilhas, the five islands of the original conquest of Goa, and the later additions of Bardez and Salcete accelerated significantly among the lower and poorer agricultural classes after the Jesuits' arrival. Conversion was stimulated by solemn mass celebrations of baptism, presents of clothes for the purpose, and their general expectations of improved social status. Brahmans and wealthy merchants, according to contemporary complaints, evaded conversion and even intimidated new Christians, officially called *cristãos novamente convertidos* (newly converted Christians).[54]

It was through "charitable" institutions, established mainly after the creation of the Goan diocese, that the new Christian communities, including that of the Portuguese settlers with their local spouses and slaves—all baptized, often in a peremptory fashion—came under firmer ecclesiastical control. Orphanages and schools were set up in Goa and Kochi in the second decade of the sixteenth century, and an official, a *juiz de orfãos* (judge of orphans), was appointed to supervise such institutions. When the Jesuits arrived, they took over most of these official positions.[55]

The confraternity of the Misericórdia was another common feature of Portuguese metropolitan and overseas towns. The exercise of Christian charity—fourteen corporal and spiritual works of mercy—facilitated communal integration, particularly in the far-removed territories where family, class, or regional ties were often tenuous due to the vagaries of commercial and military enterprises. Misericórdia served as a mutual-aid society, a sort of spiritual insurance, and was favored by royal authorities as it encouraged civil discipline and conformity, at least most of the time and when under "appropriate" leadership. Some sixteen years after the foundation of the first Misericórdia in

53 Rego, *Documentação*, 1:351.

54 Anthony D'Costa, *Christianisation of the Goa Island* (Bombay: Heras Institute, 1965), 17; Ângela Barreto Xavier, "*Conversos* and *Novamente Convertidos*: Law, Religion, and Identity in the Portuguese Kingdom and Empire," *Journal of Early Modern History* 15 (2011): 255–87.

55 Rego, *Documentação*, 1:353, 419; António de Silva Rego, *História das missões* (Lisbon: Agência Geral das Colónias, Divisão de Publicações e Biblioteca, 1949), 186–88.

Lisbon (1498), the Goan members—"brothers"—inaugurated their confraternity through celebrations of the three major patronal feasts on its calendar: the feast of the visitation, Maundy Thursday, and All Saints' Day.[56]

After 1542, at the insistence of Governor Martim Afonso de Sousa (1500–64), the confraternity took over the administration of the Goan hospital. By the second part of the sixteenth century, it was in charge of three of the four large hospitals in the city—the Hospital of All Saints, the Hospital of Nossa Senhora da Piedade, and the Hospital of St. Lazarus (for lepers)—while the Royal Hospital was given over to the Jesuits in 1591.[57]

Engaged primarily in philanthropic and funerary activities, Misericórdia was not directly involved in missionary activities but provided, in the words of Jesuit historians, "a good example" of a true Christian life (and death) to the new and prospective converts.[58] It was not before 1541 that the confraternity of the Santa Fé (Holy Faith) was established for non-European Christians, and it also included a seminary for educating the indigenous clergy. The finances for this enterprise were found by taxing the non-Christians and appropriating revenues formerly associated with the Hindu places of worship, which were on the way to being massively destroyed throughout the islands of Goa.[59]

Although the confraternity's *compromiso* (the statutes) entrusted the seminary's administration to the Franciscans, the Jesuits took it over in the early 1540s and made it famous throughout Asia. A hospital for the poor was also established by the confraternity of the Holy Faith in 1546.

The hospital was also under the Jesuits' wing and remained small, with only twenty to thirty indoor patients, until the 1560s when the number rose to sixty, but, more significantly, it opened its doors to non-Christians as well.[60] In the second part of the sixteenth century, the hospital was transferred to Margão and Rachol on the Salcete peninsula in the south. The gradual exclusion of the non-Christians and especially poor non-Christians from the "Rome of the Orient" to the margins of the Portuguese Goan *conquista*, while rich and valuable "infidels" and "heathens" continued to play a prominent role in the capital's

56 Rego, *História*, 238.

57 José F. Ferreira Martins, *História de Misericórdia de Goa*, 3 vols. (Nova Goa: Imprensa Nacional, 1910–14); Isabel dos Guimarães Sá, *Quando o rico se faz pobre: Misericordias, caridade e poder no imperio portugues, 1500–1800* (Lisbon: Comissão nacional para as comemoracões dos descobrimentos portugueses, 1997).

58 P.D. Xavier, *Goa: A Social History* (Panaji: Rajhauns, 1993).

59 Josef Wicki, S.J., ed., *Documenta Indica* (henceforth *DI*) (Rome: Apud Monumenta Historica Societatis Iesu, 1948), 1:756–70, 45.

60 Fatima da Silva Gracias, *Health and Hygiene in Colonial Goa (1510–1961)* (New Delhi: Concept Publishing, 1994).

FIGURE 2 Vestiges of the Hospital of the Poor, Goa
PHOTO: AUTHOR, 2002

commercial activities, reveals the ambiguities of the official Portuguese policy of Christianization. The liminal "mission" territories were then left to religious orders, empowered with a mixture of religious and temporal prerogatives.

One such mixed office, peculiar to Portuguese missions in the East, with a noteworthy name of *pai dos cristãos* (the father of the Christians), combined violence, persuasion, protection, and surveillance of the newly converted Indian Christians. Inaugurated in 1537, this institution's primary purpose was to safeguard the interests of the neophytes and the new converts by providing legal advice concerning their privileges and rights granted by the royal administration, settling litigations, and inflicting punishments. According to Ângela Barreto Xavier, the "father of the Christians" had the power to decide who had access to offices in the imperial order and channeled the converts to subaltern positions, such as doorman, cleaner, and similar positions.[61] It

61 Ângela Barreto Xavier, "Reducing Difference in Portuguese Empire: A Case Study from Early Modern Goa," in *Changing Societies: Legacies and Challenges*, vol. 1, *Ambiguous Inclusions: Inside Out, Inside In*, ed. Sofia Aboim, Paulo Granjo, and Alice Ramos (Lisbon: Imprensa de Ciências Sociais, 2016), 241–61, 252.

started as a secular crown office on the state payroll but was appropriated by the clergy, Jesuits included.[62] "Provisões" (Conditions) or "leis a favor da cristandade" (laws in favor of Christians) supported the "father of the Christians" in his duties. Between 1540 and 1640, these anti-Hindu laws were promulgated to create religious uniformity through strict control of ritual observances of life-cycle ceremonies.[63]

It is too often repeated that the Jesuits' arrival radically changed the religious landscape of this Christian enclave and introduced rigorous and cruel bigotry—according to the hostile historians—or unprecedented missionary zeal—in the view of Catholic apologists—in dealing with non-Christians, new converts, and the Portuguese of Jewish descent. The responsibility for these two opposing narrative plots concerning the Jesuits' presence in Asia can be traced back to the Jesuits' contemporary enthusiastic accounts and self-congratulatory historical sources.

The decade after 1540 saw an intensification of missionary efforts, although these were mostly branching outs and refinements of former trends. For example, accusations of Jesuit responsibility for the destruction of the Hindu temples are generally valid, except that by the time Xavier arrived, all of the "visible" temples on the conquered islands of Goa had already been destroyed by the joint secular sword of the governor Estevão da Gama (1505–76) and the religious sword of the Franciscan Diogo de Borba (d.1555), the preacher of the cathedral, and others. Similarly, the establishment of the Inquisition, the Santo Ofício, in Goa in 1560 is often taxed on Jesuits—Xavier's letter to King John III requesting just that in 1552 is often used as proof.[64]

---

62 Josef Wicki, S.J., *Missionskirche im Orient* (Immensee: Neue Zeitschrift für Missionwissenschaft, 1976); Patricia Souza de Faria, "O pai dos cristãos e as populações escravas em Goa: Zelo e controle dos cativos convertidos (séculos XVI e XVII)," *História* (São Paulo) 39 (2020): 1–30; Josef Wicki, S.J., ed., *O livro do "Pai dos Cristãos"* (Lisbon: Centro de Estudos históricos Ultramarinos, 1969). On the role of *pai dos Cristãos* in the seventeenth century, see Glenn J. Ames, "Religious Life in the Colonial Trenches: The Role of the *pai dos Christãos* in Seventeenth-Century Portuguese India, *c.*1640–1683," *Portuguese Studies Review* 16, no. 2 (July 2008): 1–23, here 1.

63 *Leis a favor da cristandade*, 7693, vol. 1, Directorate of Archives, Archeology and Museums, Government of Goa, Panaji.

64 Georg Schurhammer, S.J., and Josef Wicki, S.J., eds., *Epistolae S. Francisci Xaverii alliaque eius scripta* (Rome: Apud Monumenta Historica Societatis Iesu, 1996), 2:346–48. For the complicated but interlinked relations between the Jesuits and the Inquisition in South Asia, see Giuseppe Marcocci, "Jesuit Missionaries and the Portuguese Inquisition in South Asia: A Controversial History (16th–18th Centuries)," in *Intercultural Encounter and the Jesuit Mission in South Asia (16th–18th Centuries)*, ed. Anand Amaladass and Ines G. Županov (Bangalore: Asian Trading Corporation, 2014), 232–56.

However, Jesuits continued the existing policy and pragmatically followed the moods of metropolitan and local politics. As early as 1539, a "New Christian" (a Christian of Jewish origin) was burnt in Goa on account of heresy and blasphemy. The hardening of the heart against the inhabitants of Jewish descent, provoked partly by local circumstances—the presence of, and rivalry with, Jewish merchants along the Malabar Coast and in Ormuz—was also linked to a new Joanine policy of the second part of the sixteenth century in which Spanish influence began to play a considerable role in the Portuguese religious enterprise.[65]

Jesuit missionary actions in Asia were not a simple extension of Iberian ecclesiastical influence. However, the debate about the "nationality" of individual members of the Society started with the "Spanish problem" in Portugal, Rome, and the Asian missions.[66] Even before the joining of the Spanish and Portuguese crowns in 1580, the pro-Spanish policy affected the local religious climate in Goa by amplifying aggressive Catholic conversion practices in addition to ostentatious displays, solemn ceremonies such as mass baptisms or *autos-da-fé*, and by privileging pious extravagance over economic gains. According to a Jesuit writer, when warned that the forceful conversion might diminish the royal treasury, Dom Constantino de Bragança (1528–75), viceroy of Goa from 1558 to 1561, responded: "I prefer for the honor of the royal Estado and the glory of his majesty a conversion of the poorest Canarim on this island than the load full of rent and ships loaded with pepper since everything should be about the salvation of one soul."[67]

---

65 With the regency period under the dowager queen Catarina of Austria (1507–78) and Infante-Cardinal Henrique (1512–80, r.1578–80) from 1557 until King Sebastian's (1554–1578, r.1557–78) direct rule, the royal house of Portugal endeavored to modify and efface its "spice merchants" image. It began to emulate the Habsburg ideals of agrarian-based aristocracy, always ready to sacrifice commercial profits to display noble, pious actions, religious rigor, and belated chivalry—misguided as they may have been. During the Union of the Crowns (1580–1640), many Jewish merchants took advantage to flee the Iberian Peninsula and establish themselves overseas, partly following commercial opportunities, partly hoping to avoid the clutches of the Inquisition.

66 On the difficult relationship between "nationalities" in Jesuit missions in Asia, see Camilla Russell, "Becoming 'Indians': The Jesuit Missionary Path from Italy to Asia," *Renaissance and Reformation/Renaissance et Réforme* 43, no. 1 (Winter 2020): 9–50, and Liam Brockey, "A vinha do Senhor: The Portuguese Jesuits in China in the Seventeenth Century," *Portuguese Studies* 16 (2000): 125–47, here 125. On the rivalry between Portuguese *padroado* and Spanish *patronato*, see Alexandre Coello de la Rosa and João Vicente Melo, *The Jesuit Encounters with Islam in the Asia-Pacific* (Leiden: Brill, 2023).

67 *DI*, 6:318. "Mais queria pera omrra do mesmo Estado real e gloria de Sua Alteza a conversão do mais pobre canarim desta ilha, que o recheio das rendas dela e naos carregadas de pimenta, e que tudo avia d'aventurar pola salvação de huma alma." Canarim is a name

Therefore, Jesuit missionaries did not invent the religious effervescence of mid-sixteenth-century Goa, but they masterfully defined its *mise en scène* and estheticized its communal dimension.

As a transnational European organization, the Society of Jesus escapes easy generalizations. A papal bull of 1540, *Regimini militantis ecclesiae*, ratified its status as a formal religious order. By the time the founding father, Ignatius of Loyola (*c.*1491–1556), breathed his last in 1556, its members, more than a thousand in number and scattered worldwide, were engaged in all of the ecclesiastical and a good number of secular activities—foreign missions, the reform of religious communities, administration of hospitals and orphanages, education, diplomacy, and so on.[68] Relying on improvisation in the early years, not always clear about which direction to take, the Jesuits became harbingers of the new "spirit of method."[69] The order's internal organization, with particular emphasis on centralization and the control of files and information, is often likened to that of the "new monarchies" consolidated by the rulers of sixteenth-century Spain and England.[70]

However, the Jesuits' primary goal remained the Christianization of the expanding social, political, and geographical universe, and in this, they were perfect *Doppelgängers*—in Asia especially—of the other prominent social group of the sixteenth century: the merchants. They were, in short, spiritual entrepreneurs who endeavored to break open new markets, and, as a general rule, the farther from the center, the more open they were to the structures, modes, and forms of belief and sociability of the peoples with whom they came into contact.[71] Inversely, the closer to the center, such as Goa for the Asian missionary field, the Jesuits tended to monopolize all activities concerning ecclesiastical and "spiritual" enterprises and thus encroached upon prerogatives, real and imaginary, of other colonial and missionary actors.

The arrival of the first Jesuit missionaries in 1542, headed by Xavier, often referred to as the "Apostle of the Indies," and of the Dominican contingent in 1547, inaugurated a long rivalry between the Jesuits and other religious orders,

---

given by the Portuguese to the inhabitants of the Konkan coast, including Goa. Sebastião Rodolfo Dalgago, *Glossário Luso-Asiatico* (Coimbra: Imprensa da universidade, 1918), 197–98.

68 Markus Friedrich, *The Jesuits: A History* (Princeton: Princeton University Press, 2023).

69 Certeau, *Writing of History*, 159. Jean Delumeau, *Christianisme entre Luther et Voltaire* (Paris: PUF, 1971), 104–9, 278–80.

70 See Carlos Zeron, "Political Theory and Jesuit Politics," in *The Oxford Handbook of the Jesuits*, ed. Ines G. Županov (New York: Oxford University Press, 2019), 193–215, here 194.

71 Hélène Vu-Thanh and Ines G. Županov, eds., *Trade and Finance in Global Missions, 16th–18th Centuries* (Leiden: Brill, 2021).

among whom Franciscans, Augustinians and Capuchins. By 1555, a secular authority was called to intervene and subdivide the Goan field of missionary activity. Viceroy Dom Pedro Mascarenhas (*c.*1484–1555), respecting the existing ecclesiastical and territorial configurations, assigned Bardez in the north to the Franciscans and the northern part of the island of Goa (Tiswadi) to the Dominicans, while the Jesuits were in charge of the southern part and of the peninsula of Salcete and the islands of Chorão (Choddnnem) and Divar.[72]

Jesuit provincial António de Quadros (1529–72) boasted that from 1557 to 1563, the entire population of the islands of Goa—around seventy thousand inhabitants—had been won over to Christianity principally through the Society's efforts.[73] The adjacent territories north and south of the Ilhas, Bardez, and Salcete had to wait another half-century to become Christian.[74] The various missionary orders' methods of conversion remained the same: a combination of incentives—solemn baptism, expulsions, acquisition of property and titles—and threats with the use of symbolic and "real" violence: eviction from the land, prohibition to use and display local marks of prestige such as a *palanquin* (a covered litter for one passenger), and the placement of "orphans" in the Jesuit and Franciscan colleges, especially after 1567.[75] The law (*lei*) of 1559, signed by the queen in Lisbon on March 23, obliged the non-converted Brahmans to wear a distinctive sign on their clothes and to attend special afternoon lectures disputing the tenets of their religion.[76]

The five provincial councils of Goa (1567, 1575, 1585, 1592, and 1606) denounced violence in conversion. However, juridical discrimination against non-Christians and the physical force used against those who prevented the proselytizing work did not contradict the principle of peaceful and voluntary conversion. In any case, at least in principle, the Jesuits, in particular,

---

72 DI, 3:350; Rego, *Documentação*, 6, 48; Achilles Meersman, *The Ancient Franciscan Provinces in India 1500–1835* (Bangalore: Christian Literature Society, 1971), 94.

73 DI, 5:741–42.

74 Paulo da Trinidade, O.F.M., *Conquista espiritual do Oriente*, 3 vols. (Lisbon: Centro de Estudos Históricos Ultramarino, 1962–67), 1:291–307. See also Bradley T. Blankemeyer, "Conversos, Accommodation, and the Goan Inquisition: The First Five Decades of the Society of Jesus in India, between Theory and Practice," *Archivum Historicum Societatis Iesu* (hereafter AHSI) 91, fasc. 181 (2022-I): 82–119.

75 Joseph Thekkedath, *History of Christianity in India: From the Middle of the Sixteenth Century to the End of the Seventeenth Century (1542–1700)* (Bangalore: Theological Publications in India, 1982), 352. The status of "orphans" was attributed to male children whose father (not mother) had died.

76 Joaquim Heliodoro da Cunha Rivara, *Archivo portugues oriental*, fasc. 5, part 1 (New Delhi: AES, 1992 [Nova Goa: Imprensa nacional, 1865]), 384. Robert Schrimpt, "Le diable et le goupillon," in Chandeigne, *Goa 1510–1685*, 115–34, here 121.

privileged "interior conversion," the exercise of "the free will moved directly by the divine grace," with the massive Jesuit apparatus of persuasion fueling the whole process.

3.4 *Rituals and Religious Art: Estheticizing Religious Propaganda*

Religious feasts and processions in Goa and throughout Portuguese Asia were social performances of great symbolic and ideological display geared at strengthening communal solidarity while at the same time opening a "reflexive" space and encouraging the integration of new social actors. It was often after one such ostentatious event that individuals or groups, Christian and non-Christian, rushed to religious institutions of the town to ask for spiritual instruction, confession, or baptism.

A Jesuit historian described the first solemn mass baptisms performed by his co-religionists on June 29, 1557 on the St. Peter and St. Paul feast day:[77]

> The new catechumens come out of their houses well dressed with the palm tree leaf in their hands as a sign of victory and the burning candle signifying baptismal grace, accompanied by many people who were their godfathers and relatives to favor them. Many people joined this new spectacle in which drums, shawms, and tables were played with joy. As they stood in front of the [Jesuit] church of São Paulo, the procession came out and received them, with the Santa Fe collegians who were dressed in white with their cross raised, with the Benedictus sung accompanied by the organ. After them, the fathers and brothers of the college followed in rows, and at the head of the procession, the governor [Francisco Barreto (1520–73, in office 1555–58)] with the Most Reverend Patriarch of Ethiopia and the entire court, and they would receive with great joy the catechumens taking them in front. At the same time, the bells rang, the church was richly decorated, and the altars were covered with brocade ornaments.[78]

All the town's inhabitants were involved in these events. The non-Christians were forced to participate, at least as spectators, since most of the processions took a whole day, meandering from street to street, with musical instruments and general enthusiasm invading the space. The end of the ceremony was sealed by a sumptuous free meal distributed to all participants in the Jesuit college. According to Sebastião Gonçalves, upon seeing all this and learning of

77 *DI*, 3:721.
78 Gonçalves, *Primeira parte da história*, 2:328.

the privileges bestowed on the newly converted, "many gentiles came asking for baptism," and a new ceremony was arranged for the day of the Assumption of our Lady (Assumpção da Virgen Nossa Senhora) of the same year.[79]

The spectacles of solemn adult baptism multiplied on the Goan islands until the arrival from Lisbon in 1560 of the second archbishop of Goa, Dom Gaspar de Leão Pereira (?–1576). For three years, he refused to allow these elaborate, mainly Jesuit ceremonies to take place.[80] It is possible that he did that to please other religious orders and diocesan priests, whose proselytizing work was less visible because they performed these celebrations in their parishes away from the center of the Portuguese colonial social arena, and they left very few written records about them. On the other hand, the Jesuits always privileged the city of Goa to display their religious works. The archbishop's prohibition, never fully respected, was finally overruled three years later by both Pope Pius IV (1499–1565, r.1559–65) and King Sebastian (1554–78, r.1557–78), and the Jesuits continued to celebrate with great pomp the baptisms of some 2,500 souls per annum until the 1570s, when the number of adult baptisms sharply declined due to the hostilities between the Portuguese and the sultanate of Bijapur.[81] After 1575, the magnificent adult baptism scenes were no longer in fashion as almost all of the village communities on the Goan islands were Christian, although Jesuits still signaled about five hundred conversions a year until the end of the century and an even larger number for the first part of the seventeenth century.[82]

The Goan religious calendar was hardly less impressive with the decline of solemn baptism, as numerous festivities entertained, amused, edified, and, in some cases, terrified the population. Various processions and acts of public devotion during the holy week presented probably the most stunning spectacles, with penitents performing live flagellation and other mortifications, although Corpus Christi and other saints' days were equally sumptuous in decoration and theatrical inventiveness.[83] For an Italian traveler, the Roman aristocrat Pietro della Valle (1586–1652), the procession of the Corpus Christi in April of 1624 would not qualify Goa for its habitual title of the "Rome of the East" since "the Procession was made […] with many representations of mysteries by

79 Gonçalvez, *História*, 2:328.

80 *DI*, 4:20*.

81 *DI*, 6:367, 619; 7:66, 403, 668; 8:91, 337.

82 *DI*, 10:466; 11:274; 12:102, 417, 609, 899; 13:771; and Fernão Guerreiro, *Relação anual das coisas que fizeram os padres da Companhia de Jesus nas suas missões nos anos de 1600 a 1609*, 2nd ed. (Coimbra: Imprensa da Universidade, 1930), 1:4.

83 Rego, *História das missões*, 1:495–96.

persons disguised, fictitious animals, dances and masquerades; things which in our Countries would more suit with Villages than great Cities."[84]

Nevertheless, a year later, the nine-day celebration of Xavier's canonization (February 10–19, 1624) acquires in della Valle's description a dimension of the most solemn festivity with "good" music, "gallant" dances, and "various contrivances of Charriots [*sic*], Ships, Galleys, Pageants, Heavens, Hells, Mountains and Clouds," and even this haughty Roman aristocrat participated in the procession of the "notables" of the city wearing a specially designed costume.[85] If one of the goals of the theatrical religious presentations was to impress the non-Christians, which the Jesuits repeatedly affirmed in their letters, these were not entirely successful in the city of Goa because, in 1600, it remained solidly non-Christian with 20,000 Hindus.[86]

The material incarnation of Jesuit religious sensibility is found in church architecture, religious objects, and art. A complete account of the architectural and artistic production that the Jesuits commissioned, patronized, and employed in the Portuguese colonial settlement, missions, and beyond would require massive shelf space. Unlike churches that remained perforce rooted in one place and always experienced multiple renegotiations with local artisans, dependent on the availability of materials and ecological preconditions, such as heat and rain, other objects—retables, paintings, relic coffers, and liturgical and devotional articles—traveled widely.[87] Jesuit iconographies, preferring Christological and Marian programs, are often composite with European elements essential for one figure with Japanese or Indian elements appearing next to them. Contradicting the early label of "Jesuit style," art historians studying Goan churches preferred "Indian baroque" or "modo Goano" (Goan style).[88]

The turning point in the evolution of Jesuit architecture and artistic investments was 1622, which was important because of the canonization of the first

84 *The Travels of Pietro della Valle in India* (New Delhi: Asian Educational Services, 1991 [London: Hakluyt Society, 1892]), 1:167.

85 *Travels of Pietro della Valle*, 2:410–13.

86 Souza, *Medieval Goa*, 115. The number of Hindus was calculated on the basis of the tax they were required to pay. There may have been around seventy-five thousand Christians in total.

87 Josef Wicki, "Jesuitenmaler und -bildhauer in Indien im 16. Jahrhundert," *Neue Zeitschrift für Missionswissenschaft* 38 (1982): 30–39.

88 Paulo Varela Gomes, *Whitewash, Red Stone: A History of Church Architecture in Goa* (New Delhi: Yoda Press, 2011); Maria Cristina Osswald, *Written in Stone: Jesuit Buildings in Goa and Their Artistic and Architectural Features* (Saligao: Goa 1556 and Golden Heart Emporium Book Shop, 2013); José Pereira, *Baroque Goa: The Architecture of Portuguese India* (New Delhi: Books and Books, 1995); Pereira, *Churches of Goa* (New Delhi: Oxford University Press, 2001).

FIGURE 3 The church of Bom Jesus and sacristy, Goa
PHOTO: AUTHOR, 2002

two Jesuit saints, Ignatius of Loyola and Francis Xavier.[89] Bom Jesus, the iconic Jesuit church in Goa, which took about a decade to be built, was consecrated on May 15, 1605 and stands adjacent to the professed house (see fig. 3). Like many Jesuit churches, Bom Jesus became a "museum" of sacrality as patrons gifted or commissioned objects for its interior. Among the most famous are the chapel niche with marble tomb, imported from Tuscany, and the silver casket containing Xavier's body made by local silversmiths.[90]

In the long run, the structural elements and iconography of Goan religious monuments, Jesuit included, were repurposed in Indian Christian architecture,

89 Simon Ditchfield, "Thinking with Jesuit Saints: The Canonization of Ignatius Loyola and Francis Xavier in Context," *Journal of Jesuit Studies* 9, no. 3 (2022): 327–37.

90 On Marcello Mastrilli, who commissioned the silver casket for Xavier's body, see Ines G. Županov, "Passage to India: Jesuit Spiritual Economy between Martyrdom and Profit in the Seventeenth Century," *Journal of Early Modern History* 16 (2012): 121–59, here 39. On Foggini's marble tombs, see Carla Sodini, *I Medici e le Indie Orientali: Il diario di viaggio di Placido Ramponi emissario in India per conto di Cosimo III* (Florence: Leo Olschki Editore, 1996); Osswald, *Written in Stone*, 81.

commissioned by Indian priests and executed by Indian builders.[91] Since Jesuits barred Indians from joining the Jesuit order—with the sole exception of Pedro Luís Bramane (*c.*1532–96)—these churches conceived and built by Indian Christians are celebrated as the work of Oratorians.[92]

Perhaps the most spectacular history of the reception of Christian iconography is that of Christian motifs in the Mughal paintings.[93] Jesuit missions at the Mughal court banked on the power of images to tell the story of Christ and entice spiritual conversion. To their disappointment, the forms and imageries were readily taken but not their Christian content and intention. Without Portuguese colonial coercion to back their defined and unified religious meanings, the images proved ineffective in the Jesuit project of the Christian conversion of the Mughals. The Jesuits remarked with sorrow that the Mughal emperor Jahangir (1569–1627, r.1605–27) merely used them to enhance his dynasty's prestige and shore up imperial power.

3.5 *Indigenization of Christianity and the Inquisition*

The simultaneous resistance to conversion and the growing number of Christians posed a new problem: Were these conversions sincere or only a shield for secret "pagan" practices? The ecclesiastical hierarchy, already casting a menacing shadow over the families of *cristãos novos* (Christians converted from Judaism) settled in Kochi and Goa, proved to be doubtful of Hindu converts, defining them as second-class Christians and often refusing to ordain

91 Sidh Losa Mendiratta, "From Rome to Goa: The Question of the First Goan Church," in *Palimpsests of Religious Encounter in Asia, 1500–1800*, ed. Mia M. Mochizuki and Ines G. Županov (Leiden: Brill, in press). On a strong statement on Indian agency involved in the production of Christian art, see Erin Benay, *Italy by Way of India: Translating Art and Devotion in the Early Modern World* (Turnhout: Harvey Miller Publishers, 2021).

92 Lorhany Cordeiro Ribeiro, "'Chronologia da Congregação do Oratório de Goa': Uma construção de memória (século XVIII)," paper presented at XXVII Simposto Nacional de Historia (Natal, July 22–26, 2023); Ines G. Županov, "Goan Brahmans in the Land of Promise: Missionaries, Spies, and Gentiles in 17th–18th-Century Sri Lanka," in *Re-exploring the Links: History and Constructed Histories between Portugal and Sri Lanka*, ed. Jorge Flores, South China and Maritime Asia Series (Wiesbaden: Harrassowitz and the Calouste Gulbenkian Foundation, 2006), 171–210; Ângela Barreto Xavier, *A invenção de Goa* (Lisbon: Imprensa de Ciências Sociais, 2008); Županov, *Missionary Tropics*, 259–70.

93 Mika Natif, *Mughal Occidentalism: Artistic Encounters between Europe and Asia at the Courts of India, 1580–1630* (Leiden: Brill, 2018); Gauvin Alexander Bailey, *The Jesuits and the Grand Mogul: Renaissance Art at the Imperial Court of India, 1580–1630* (Washington, DC: Freer Gallery of Art, Arthur M. Sackler Gallery, Smithsonian Institution, 1998); Ebba Koch, "The Influence of the Jesuit Missions," in *The Phenomenon of "Foreign" in Oriental Art*, ed. Annette Hagedorn (Wiesbaden: Reichert, 2006), 117–30.

even *mestiços* (born to Portuguese fathers).[94] The Third Provincial Council of Goa (1585) had decreed that the adult converts could receive ordination only fifteen years after the baptism and that they were to be at least thirty. The Fifth Provincial Council (1606) added a local "caste" flavor to these already highly selective restrictions: only Brahmins, *prabhus*, and other "noble" castes were to be admitted to the priesthood.[95]

Indigenous diocesan priests employed in various Goan parishes rarely acquired ecclesiastical benefices, those being reserved for the Portuguese.[96] Nevertheless, these "parish jobs" were much coveted, and in the seventeenth century, Indian diocesan priests resented the presence of religious orders who still detained nearly two-thirds of the parishes in their hands.[97]

The religious orders were generally more sympathetic to their new converts although the rules of the purity of blood applied to all Indians. Moreover, very few Hindus and *mestiços* were permitted to join any religious order before the eighteenth century, with the exception, though rare, of the Society of Jesus, and if they did, they remained in a subordinate position and a lower grade.[98] The lower status was also reserved for the Portuguese of Jewish ancestry, despite Loyola's philosemitism and the fact that prominent Jesuits in Europe were of New Christian blood, such as Diego Laínez (1512–65), the second Superior General of the order (in office 1558–65).[99] After 1622, the newly established Propaganda Fide in Rome worked to undermine the Portuguese Padroado, which was considered ineffective, by stimulating the formation of the local clergy and even conferring higher ecclesiastical benefices on Goan priests.[100] The case of Mattheus de Castro (*c.*1569–1679), a Goan Brahman, is often taken as

94 José A.R. da Silva Tavim, "From Setúbal to the Sublime Porte: The Wandering of Jácome de Olivares, New Christian and Merchant of Cochin (1540–1571)," *Santa Barbara Portuguese Studies* 2 (1995): 94–134.

95 Joaquim Heliodoro da Cunha Rivara, *Archivo portuguez oriental*, 6 fasciculos in 10 parts, fasciculo 4 (New Delhi: Asian Educational Services, 1992).

96 Carlos M. de Melo, S.J., *The Recruitment and Formation of the Native Clergy in India* (Lisbon: Agencia geral do Ultramar, 1955); Josef Wicki, "Der einheimische Klerus in Indien," in *Der einheimische Klerus in Geschichte und Gegenwart*, ed. Johannes Beckmann (Schöneck-Beckenried: Administration der Neuen Zeitschrift für Missionswissenschaft, 1950), 17–72.

97 Thekkedath, *History of Christianity in India*, 402.

98 Charles R. Boxer, *The Church Militant and Iberian Expansion, 1440–1770* (Baltimore: Johns Hopkins University Press, 1978), 12–14; Josef Wicki, S.J., "Pedro Luis, Brahmane und erster indischer Jesuit (ca. 1532–1596)," *Neue Zeitschrift für Missionswissenschaf* 6 (1950): 115–26.

99 Robert Aleksander Maryks, *The Jesuit Order as a Synagogue of Jews: Jesuits of Jewish Ancestry and Purity-of-Blood Laws in the Early Society of Jesus* (Leiden: Brill, 2010).

100 See articles in Josef Metzler, O.M.I., *Sacrae Congregationis de Propaganda Fide Memoria Rerum: 350 Years in the Service of the Missions*, vol. 1/1 (1522–1700) (Rome: Herder, 1972).

an example, although his mandate as a bishop was questioned and opposed by the Goan ecclesiastical hierarchy.[101] It was not until the last decades of the seventeenth century that the Goan diocesan priests, headed by José Vaz (1651–1711), pulled their ranks together and founded their congregation—Oratório do Santa Cruz dos Milagres—which was finally approved in 1686 by the pope and the king of Portugal under the rules of the Oratory of St. Philip Neri—and all this despite the opposition of the Goan archbishop.[102]

Of the twelve archbishops of Goa from 1560 until the end of the seventeenth century, not all were adamantly against indigenous clergy. A famous Augustinian archbishop, Dom Aleixo de Menezes (1595–1609), appointed Indian priests to various parishes in Goa, Kanara, and the Bassein region. His ordinations en masse of St. Thomas Christians during the Synod of Udayamperoor (Diamper) signaled his "indigenization" policy of ecclesiastical offices stimulated by similar Jesuit success stories in Japan. One should also not forget that his principal informant was the Catalan Jesuit Francesco Ros [Roz] (1584–1624), who resided among St. Thomas Christians and was sympathetic to "adaptationist" experiments in the Madurai mission (from 1606 onward) that were about to open a major dispute within the ecclesiastical ranks in India.[103]

There was no consistent policy, however, on the recruitment of indigenous clergy, and the prelate who replaced Menezes, Christovão de Sá e Lisboa (in office 1616–22), of a Hieronymite order (Ordem de São Jerónimo), swore on the missal never to ordain any indigenous priest and denounced vehemently the method of accommodation. What he was tacitly denouncing was also the incessant papal efforts to circumvent the Portuguese Padroado by encouraging missions outside the direct control of the Estado da Índia amid the "heathen" and "infidel" kingdoms. The jurisdictional muddle that emerged from this struggle marked the seventeenth and eighteenth centuries until the marquis of Pombal (1699–1782) ensured that the Goan clergy officially achieved

101 Ângela Barreto Xavier and Ines G. Županov, "Ser brâmane na Goa da Época Moderna," *Revista de história* 172 (São Paulo) (January–June 2015): 15–41, http://dx.doi.org/10.11606/issn.2316-9141.rh.2015.98757 (accessed September 2, 2024); Theodore Ghesquière, *Mathieu de Castro, premier vicaire apostolique aux Indes* (Louvain: Revue de la Bibliotheque de l'histoire ecclesiastique [fasc. 20], 1937).

102 Viriato António Caetano Brás de Albuquerque, "Congregação do Oratorio de S. Felippe Nery em Goa," *O oriente portuguez* 2, no. 7 (1905): 310–26, here 310. Simon Gregory Perera, *Life of the Venerable Father Joseph Vaz* (Galle: Loyola House, 1953 [1943]); M. da Costa Nunes, *Documentação para a história da Congregação do Oratório da Santa Cruz dos milagres do clero natural do Goa* (Lisbon: Centro de Estudos Históricos Ultramarinos, 1966); Cosme Jose Costa, *Life and Achievements of Blessed Joseph Vaz* (Goa: Pilar Publications, 1996).

103 Francisco Ros (archbishop of Cranganore, today Kodungallur) to Claudio Acquaviva, November 19, 1613, ARSI, Goa 51, fols. 165–97.

equality vis-à-vis their European counterparts.[104] Another target of Pombal's reforms was the Inquisition, which he abolished (1774), although, after he fell from power, it was briefly resuscitated until 1820.

The Portuguese Inquisition, established *de facto* in 1547, was a latecomer compared to its Spanish model and counterpart (1478). It might be that this crucial half-century of calm helped the Portuguese overseas empire prosper economically through the financial and commercial contributions of the New Christian trading networks. Nevertheless, the Inquisition was originally King Manuel's project, more for political than religious reasons. It was set up precisely to disempower the New Christians against the grain of economic indications, which proved their importance for producing wealth and prosperity for the state and the nation. Even if individual Portuguese high officials, including the kings, were aware of the importance of the New Christians for the economy, the social and cultural/religious imperatives overruled all pragmatic concessions.[105]

Often associated with the second "Spanish" phase of John III's reign, the Santo Ofício found its way to Goa only in 1560 during the regency of the dowager queen Catarina of Austria (1507–78, r.1557–62) and thrived for almost two and a half centuries despite the waves of opposition from the secular governments and even the clergy and archbishops. Conceived as a royal weapon of centralization—John III's brother, Cardinal Henrique (1512–80), held the office of inquisitor-general for forty years (1539–80)—against particular interests of just about everybody else in the kingdom, the implantation of the Inquisition in Goa—its jurisdiction often overlapping with that of the secular authorities and provoked endless disputes. This institution eventually grew to become a state within a state with elaborate bureaucracies and clients—*familiares*, recruited from all social groups and primarily involved in the preliminaries such as informing, denouncements, and spy-work—accompanying the decision-making process of the General Council and the four inquisitorial courts of Lisbon, Evora, Coimbra, and Goa.[106]

To the usual list of "crimes" attributed to "crypto-Jews" and Protestants—heresy, blasphemy, sodomy, homosexuality, apostasy, etc.—tried at the "table" (*mesa*) of the holy house (*santa casa*), as it was commonly known, Goan

104 Charles R. Boxer, *The Portuguese Seaborne Empire, 1425–1825* (London: Hutchinson, 1969), 265–57. Claudio Lagrange Monteiro de Barbuda, ed., *Instrucções com que El-Rei D. José I mandou passar ao Estado da India, o governador e capitão general e o arcebispo primaz do Oriente no anno de 1774* (Pangim: Na Typographia nacional, 1844).

105 Henry Kamen, *The Spanish Inquisition* (London: White Lion Publishers, 1965), 217–18.

106 António Henrique de Oliveira Marques, *History of Portugal: From Lusitania to Empire*, 2 vols. (New York: Columbia University Press, 1976), 1:289.

inquisitors added and created many more offenses, published in the *Regimento do Santo Officio da Inquisição dos reynos de Portugal* (Rules of the Holy Office of the Inquisition of the kingdoms of Portugal [1640]), to include non-Christian, Hindu, and Muslim practices like the choice and preparation of food—such as "cooking rice without salt"—and dress code, and, more importantly, the organization of calendrical celebrations and life-cycle ceremonies.[107] Similarly, although technically only Christians were the target of the Holy Office, under the pretext of obstructing conversion, even Muslims and Hindus could fall under its jurisdiction.

Despite its busy working schedule, financed by the local government, in setting up processes—from 1562 to 1774, there were 16,202 registered court cases—trying them, and organizing awe-inspiring *autos-da-fé*, only about two hundred people were burnt at the stake. More important was the extent to which the tribunal confiscated the local New Christian families' property and riches to feed its machine.[108] Seventeenth-century visitors such as François Pyrard de Laval (*c.*1578–*c.*1623), Charles Gabriel Dellon (1649–*c.*1710), and many others denounced the economic aspects of inquisitorial purpose and the office's administrative and authoritarian behavior.[109] Jesuit attitudes and actions toward the Goan Inquisition were mixed. Valignano found the Inquisition incompatible with the Jesuit purpose in Asia, while many Portuguese Jesuits saw nothing wrong with it.[110] In religious form and sensitivity, the national distinctions between Italian and Spanish Jesuits grew throughout the sixteenth century. The scope and shape of orthodoxy and orthopraxy were tested through those inhuman institutions geared to control the population through fear and violence. Jesuits may not have approved of the Inquisition's strategies, not only because of its focus on punishment but also because of its disregard for European moral theology. Between 1556 and 1573, the Portuguese Jesuit Francisco Rodrigues (1515–1573), despite his physical disability, worked

107 Anant K. Priolkar, *The Goa Inquisition* (Bombay: Bombay University Press, 1961), 87–113; António Baião, *A Inquisição de Goa, tentativa de história da sua origem, estabelecimento, evolução e extinção*, 2 vols. (Lisbon: Academia das Ciencias, 1930–45); Miguel Rodrigues Lourenço, "On *Gentilidade* as a Religious Offence: A Specificity of the Portuguese Inquisition in Asia?," in *Norms beyond Empire: Law Making and Local Normativities in Iberian Asia, 1500–1800*, ed. Manuel Bastias Saavedra (Leiden: Brill/Nijhoff, 2020), 207–48.

108 Charles Amiel, "Les archives de l'Inquisition portugaise: Regards et réflexions," *Arquivos do Centro cultural português* 14 (1979): 421–43.

109 Charles Dellon, *The History of the Inquisition as It Is Exercised at Goa* (London: Printed for James Knapton, at the Queens Head in St. Paul's Churchyard, 1688); François Pyrard de Laval, *Voyages aux Indes orientales* (Paris: Louis Billaine, 1615).

110 Blankemeyer, "Conversos, Accommodation, and the Goan Inquisition," 86.

hard to standardize liturgy, doctrine, and dogma and resolve moral issues that cropped up in Goa and the frontier missions. He was not working against the Inquisition, but—faced with the limits of European ecclesiastical law in Asia—he strained his theological mind and imagination in the hope of establishing certainty and casuistry in the context of the Portuguese empire.[111]

After the peak of its activity in the seventeenth century, the Inquisition in Goa was increasingly referred to as proof of Portuguese backwardness and religious bigotry by the rival European powers in the Indian Ocean. The Inquisition became identified with the Jesuit presence in the popular hostile imagination.

4 Missionary Frontiers

From the mid-sixteenth century, Portuguese factory (*feitoria*) settlements dotted the west and the east coast of India and Southeast Asia and, later on, Japan and China. The settlers endeavored to organize their religious life, imitating the Goan Catholic effervescence. Most settlements had limited and short-lived success due to the political, economic, and social conditions, while a few survived long into the modern period. Around the time when Goa was elevated to the rank of archbishopric (1558), two dioceses were created—Kochi and Melaka—followed by Macau (1576), Funai in Japan (1588), Angamaly on the Malabar Coast (1594; it became an archbishopric in 1608), and Mylapore (1600).[112] In addition to being in charge of the diocesan priests, under the jurisdiction of the bishops, the Portuguese Padroado was also obliged to provide funds for the upkeep of the missionaries belonging to different religious orders. Franciscans, Dominicans, Jesuits, and Augustinians established their missions, colleges, monasteries, and other institutions before the end of the sixteenth century. A second wave of missionary orders—Carmelites, Capuchins, Italian Oratorians, and Theatines—arrived in the seventeenth century, directly

111 See Bastias Saavedra, *Norms beyond Empire*, and Rômulo da Silva Ehalt's book project and postdoctoral work in progress at the Max Planck Institute for Legal History and Legal Theory, "Evidences of Truth: Francisco Rodrigues, S.J. (1515–1573) and Normative Knowledge Production in Early Modern Portuguese Asia." Romulo da Silva Ehalt, "Casuistry in the Tropics: The Moral-Theological Pragmatics of Francisco Rodrigues in Portuguese Asia (Sixteenth and Seventeenth Centuries)," *Revista da história da sociedade e de cultura* 19 (2019): 399–418, https://doi.org/10.14195/1645-2259_19_16 (accessed September 19, 2024).

112 João Paulo Oliveira e Costa, "Em torno da criação do bispado do Japão," in *O Japão e o Cristianismo no sèculo XVI: Ensaios de história Luso-Nipônica* (Lisbon: Sociedade Histórica da Independência de Portugal, 1999), 129–57.

financed by and responsible to the Propaganda Fide. Although, in theory, they were sent to "help out" the Portuguese Padroado and were employed in the fields outside of the ecclesiastical grid, the newcomers were often seen as intruders by the Portuguese and treated as such. Catholic missionary fields away from Goa and subject to local indigenous rulers remained forever unstable, segmentary, and in permanent competition with other indigenous and/or foreign religious institutions and actors. At the same time, the distance from the center of Portuguese ecclesiastical and secular power allowed for social and cultural experiments and accommodation to local customs. The "frontier" missions were powder kegs of innovation in terms of strategies of conversion as well as laboratories of knowledge about non-Christian religious theologies and practices. These were also "linguistic" missions because proselytism switched to local and native languages from the Latin and Portuguese imposed in Goa as a "lingua franca" of Christianity. Each mission was, for this reason, different from another, even if the translation of Christian liturgy and pious works of literature labored to unify Asian Christianity while simultaneously promoting diversity and cosmopolitan horizon and reach.

4.1 *Portuguese "Reform" and Division of the Syrian Christians of Kerala*

The "discovery" of St. Thomas or Syrian Christians on the Malabar Coast was considered providential by Pedro Álvares Cabral (*c.*1467–*c.*1620) and his successors engaged in Asian pepper empire-building. The privileged position of this Christian group within the local social and political fabric of sixteenth-century Kerala—numbering between eighty thousand and two hundred thousand in the course of the sixteenth century—due to its corporate control of commercial enterprises, its tradition of martial prowess, and "noble" or "purity-conscious" lifestyle, opened the way for the Portuguese traders to profit from the local market opportunities. At the same time, St. Thomas or Syrian Christians accepted Portuguese patronage to enhance their economic and symbolic prestige.[113]

The centralizing nature of the Estado da Índia's political and colonial intentions quickly came into conflict with the existing segmentary power relations in Kerala, which had previously left St. Thomas Christians with a high degree

113 The most erudite recent statements on the Syrian Christians in India are by István Perczel. See István Perczel, "Syriac Christianity in India," in *The Syriac World*, ed. Daniel King (London: Routledge, 2018), 653–97; Perczel, "Cosmopolitismes de la Mer d'Arabie: Les chrétiens de saint Thomas face à l'expansion Portugaise," in *Cosmopolitismes en Asie du Sud: Sources, intinéraires, langues (XVIe–XVIIIe siècle)*, ed. Corinne Lefèvre, Ines G. Županov, and Jorge Flores, Collection Puruṣārtha 33 (Paris: Éditions de l'École des hautes études en sciences sociales, 2015), 143–69.

of autonomy. Through religious patronage, the Portuguese endeavored to gain control of this Indian community, which claimed as its founder one of Christ's disciples, St. Thomas, and had maintained ecclesiastical connections with the independent West Asian churches since the fourth century. These ancient religious ties came to be branded by the Portuguese ecclesiastical hierarchy as illegitimate since the doctrine of the Syrian patriarchs was known to be based on Nestorian teaching and therefore "heretic." Furthermore, according to the regulation of the Padroado, the appointments of the bishops were the prerogatives of the Portuguese king and the pope, and thus, all "foreign" ecclesiastical officials sent by the West Asian patriarchs were potentially seen as transgressors. However, since the Estado da Índia never militarily "conquered" the Malabar Coast and could thus never claim territorial sovereignty, ecclesiastical obedience to the local Christian hierarchy remained a moot point.[114]

During the first half of the sixteenth century, Portuguese relations with St. Thomas Christians—headed by their Syrian bishop Mar Jacob (d.1554), who arrived at Cranganore in Kerala in 1504 and remained there until his death around 1554—appear to have been relatively harmonious. There were two significant reasons for this initial calm. The first is the lack of European missionaries. A few Franciscans and Dominicans who did apply themselves to proper pastoral work immediately signaled the strangeness of social and religious customs and the "errors" in the liturgy and Christian doctrine, but they remained divided over how to go about correcting them. The second reason was that overzealous "hard-liners" such as the Franciscan Alvaro Penteado (in India from 1511 to 1533) lost out temporarily to the "softer" line of the Dominican João Caro (in India 1512/22, d.1527), who encouraged Mar Abraham (d.1597), Syrian bishop and metropolitan of Angamaly—who first came to India in 1556 and died in 1597—to claim a certain degree of religious autonomy.[115] This was,

114 Placid J. Padipara, C.M.I., *The Hierarchy of the Syro-Malabar Church* (Alleppey: Prakasam Publications, 1976); Sidney George Pothan, *The Syrian Christians of Kerala* (New York: Asia Pub. House, 1963).

115 The Portuguese never succeeded in dominating or replacing local kings: the pope was far away, and his representatives (Dominicans, Franciscans, Jesuits, etc.) were endlessly bickering between themselves and the traditional ecclesiastical elite of the St. Thomas Christians (hereditary priestly lineages, traditional archdeacons, spiritual/martial preceptors, and West Asian bishops), who rightly suspected the European intruders of plotting to deprive them of their age-old privileges. See Mathias Mundadan, C.M.I., *History of Christianity in India: From the Beginning up to the Middle of the Sixteenth Century (up to 1542)* (Bangalore: Church History Association of India, 1989), 298.

however, only the beginning of similar "triangular" relationships riddled with shifting alliances between various European and Indian actors.[116]

The general trend of Portuguese political and religious initiatives concerning the St. Thomas Christians was to firmly attach them to the royal Padroado, to expurgate "heretical" accretions found in their Syrian liturgy, to "Europeanize" their social customs and religious celebrations, and to discredit the authority of the West Asian bishops. Despite what was thought of as a considerable effort from the European religious to "Latinize" the Syrian Christians and unite them with the Roman church, they continued to privilege their local and older social and religious ties.[117]

Throughout the second part of the sixteenth century, the Jesuits came to dominate the missionary scene along the Malabar and Fishery Coast, and some of them "specialized" in this particular field. Ros, for example, who became the first archbishop of the Angamaly seat (1608), acquired impressive linguistic expertise in Malayalam and Syriac during his forty-year ministry to the St. Thomas Christians.[118] Under the Jesuit helm, the European ecclesiastical pressure on the St. Thomas Christians increased from the 1550s onward. Although, in 1553, communion was established between the Malabar church and the Roman church, the Jesuits continued to harass St. Thomas Christian prelates and objected to the use of the Syriac language and the East Syrian ecclesiastical rites. The provincial councils of Goa issued special decrees to regulate the St. Thomas Christian case. The third, held in 1585, issued a strong opinion on the defective sacramental rite of ordination practiced by Syrian bishops.[119] Under such external weight and fed by rumors and suspicions, the community of St. Thomas Christians began fracturing into factions of those

116 Georg Schurhammer, s.j., *The Malabar Church and Rome during the Early Portuguese Period and Before* (Trichinopoly: St. Joseph Industrial School Press, 1934).

117 The European missionaries, Jesuits in particular, established colleges for the training of the clergy (in Kodungallur in the 1540s; in Vaipikotta [today Vypeekotta] in the 1580s) and endowed new and old churches (about sixty in 1578).

118 Irénée Hausherr, ed., *De erroribus nestorianorum qui in hac India Orientali versantur, auctore P. Francisco Roz, s.j.*, Orientalia Christiana 11:1, no. 40, (Rome: Pont. Institutum Orientalium Studiorum 1929), 1–35; Anthony Mecherry, s.j., *Testing Ground for Jesuit Accommodation in Early Modern India: Francisco Ros, s.j. in Malabar (16th–17th Centuries)* (Rome: Institutum Historicum Societatis Iesu, 2019); István Perczel, "Accommodationist Strategies on the Malabar Coast: Competition or Complementarity?," in Županov and Fabre, *Rites Controversies in the Early Modern World*, 191–232.

119 Mecherry, *Testing Ground*, 71, 99. The Portuguese authorities withheld Gregory XIII's (1502–85, r.1572–85) confirmation of Archdeacon George (Giwargis) of Christ (d.1586) as a bishop of Palayur and never handed over five hundred ducats as an annual grant sent by the Portuguese king.

who were *pro* or *contra* "Latinization."[120] An additional historical contingency that facilitated the splintering of this Christian community, which traditionally possessed an endemically unstable religious leadership, was the split (1553) within the Chaldean Church itself.[121] Hereafter, one patriarch acknowledged the union with Rome, and the other denied it.[122] Abraham, who went from being a Nestorian bishop to being confirmed by the pope, returned to his diocese after being forced to travel to Europe. He used various strategies to remain in power despite the Jesuit opposition until he died in 1597.[123]

However, this highly conflictual situation came to a sudden, albeit brief resolution through the highhanded gesture of a young and zealous Goan archbishop, an Augustinian, Dom Frey Aleixo de Menezes (1559–1617). Imbued with religious idealism comparable to that of Xavier half a century earlier among the Parava Christians of the Fishery Coast, this noble Portuguese prelate stormed the sacred territory of the Syrian Christians and imposed a complete Latinization of liturgy and customs at the Synod of Udayamperoor (Diamper) in 1599. Through a combination of political menace, (presumed) personal charisma, and downright bluff, he managed to bully even the archdeacon, the most adamant opponent to European ecclesiastical intrusion.[124] However, the moment of union was as short-lived as the archbishop's year-long stay in the area. The religious leadership under the Jesuit bishops, from Ros to Francisco Garcia (1580–1659, in office 1641–59), continued to be unstable, while other religious orders tried to break this and other Jesuit monopolies by encouraging opposing factions among the St. Thomas Christians. Garcia's quarrel with Archdeacon Parambil Thoma Kathanar (*c.*1610–70, in office 1653–70), from the Pakalomaṭṭam family, escalated until the so-called Oath of the Slanting Cross (*kūnan kuriśu satyam*). The archdeacon rejected the obedience of the

120 Latinization means the use of the Latin language in all ecclesiastical ceremonies and rites, as well the "correction" of the liturgy and calendar of the Church of the East.

121 After internal conflicts within the Church of the East, Patriarch Yukhannan Sulaqa (in office 1553–55) went to Rome and was confirmed by Pope Julius III (1487–1555, r.1550–55). The union with the Roman church created two branches of the church. The Uniate line split further in the eighteenth century. Mecherry, *Testing Ground*, 11; Joseph Habbi, "Signification de l'union chaldeenne de Mar Sulaqa avec Rome en 1553," *L'Orient Syrien* 11 (1966): 117–21.

122 Thekkedath, *History of Christianity in India*, 37.

123 Brown, *Indian Christians of St Thomas*, 26.

124 António de Gouvea, *Jornada do Arcebispo de Goa Dom Frey Aleixo de Menezes Primaz da India Oriental, religioso da ordem de S. Agostinho* [...] (Coimbra: Diego Gomez Loureyro, 1606); António de Gouvea, "Synodo diocesano da igreja e bispado de Angamale dos antigos cristãos de Sam Thome [...]" (Coimbra: Na officina de Diogo Gomez Loureyro Impressor da Universidade, 1606).

Portuguese and the Jesuits, and the result was a schism within the Christian community in 1653. He was elected and consecrated by the "rebel" faction as their bishop, Mar Thoma I (d.1670).[125] Two-thirds of the Christians returned to the Roman fold in 1662, mainly through Discalced Carmelite efforts. In fact, from 1622, the Propaganda Fide—with the barely dissembled intention to replace the Portuguese Padroado and the Jesuits—started sending Italian Discalced Carmelites as vicars apostolic among the Syrian Christians. The Discalced Carmelites and Dominicans covertly supported factions of St. Thomas Christians opposed to the Jesuits, who lost all authority among the Christians after 1653. Moreover, under the Dutch occupation of Kochi and the surrounding area, the Discalced Carmelites, sent by the papacy, were allowed to continue the mission among St. Thomas Christians.

The reasons for the Jesuit loss of the mission among St. Thomas Christians were circumstantial and political. The conversion and "pacification" of the St. Thomas Christians who inhabited the Serra—that is, a mountain where they grew pepper between the Western Ghats and the Arabian Sea—had been challenging for the Jesuits, who were, in the early second half of the sixteenth century, still newcomers to India and the missionary field beyond the Portuguese colonial frontiers. It is precisely in confrontation with the peculiar *long durée* ecclesiastical situation in which St. Thomas Christians imported foreign bishops to consecrate local priests and sanctify the community that the Jesuit missionaries developed the famous method of accommodation. Ros, who learned Syriac and Malayalam, was probably the first Jesuit to connect the dots between language and religious practices. He understood the importance of liturgical Syriac, which permanently sanctified the community that lived for a few centuries in a disconnected diasporic space, surrounded by "friendly" religious others. When Portuguese and Latin could not substitute Syriac, the pragmatic decision to accept Syriac as a "true" Catholic doctrine vehicle was the first step toward accommodation.[126] The second was to tweak and repurpose the rites and customs, some of which were Nestorian, hence schismatic and heretic. It was a difficult task because of the continuous, if sporadic, arrival of the Syrian bishops, whose authority mostly trumped that of the Jesuits, and because of the lineage structures based on the distinction between "higher" and "lower" status within the community.[127] The Jesuit missionaries played

125 Brown, *Indian Christians of St Thomas*, 92–109.

126 Ines G. Županov, "*Antiquissima Christianità*: Indian Religion or Idolatry? (17th–18th c.)," *Journal of Early Modern History* 24 (2020): 471–98.

127 Oral tradition attributes to St. Thomas the conversion of the Brahmans and the foundation of seven Christian settlements in Malabar: Cranganore (Muziris), Palayur

all the cards available. They tried to undermine the authority of the "ancient" priestly families and opened a college where any St. Thomas Christian boy, not only those considered of "priestly" families, could learn the Syriac language and literature. Unlike in Goa, however, religious coercion led to trouble, revolt, and division among St. Thomas Christians. When Nobili encountered a similar situation in Madurai, in the Tamil country, where no coercion or persuasion was possible or advisable, his counsel and support was precisely Ros, who had long experience among St. Thomas Christians in Kerala. Unlike in the Madurai mission, the most important and invincible enemy was not "Hinduism" but other varieties of Christianity. With the arrival of the Protestants, St. Thomas Christians had an even wider field of choices to translate their communal and spiritual aspirations into a preferred institutional framework.

4.2 *Parava Christians: a Case of "Communal" Conversion*

Except for the St. Thomas Christians, initially all other "new" Christians in South India belonged to ritually low-status groups very often engaging in "polluting" activities—according to the elite literati normativity—such as manual labor and fishing. There were token Brahmans and some Nayar lineages who accepted European religious patronage for exceptional reasons, but they remained very few throughout the period.[128]

The "romantic" plot of evangelizing the Paravas was one of the shining Jesuit master narratives of conversion because it is an essential part of the biography of St. Francis Xavier, the first Jesuit missionary in Asia. In the early seventeenth century, in his history of the Jesuit missions in India, Sebastião Gonçalves referred to Xavier as *negoceador das almas*, a soul merchant who came in search of "precious stones that are the souls of the infidels, that polished through the holy baptism [...] turn into even more precious [stones] such as carbuncles, diamonds, sapphires, emeralds and pearls created in the deep of the sea."[129]

A commercial aspect of the Jesuit proselytizing was, thus, underlined in his text by a figurative equation of "infidel souls" and "precious stones." There is, undoubtedly, some truth in his statement since Paravas can *de facto* be likened

(Palur), Paruru (Kottakayil), Kokkamangalm, Niranam, Nilakkal (Chayal), and Kollam. Pius Malekandathil, "St. Thomas Christians: A Historical Analysis of their Origins and Development up to 9th Century AD," in *St. Thomas Christians and Nambudiris, Jews, and Sangam Literature: A Historical Appraisal*, ed. Bosco Puthur (Kochi: LRC Publications, 2003), 1–45, here 4; Brown, *Indian Christians of St. Thomas*, 51–54.

128 Nayars were a matrilineal, warrior grouping of castes in Kerala. Just like Brahmans, they claimed the highest status in early modern Kerala.

129 Gonçalves, *História*, 1:133.

to pearls in a metonymical sense. They were one of the pearl and conch-shell fishing coastal groups in the Gulf of Mannar, or, as the Portuguese would evocatively name it, "Costa da Pescaria," or the Fishery Coast.[130] This particular skill was the currency with which they attracted Portuguese patronage and protection that went hand in hand with evangelization.

The Paravas' conversion to and subsequent persistence in Catholicism was, at least in its early phase of the sixteenth century, the result of a conjunction of political, economic, and cultural factors, all of which threatened to undermine the Paravas' corporate economic activities.

The Portuguese presence along the South Indian coast and their naval skirmishes in the 1520s with the Mappilas and Maraikkayars, Muslim trading groups that controlled the pearl-fishery revenues and the bulk of other seaborne trade from the Coromandel Coast, disrupted the region's social and economic balance.[131] The Portuguese determination to edge out the Muslims from the local trade networks by diplomacy or arms enabled the Paravas to negotiate a more favorable niche in the regional division of pearl trade profits. The "pearl" politics in the Gulf of Mannar were complicated, with shifting alliances between various local groups, the rulers of the Sri Lankan kingdoms of Kotte and Jaffna, and the competing Muslim chieftains on the Fishery Coast in Palayakkayal to the south and in Kilakkarai to the north. The Portuguese could ultimately exploit these divisions, although not without setbacks, coming at times from their internal quarrels.[132]

At that time, the Parava fishing community was subjected to different local authorities, Hindu in Vaippar and Vembar, and Islamic in Palayakkayal and Kilakkarai. In 1532, according to a story with a typical overture plot for a communal conflict—of a woman insulted by a Muslim and her husband mutilated in an effort of revenge—tension rose between Parava and Muslim divers from Palayakkayal. However, from an insult to conversion, four years had passed, and incidentally, the initiative of this political move, that is, to convert to the

---

130 The conch shells or chanks were considered emblems of Lord Shiva and were in demand from early times. They were also used in Bengal for the carving of the bangles. James Hornell, The *Sacred Chank of India: A Monograph of the Indian Conch (Turbinella pyrum)* (Madras: Govt. Press, 1914); Susan Bayly, *Saints, Goddesses, and Kings: Muslims and Christians in South Indian Society 1700–1900* (Cambridge: Cambridge University Press, 1989), 322.

131 Jorge M. Flores, "'Cael Velho,' 'Calepatanão,' and 'Punicale': The Portuguese and the Tambraparni Ports in the Sixteenth Century," *Bulletin de l'Ecole française d'Extrême-Orient* 82 (1995): 9–26.

132 Chandra Richard de Silva, "The Portuguese and Pearl Fishing off South India and Sri Lanka," *South Asia* 1, no. 1 (March 1978): 14–28, here 18–20.

religion of the Portuguese, came from an "outsider." According to the Jesuit sources, this idea came from João da Cruz (dates unknown) from Kozhikode, called variously a "Chetti" (a merchant) or a "Malabar" (a Keralite).[133]

As Sebastião Gonçalves pointed out, in 1536, when a delegation of eighty-five Parava leaders, *paṭṭamkattiyār* (பட்டம்கட்டியார்), officially presented their request to be baptized to Captain Pero Vaz de Amaral (in office 1532–36) in Kochi, they offered eight pearls worth twenty thousand *fanões* and some valuable cloth. The gifts were refused, at least in the text, but the baptism took place immediately, and a few clerics were sent to the Fishery Coast headed by the vicar general, Miguel Vaz Coutinho (in India 1533, d.1547).[134] In some thirty villages, twenty thousand Paravas were baptized.[135] As for Cruz, in 1537 he requested from the Portuguese authorities the captaincy on the Fishery Coast and the right to import horses to Kollam to repay his conversion scheme.

However, when Xavier arrived in the area in 1542, himself a missionary novice, he commenced a proper Catholic indoctrination and secured the field for the Jesuit monopoly for over half of the century. The Estado da Índia's weak presence, the rivalry with local political predators, and the Jesuits' sustained "spiritual" control, combined with the Paravas' pre-existing social and family structure, produced a coherent and tightly knit community, an endogamous caste with solid leadership and uniform religious and domestic customs, despite inevitable internal factional struggles.[136]

The emerging Parava elite soon realized that Catholicism could be used to transform their kinship system into a political structure resembling a South Indian "little kingdom."[137] For this particular task, they needed an influential god/father figure capable of bestowing a permanent sense of legitimation on the "noble" lineages headed by the *jāti talaivaṉ* (ஜாதி தலைவன், the caste headman) and his progeny. The confluence of Jesuit proselytism with Xavier

133 Patrick A. Roche, *Fishermen of the Coromandel* (New Delhi: Manohar, 1984), 54; see also Markus P.M. Vink, "Between the Devil and the Deep Blue Sea: The Christian Paravas; A 'Client Community' in Seventeenth-Century Southeast India," *Itinerario* 26, no. 2 (July 2002): 64–98, doi: 10.1017/S0165115300009141 (accessed September 19, 2024); João da Cruz converted to Catholicism in 1536.

134 *Epistolae S. Francisci Xaverii*, 1:244.

135 Gonçalves, *História*, 1:138.

136 Susan Bayly Kaufmann, "A Christian Caste in Hindu Society: Religious Leadership and Social Conflict among the Paravas of Southern Tamilnadu," *Modern Asian Studies* 15, no. 2 (1981): 203–34.

137 The concept of the "little kingdom" has been used in a number of scholarly studies in order to define the segmentary political structure of pre-modern South India. See, for example, Nicholas B. Dirks, *The Hollow Crown: Ethno-history of an Indian Kingdom* (Cambridge: Cambridge University Press, 1987); Pamela Price, *Kingship and Political Practice in Colonial India* (Cambridge: Cambridge University Press, 1996).

elevated to the role of Parava tutelary deity and socio-political interests of the Parava elite, partly created by the Jesuits, succeeded in the next few decades in reformulating the Paravas' corporate identity, internal social relations, and cultural meanings.[138]

While Xavier, besides cutting a father figure, also brought a gift of "miracles," Henrique Henriques (1520–1600), a Jesuit missionary who came to the Fishery Coast in 1549 and stayed on until the end of his life in 1600, gave a gift of "Tamil Christian" speech and captured it in writing. Not only did he write the first Tamil grammar and dictionary for the missionaries' use—for them to learn what everybody thought was a challenging language, notably its phonetics—he also wrote and published pious books for the edification of the Tamil Christians.[139]

By 1552, most of the thirty churches along the Fishery Coast had Henriques's "A Short Compendium in Malabar [i.e., Tamil] Language concerning the Creation of the World, Angels, Men Hell, Heaven, Sin, and Grace."[140] In 1567, Henriques founded a Tamil college in Punnaikkayal in which, in addition to Christian doctrine, music and various languages—Portuguese, Tamil, and Latin—were taught to the Parava youths. It was a long way from Xavier's initial indifference to the indigenous secular education and the reliance on memorization by rote. Paravas were, however, never mere recipients in the language transactions, neither with Xavier nor with Henriques. Moreover, they financed the Jesuit printing works. Henriques wrote in the preface to his "Small Catechism" (*tampirāṉ vaṉakkam*) in Tamil:

> You have desired to have several books that will teach you and your descendants the path to heaven, and therefore you have contributed large sums of money toward the printing. Therefore, we are giving you these books as a gift. Because you have spent large sums of money and established the press, you have gained respect and praise before the world.[141]

---

138 Ines G. Županov, "Prosélytisme et pluralisme religieux: Deux expériences missionnaires en Inde aux XVIe et XVIIe siècles," *Archives de sciences sociales des religions* 87 (1994): 35–56.

139 Xavier S. Thani Nayagam, "The First Books Printed in Tamil," *Tamil Culture* 3 (1956): 288–308. Georg Schurhammer, S.J., and G.W. [George William] Cottrell Jr., "The First Printing in Indic Characters," in Georg Schurhammer, *Orientalia* (Rome: BIHSI, 1963), 317–27.

140 Henriques to Loyola, Kochi, January 27, 1552, *DI*, 2:309.

141 Henrique Henriques, *Doctrina Christam* [...] தம்பிரான் வணக்கம் [*Tampirāṉ vaṉakkam*] [Salutation to God] (Coulam [Kollam]: Collegio do Salvador, 1578), 3. Also called the *Small Catechism*.

In time, as more stable, although not necessarily correct knowledge about each other alleviated the translation problem, Henriques acknowledged the help given to him "by some natives versed in the language" in writing his Tamil books.[142]

The Tamil written word became a stem from which the Christian message was to sprout and blossom. And it did. The language of Tamil Christian piety, a mixture of Parava Tamil idiom and transliterated Portuguese terms for Christian concepts considered untranslatable, was appropriated by indigenous imagination and poured into popular folk songs.[143]

The re-orientation of the communal life in and around churches, the growing popularity of Christian pilgrimage sites, and lavish Christian festivals such as the Corpus Christi became the hallmark of Parava life. The rich Parava merchants financed the building and endowments of the churches. Stone churches eventually replaced the shrines built in Xavier's time resembling fishermen's huts and made of dried palmyra leaves. A certain Manuel da Lima (dates unknown) was responsible, according to Xavier, for the construction of the church in Kombukireiyur in 1544.[144] For the interior ornaments of the church, Henriques was amazed to see that his Christians bought "rich ornaments, better than they ever had," even when the seasonal pearl-fishing, *pescaria do aljofar*, failed.[145]

The churches were not only enriched by decorations, according to the Jesuit visitor, Valignano, but also by a network of indigenous missionary assistants, such as a *merigno* (law officer), a *canacapali* (catechist/sacristan), and a *topaz* (interpreter), who helped some dozen Jesuits tend to their flock.[146]

Besides hereditary notables—*aṭappaṉ* (அடப்பன்), *paṭṭamkaṭṭi* (பட்டம்கட்டி), or *mūpan* (மூபன்)—a whole new ecclesiastical structure was created by the Jesuits and often recruited from prominent Parava families. A *modom* (ecclesiastical overseer), *kanakkapillai*, *ubadesiyar* (sacristan), and *vathiyar* (teacher) joined the secular authorities in controlling all aspects of

142 *Doctrina Christam* [...] கிரிசித்தியானி வண்ணகம் [*Kiricittiyāṉi vaṉakkam*] [Salutation to Christians] (Cochim: Collegio de Madre de Deos, 1579) or the *Big Catechism* and his monumental *Flos sanctorum* (printed in 1586 in Punnaikkayal). See Roche, *Fishermen of the Coromandel*, 51.

143 *DI*, 12:718.

144 *Epistolae S. Francisci Xaverii*, 1:206–8. The first stone church was built on the island of Mannar in 1521. Thekkedath, *History of Christianity in India*, 166.

145 Henrique Henriques to Sociis Lusitanis, Tuticorin, December 30, 1566, *DI*, 7:169.

146 Alessandro Valignano, "Della grandeza, divisione et sito di questa provincia et delli collegii et case che in essa teniamo," Malacca, November 22–December 8, 1577, in *DI*, 13:43. Ines G. Županov, "Jesuit Proselytism versus Resilient Religious Pluralism: Two South Indian Missions in the 16th and 17th Centuries," in Amaladass and Županov, *Intercultural Encounter*, 199–231, here 213.

Parava social and cultural life—economic activities, marriage contracts, communal solidarities, and so on.[147] The growth of an indigenous politico-ecclesiastical order facilitated the growth of the Parava Catholic caste.

Jesuit missionaries recorded the changes taking place, such as the Paravas' eagerness to confess and receive communion, and attributed them to divine gifts rather than the enhanced sense of caste-like reciprocity and tightening of the communal moral economy.

If Xavier's role, and that of other Jesuit missionaries, was of a "spiritual" father of the Parava Christian community, the church, in the sense of a fine texture of economic, social, and spiritual relations, became its "mother." The church socialized the Paravas' dominant cultural principles into distinct ideas and actions. At the same time, a set of particular cultural meanings bound Paravas to the larger Hindu macrocosm. As the church as an institution grew in importance among the Paravas, its social function started to resemble the South Indian temple. It became the "storage" of communal and regional status and power relations.[148] As Jesuits noted with surprise, investing in church ornaments, even when it meant almost starving, was also an investment in prestige and status that could be cashed as an economic asset in the long run. A very elaborate system of "Christian" honors, *mariyātai* (i.e., respect), or graded privileges was created and acted out during the important religious festivals. More importantly, the Parava elite groups, those who managed to distance themselves from traditional fishing, diving, and boat-handling occupations and entered, with the help of the Portuguese, into the wider inter-Asian trade network, enthusiastically encouraged the new church system that sanctioned and legitimized their ascending aspirations.[149]

When, in 1582, Jesuits received the statue of the Virgin Mary from Manila for the church in Tuticorin and christened it the Nossa Senhora das Neves (Our Lady of the Snows), or Panimaya mātā (பனிமய மாதா) in Tamil, the Paravas finally acquired their "mother." Enshrined in the church called Periyakovil (the Big Temple) or Mātākovil (the Mother Temple), she was to nurture the Paravas' sense of corporate identity and enhance the role of the Parava elite, in particular that of the *jāti talaivan̲*.[150] He became a chief protector and donor (*yajamāna*) of the "Mother's" church and, by the early seventeenth century,

147 Roche, *Fishermen of the Coromandel*, 48.

148 Arjun Appadurai, *Worship and Conflict under Colonial Rule: A South Indian Case* (Cambridge: Cambridge University Press, 1981).

149 The confraternities organized by the missionaries emphasized and reflected intra-community stratification. See Josef Wicki, S.J., "The Confraternity of Charity of Henrique Henriques," *Indian Church History Review* 1, no. 1 (1967): 3–8. See also Roche, *Fishermen of the Coromandel*, 52.

150 The official name of the church is Our Lady of Mercy.

had an exclusive right to be seated beneath the statue and to have it bejeweled on the occasion of his installation or marriages in his family.[151] The festival of Our Lady of the Snows (August 5) confirmed the distribution of the ceremonial rank and precedence, and even non-Christian, non-Parava client groups were incorporated into the process.[152]

The Jesuit missionaries also adopted the Hindu custom of *viruntu* (விருந்து), a feast the temple authorities gave to the most prominent patrons. In the long run, this custom of commensality created a permanent division among the Paravas, separating those who ate at the table, the *mejaikārars*, from those who did not, the *kamārakkārars*, who were considered ritually inferior. The *mejaikārar* lineages of wealthy traders constituted an endogamous group intermarried with the *jāti talaivaṉ*'s family and preserved their elite status well into the nineteenth century, when a new set of circumstances brought the two groups into an intra-*jāti* conflict.[153]

Ever since Cruz—the first to hold the title—the office of the *jāti talaivaṉ* became hereditary, and the Cruz lineage assumed the status of Parava "royalty." By the eighteenth century, the Parava community functioned as a South Indian "little kingdom." The Jesuits were gone, and the Dutch and later British replaced the Portuguese, but the structure of the authority and solidarity remained firmly tied around the Paravas' "Catholic" rituals, ceremonies, and beliefs.

By the eighteenth century, some Paravas formed an elite and powerful maritime trading clan. The combination of Christian discipline and the tight-knit pre-existing Parava kinship organization, typical of many specialist occupational groups in the region, favored the successful caste-based conversion. The situation differed significantly from the "volatile" Tamil hinterland, where *bhakti* or devotional worship encountered Christianity with different emotional and epistemic tools. As clients of the Portuguese colonial authorities, Paravas prospered as merchants and migrated to other areas of South India—to Ramnad, Madurai, Tranquebar, and other places on the Coromandel Coast and the Tamil Nadu interior. Catholicism traveled with them, with or without the European priests. Christianity progressed through indigenous "gurus" (religious teachers) and their devotees who were not always aware of the Roman Catholic tradition, nor did they care to belong to a larger Christian community based around the fixed ecclesiastical institutions. By the end of the sixteenth

151 Kaufmann, "Christian Caste in Hindu Society," 211.

152 Non-Christians belonging to the Parava patronage network also invested in other regional churches and celebrated Christian festivals. See, for example, *DI*, 12:670 and *DI*, 11:816.

153 The Jesuits were expelled from the Gulf of Mannar in 1759, but the tradition of *viruntu* continued under the patronage of the *jāti talaivaṉ*. Kaufmann, "Christian Caste in Hindu Society," 221.

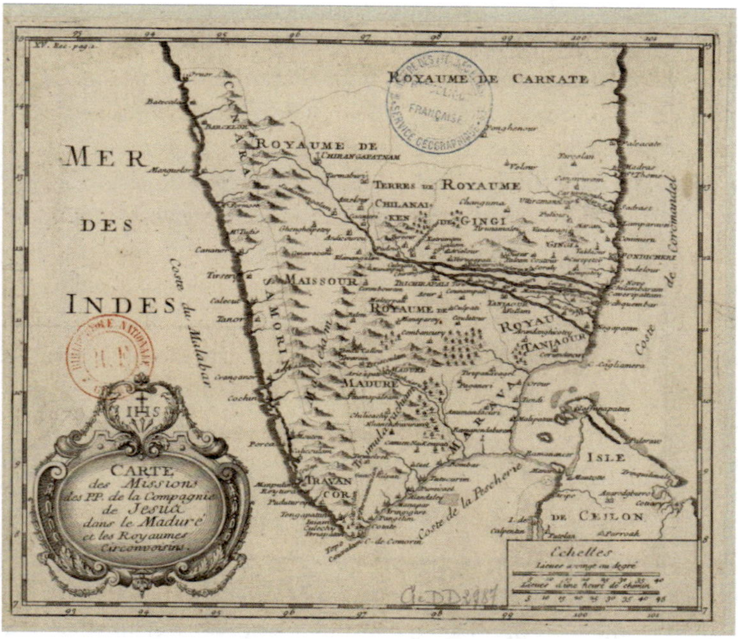

FIGURE 4 "Carte des missions des P.P. de la Compagnie de Jésua dans le Maduré et les royaumes circonvoisins, 1600–1799," Bibliothèque nationale de France, https://gallica.bnf.fr/ark:/12148/btv1b84466697d

century, southern coastal Kerala and Tamil Nadu had forty-five thousand baptized Roman Catholics.[154] The famous inland Madurai mission started as an extension of the mission among the coastal Parava fishermen (see fig. 4).

4.3 *The Madurai Mission: Jesuit Controversial Social and Religious Experiments (1606–1660s)*

In the 1590s, a Jesuit mission for the Parava trading community was established in Madurai, the capital of the Nayaka kingdom in the heart of the Tamil country.[155] It was owing to the Portuguese horse trade, much coveted by the Hindu rulers, that permission was granted to the "Paraṅki (பறங்கி)" authorities to build a

154 Excluded from this count are St. Thomas Christians, who numbered around 150,000 at the time. James C. Houpert, *A South Indian Mission: The Madura Catholic Mission from 1535–1935*, 2nd ed. (Trichinopoly: St. Joseph Industrial School, 1937), 22; Bayly, *Saints, Goddesses and Kings*, 280.

155 For about a hundred Paravas and an occasional Portuguese horse trader. Thekkedath, *History of Christianity in India*, 212. The Madurai Nayaks were Telugu rulers from around 1529 until 1736. R. Sathyanatha Aiyar, *The History of the Nayaks of Madura* (Madras: University of Madras, 1980).

church with a presbytery and a school in this famous temple city and center of Tamil culture.[156] Gonçalo Fernandes Trancoso (1541–1619), an ex-soldier in the Portuguese army, formed as a spiritual coadjutor by Henriques, a Jesuit superior of the Fishery Coast, was the first and the only Jesuit in the mission until 1606 when Nobili, started his famous "accommodationist" experiment.

If Xavier had to deal with the Paravas' problematic corporate self in search of identity and patronage, Nobili could be said to have dealt with individual selves in search of identity, patronage, and salvation. "Salvation" is also a form of patronage in which terrestrial relationships are seen as only a reflection and a defective configuration of the perfect other-worldly ideal. The "new" Madurai mission, established by Nobili and separated from the "old" Fernandes Trancoso's church and residence, was an Italian, cosmopolitan, baroque, and utopian project and, more importantly, often opposed to Portuguese colonial aspirations. For non-Portuguese Jesuit missionaries, one thing was evident by the end of the sixteenth century—Christianization did not equal Portugalization.

According to Nobili, the Paravas, who adopted some visible Portuguese characteristics such as names and certain symbols on ceremonial occasions—the cross of Avis, for example—jeopardized the Jesuits' planetary and lofty goals of evangelization by associating Christianity with the "low-caste," polluting activities (fishing), and lifestyle (drinking alcohol, eating meat, etc.) of the Parava fishermen. In a move similar to Xavier's, which identified elite individuals or groups and made them the first targets of conversion, in Madurai, the young Italian missionary selected the Brahmans for their spiritual and theological expertise and local chieftains for logistical military support.

Centered on the Minakshi temple and Nayaka's palace, the political power network in Madurai was more complex than that on the Fishery Coast. A zealous missionary had a more difficult task than Xavier. The populace was not simply "indifferent to heaven," but, in addition, there were other religious specialists who saw their ritual and sacred territory encroached upon by the foreign, *paraṅki*, holy man. Nobili's reports were cautiously critical of the Brahmans in general, who, in his view, resembled the ancient Jews.[157] On the other hand, he thought that the Brahmans were "confused" about him. Was

---

156 *Paraṅki* or *Parangi* (*frangue*, *fringue*, *firingi*, *firanghi*, etc.) was a generic term for foreigners in India, coming from the West, derived from the Latin "francus." Jesuits spell it in different ways: *parangui*, *prangue*, etc. In seventeenth-century South India, it was mostly used to designate Christians. See Sebastião Rodolfo Dalgado, *Glossário Luso-Asiático* (Coimbra: Imprensa da Universidade, 1919), 406.

157 Ines G. Županov, "Aristocratic Analogies and Demotic Descriptions in the Seventeenth-Century Madurai Mission," *Representations* 41 (1991): 123–48.

he a holy man/*sannyāsī* (in Sanskrit, *caṉṉiyāci* in Tamil) or a fraud/*paraṅki*, Indian or European, chaste or vile? He also attracted hostility from the local religious specialists. In his letters, he skillfully staged the accusations against himself. For example, at a trial of his Brahman teacher, Śivadharma (or Shivakannan [dates unknown]), renamed Bonifacio Xastri after conversion, the Brahmans brought out a catalog of Nobili's "blasphemous statements" against Brahman religion: that it was a "tissue of lies," that giving alms to the Brahmans and taking sacred baths in Rameshwaram or the Ganges did not bring eternal bliss, that kings were higher in nobility than the Brahmans, and that nobody in the Tamil country knew the true God, and, therefore, nobody could be saved.[158]

Although this ventriloquist statement was addressed to his European audience to fend off accusations about his accommodation method, it was the experiments with South Indian social and cultural models that provoked doubts and confusion about his origins and intentions in Madurai. In one *ōlai*, a strip of the palm leaf used for writing hammered to a tree before his church, he made public his origins as that of a Roman *rājā* (king) by birth and a Brahman by profession.[159] Whatever this could have meant to his Tamil audience, this strange genealogy, from a Hindu point of view, showed that Nobili was aware of the rumors' power and probably thought it was more effective to spread an excess of meaning than a lack.

Gonçalo Fernandes Trancoso, Nobili's companion in the field, was the first to denounce him for "going native." Not only did the young Italian missionary sever all his ties with the "old" Madurai church—not permitting Paravas to attend his Mass, not communicating publicly with Fernandes Trancoso, while at the same time eating, dressing, and behaving like a Brahmin hermit (see fig. 5); he also, according to Fernandes Trancoso, refused to be associated with *paraṅkis*.

Finally, Nobili's refusal to follow the Parava model of Catholicism reflected his conception of religious conversion as an individual and intellectual process that should affect first the most learned (Brahmans) and the most noble (kings) like himself who would then spearhead the transformation in a trickle-down movement of cultural change.

Like Xavier, he became a spiritual preceptor, a guru, and a miracle worker, but unlike his famous predecessor, his supernatural powers attracted mostly individual conversions. In his missionary reports, it is clear that most of his

158 Nobili to Laerzio, Madurai, February 20, 1609, in Laerzio to Acquaviva, [Italian] Kochi, November 20, 1609, ARSI, Goa 54a, fols. 2–6 and fols. 17–75.

159 Laerzio to Acquaviva, Kochi, December 8, 1610, ARSI, Goa 54a, fols. 76–92.

FIGURE 5 A Jesuit eating in Madurai. Aquarelle. Source: manuscript confusingly mislabeled *Usages du Royaume de Siam: Cartes, plans et vues en 1688* [peinture], 1688–1700, Bibliothèque nationale de France, https://gallica.bnf.fr/ark:/12148/btv1b55007288r/f87.item

converts belonged to small groups of disgruntled, young Brahmans who, at the time of meeting Nobili, had either or both financial and spiritual problems and of other "high caste," "noble" young men facing similar uncertainties, and of dethroned or contesting *pāḷaiyakkārars* (பாளைக்காரர்); in British usage, *poligars*) or military chiefs, and, more generally, of various men and women facing social, psychological, and biological life-cycle crises. These were all unstable conversion individuals or groups, and despite their "promise" to influence their relatives and kinsmen, the backsliding and opposition from their families were a constant menace.[160]

The *sannyāsī* missionary model, was based on this indigenous Tamil conception of a holy man whose position on a threshold space between the social and the divine was, in fact, the fulcrum of a "political" network. The problem was

160 Pierre Dahmen, s.j., ed., *Robert de Nobili, l'apôtre des Brahmes, première apologie, 1610* (Paris: Edition Spes, 1931); Savarimuthu Rajamanickam, s.j., *The First Oriental Scholar* (Tirunelveli: De Nobili Research Institute, 1972).

that in early modern South India's fluid, segmentary political situation, leadership and "holiness" were up for grabs by numerous exalted spiritual gurus, inspired by a syncretic *mélange* of Islam, popular Hinduism, and Christianity. The ability to gather followers, directly connected with raising funds, performing miracles, and distributing honors, produced patronage networks in which the leader sometimes becomes dispensable. A rival leader, often a disciple, might easily dethrone him.[161]

The Christian life story of Nobili's Sanskrit teacher Śivadharma, a Brahman who was also his informant about all aspects of Brahman culture and learning, exemplifies the problems a solitary missionary faced in Madurai.[162] In Nobili's early letters, he is portrayed as a young, "pagan" philosopher, demonstrating Christian dogmas to his Brahman teachers with the simplicity and tenacity of a "primitive" Christian.[163] Less than a decade later, another side of his character and intentions transpires from a document containing a recantation from some of the converts who had plotted against him a few years earlier. According to the *Testimónio* of 1617, Boniface and a few other exemplary converts, often mentioned as missionary's almost angelic flock, schemed to eliminate the Jesuits and take over the administration of the church.[164] Economic reasons were evoked as the main incentive for conversion, and this *coup d'état* of the local Christians was partly orchestrated behind the scenes by Nobili's Jesuit adversaries in the old (Fernandes Trancoso's) Madurai residence. Bonifacio admitted that a rival Jesuit faction promised him fifteen *fanams*.

Unreliable as they are, these Jesuit reports disclose the intentions and motivations of various local actors precisely when trying to hide or attribute them to a rival party. One of them is that converts were paid for their services in the new residence and church, while in the old Fernandes Trancoso's church, the Paravas continued to contribute to its upkeep.[165] Despite the Padroado's

161 See Bayly, *Saints, Goddesses, and Kings*; Mattison Mines and Vijayalakshmi Gourishankar, "Leadership and Individuality in South Asia: The Case of the South Indian Big-Man," *Journal of Asian Studies* 49, no. 4 (November 1990): 761–86.

162 Margherita Trento studied Śivadharma's biography in more detail. See Margherita Trento, "Śivadharma or Bonifacio? Behind the Scenes of the Madurai Mission Controversy (1608–1618)," in Županov and Fabre, *Rites Controversies in the Early Modern World*, 91–121.

163 Laerzio to Acquaviva, Kochi, December 20, 1609, ARSI, Goa 54a, fols. 2–16 and 17–75.

164 *Testimónio* (by Carnayake Bramane and Bonifacio Xastri) for Archbishop Ros and the rector of the College of Cranganore (Kodungallur), Francisco de Oliveyra, 1617, [Port.] ARSI, Goa 51, fols. 261–65.

165 The method of accommodation was generally considered an expensive project, and this was one of the main arguments against the new Madurai mission advanced at the theologians' consultation in Kochi (1610). Moreover, among Antonio Vico's correspondence, there were a few "private" letters in which he tried to claim his Italian inheritance for

promised financial support, a typical feature of all Jesuit missions was a chronic cash shortage. This problem was even more visible in the new Madurai mission since the missionaries consciously competed with the Brahman establishment.[166] A rich and ostentatious Minakshi temple in Madurai, which served as a focus of social and ritual order, was what Nobili dreamed of replacing with his church. Dreams, alas, were all he could afford and propose to his converts.

Just like Śivadharma, who appeared to have been recruited by Nobili at the time of his financial and spiritual crisis, two brothers, renamed as Visuvasan (also known as Fidelis) and Aleixo saw in the missionary a way out of their difficulties. From fragmentary sources in which the ups and downs of their Christian destinies were carefully silhouetted by the missionaries, alternating between praise and blame of their converts, these two, probably Telugu youths seemed to have been attracted to the "new Madurai mission" on both personal, financial, and social grounds. They were both desperately searching for a spiritual guru; their mother was a poor widow, and they were probably unable to have their presumed or desired social status—claimed to have been of Nayaka lineage, that is, "aristocratic"—fully acknowledged.

Nobili's role as a spiritual guru, a model of religious and social action current in early modern India, helped local "misfits" establish a niche for themselves in the larger society of Madurai. This role resembles a Tamil *periyār*, a "big man," a spiritual leader described by Mattison Mines (1941–2016) and Vijayalakshmi Gourishankar.[167] This South Indian "political" figure was and still is a combination of both sacred and profane qualities. As such, the *periyār* creates new social distinctions for those willing to enhance their status or find a new patron. Reminiscent of a medieval South Asian charismatic king, he is a quasi-divine, altruistic being, distributing benefits and creating his *maṇḍala*, socio-political structure.[168] The *sannyāsī* missionary model, devised by Nobili,

financing the mission. Most of these topics are developed and referenced in Ines G. Županov, *Disputed Mission: Jesuit Experiments and Brahmanical Knowledge in Seventeenth-Century India* (New Delhi: Oxford University Press, 1999).

166 In a letter to Robert Bellarmine (1542–1621), Nobili complained that the (Portuguese) king did not provide adequate support to his mission. He demanded, therefore, that the papacy and the Jesuit curia directly support the Madurai mission just as they did in Japan. Nobili to Bellarmine, Madurai, November 13, 1610, ARSI, Goa 51, fols. 170–71.

167 For an interesting discussion connecting individuality, leadership, and renunciation in South India, see Mines and Gourishankar, "Leadership and Individuality in South Asia," 76.

168 Stanley J. Tambiah, *World Conqueror and World Renouncer: A Study of Buddhism and Polity in Thailand against a Historical Background* (Cambridge: Cambridge University Press, 1976). The concept of *maṇḍalas* or "circles" comes from Kautiliya's political treatise, the

was based on this indigenous Tamil conception of a holy/political man whose threshold space between the social and the divine was the locus of the "universal" order.

Aleixo's and Boniface's *coup d'état* was such an endeavor to dispossess Nobili and take over his "sacred *maṇḍalas*." Aleixo and his brother already operated as his clients, "little kings" or administrators. According to the *Testimónio*, they embezzled money from local Jesuit revenues they were given to collect.[169]

By the 1620s, Nobili and his Italian missionary companion Antonio Vico (1576–1638), surrounded by their shifting population of converts, formed a relatively autonomous group in the fluid world of South Indian politics. The ideal, of course, was to form a *maṇḍala* and transform it into a community and then try adding other *maṇḍalas*. For this purpose, Nobili incessantly tried to recruit local military chieftains or *pāḷaiyakkārars* to become his badly needed "secular arm." Again, his efforts paid off only with the dispossessed, disgruntled, or aspiring political actors. According to missionary correspondence, Erumaichetti (dates unknown), a younger brother of a deceased, important "noble" Telugu chieftain called Nagaichetti (dates unknown), "broke" into "loud sobs and shed an abundance of tears" when he was told about the punishment of hell that his older brother would endure having failed to follow "the law of God and the way of salvation." He expressed the desire to embrace the Jesuit way of salvation as soon as he settled a difficult succession affair in which he was involved.[170] However, as soon as Erumaichetti's "career" crisis was resolved, which consisted, among other things, of a payment of "seventy thousand *scudi* as investiture fee to the Nayak who added other lands to those which that young man has inherited from his brother," he faded away from Nobili's correspondence after a few instances of downright hostility to the missionary.

In his peregrinations through the Tamil country, Nobili managed to attract other *pāḷaiyakkārars*, but his encounters all seemed to follow the same pattern. As soon as their political and strategic situation improved, they opted for Hindu religious specialists rather than Nobili. Jesuits offered extraterrestrial "patronage" that worked well as a consolation only when the earthly one was lacking.

Not all of his converts were "high caste," but all aspired to improve their social status through connection to their "spiritual preceptor." Amator, or Iesupattan, was an over-enthusiastic Christian. "His devotion and strength

---

Arthaśāstra (fourth century BCE). Each circle represented a political and geographical territory of a small king.

169 ARSI, Goa 51, fols. 261–65.

170 Laerzio to Acquaviva, Kochi, November 20, 1609, ARSI, Goa 54a, fols. 17–75.

of character," wrote Nobili, "is such that I cannot help wondering at it myself. He is so inflamed with the desire of suffering and dying for the faith of Christ that he speaks and thinks of nothing else."[171] However, before Amator became Christian, Nobili admitted, he was an equally devout worshipper of idols.[172] His piousness was so great that, before he and his father Gnani converted to Nobili's religion, they supported a *paṇṭāram* who lived in their house.[173]

For Amator and Gnani, Jesuit "ritual community," which was still in formation and had a relatively open membership, provided an expeditious way to enhance their extended family's ritual status. The *paṇṭāram* was dismissed, and Nobili took his place. Although Jesuit documents that reveal his life story dramatize some and suppress other details of his Christian actions, Amator's life crisis corresponded to the status and identity crisis of his kith and kin grouping. The role and position of women, in particular, appeared to have been reformulated to fit new, desired standards of purity and elevated status. Most exemplary missionary stories about Amator's miraculous effects on his wife, nieces, and other female relatives are anchored around the dispossession of women of all extraordinary powers, from simple "stubbornness" to "demonic" possession.[174]

A decade later, summing up a brief necrology of Amator's Christian deeds and virtues, Vico mentioned abolishing polygamy—or polyandry?—in his caste as his last and most important endeavor. Under Vico's indignant pen, this custom assumed a form of "demonic impurity" practiced by those who possessed "degraded intelligence" and reveled in an "abominable promiscuity."[175] At the caste meeting in Tiruchirappalli, Amator managed "to captivate their [the caste headmen's] minds and hearts gradually with his persuasive eloquence," and "burning with undaunted courage, he appealed successively to their reason, their sense of natural decency, public good, and above all he touched that chord that vibrates in every Indian heart: the honor of the family." Furthermore, Vico related that the headmen adopted the principle

---

171 Laerzio to Acquaviva, Kochi, [Italian], November 20, 1609, ARSI, Goa 54a, fols. 17–75.

172 In his Latin treatises, Nobili refuted by way of theological explanation the accusations of his Jesuit adversaries that it was he who was finally "convinced" and turned into a "pagan" rather than his converts. All a missionary had to do was to change the *finis* (an end, a goal, a finality) of a given social custom or cultural expression. And that is what Nobili did from then on, turning every "pagan" custom into a Christian practice.

173 *Paṇṭāram* is a non-Brahman, *Veḷḷāḷa* ritualist.

174 Vico to Laerzio, Madurai, August 31, 1611, in Laerzio to Acquaviva, Kochi, November 25, 1611, ARSI, Goa 54a, fols. 93–129, and Nobili to Vico, June 17, 1610, in Laerzio to Acquaviva, Kochi, December 8, 1610, ARSI, Goa 54a, fols. 76–92.

175 Vico to Palmeiro, Madurai, November 1620, ARSI, Goa 18, fols. 11–12.

of monogamy as a law and established rigorous penalties in case of adultery. Nayak approved all these various provisions and communicated them to the "judges of customary law who are responsible for their execution."

By using the European juridical language of the seventeenth century, what Vico described here resembles a process anthropologists variously described in the twentieth century as "Sanskritization" (Srinivas) or moving up the social scale by selecting and adopting elements of what was considered as prestigious lifestyles.[176] Since important historical data are irrevocably missing from Vico's narrative, all reconstructions of the process are necessarily incomplete and imperfect. Nevertheless, a few significant indications of the indigenous strategy of status elevation resurfaced in Vico's obituary.

From the patchwork of Western accounts that prefigured the problem of polygamy in a variety of ways and invariably imposed their ethical and epistemological framework on the description itself, it is difficult to discern the role that the practice of polygamy played in status negotiations among the Tamils. According to Vico, Amator's efforts to introduce monogamy were, in large part, the result of his conversion to Christianity. However, on the other hand, the "shaming technique" that Amator used to persuade the headmen of his caste, still "pagan," appealing to the sense of caste honor and making "their ears tingle with shame," could not have been efficient without an underlying value grid that promoted maybe not monogamy as such but something like sexual restraint. Adopting monogamy with the stress on "conjugal fidelity" and "rigorous punishment of adultery" and having it approved by the Nayaka king, Muttu Virappa Nayaka (r.1609–*c*.1623), undoubtedly meant that the caste as a whole tried to claim a new, elevated status by espousing, through Jesuit Sanskritized Christianity, what Louis Dumont (1911–98) termed as the "Brahmanic pattern."[177]

By the 1630s, attempts to convert Brahmans and other "high castes" had largely been abandoned, mainly for economic reasons. Henceforth, the missionaries in Madurai focused on those groups that showed an eagerness to improve their ritual status through conversion and adherence to a spiritual leader. A new missionary model was devised for this purpose—the *paṇṭāracāmi*

176 M.N. [Mysore Narasimhachar] Srinivas, *Social Change in Modern India* (Berkeley: University of California Press, 1966).

177 Vico to Palmeiro, Madurai, November 1620, ARSI, Goa 18, fols. 11–12. See Louis Dumont, *Homo hierarchicus* (Chicago: University of Chicago Press, 1970; trans. from French [Paris: Gallimard, 1971]), 112–29. Dumont found two contrasting patterns: Brahmanic (monogamous except in cases of barrenness) and royal (polygynous). As for the middle castes, he found that sororal polygyny was in use, although limited according to the economic resources.

(from *paṇṭāram*, a Śaiva religious mendicant), an adapted imitation of a local non-Brahman ritual specialist.

According to Sanskritic tradition and various South Indian schools of theism to which Nobili, the theologian, was naturally inclined, all manifestations of the divine and supernatural had their sole source in the supreme deity. By mistaking these philosophical texts for Indian "laws" and "prescriptions" for religious behavior and all other accounts and practices as their corruptions, Nobili focused in his proselytizing on local "doctors," the Brahmans, and presumed that their conversion would necessarily cause the Christian message to trickle down into all the other degenerate practices of the lower, "impure" castes.

It took the Jesuits at least two decades to understand that this approach was inadequate, that the Brahmans were not the key figures for global conversion, and that there were other models of holiness and authority. In the course of his life, he experimented with all of them—Brahman *sannyāsī*, *paṇṭāracāmi*, guru, *muṉi*, and so on.

4.4 *Marava Country: Mass Conversion to Martyrdom*

As the militarized clans of Kaḷḷars and Maravas were in the process of regrouping and becoming more caste-like in the second half of the seventeenth century, Jesuit missionaries were able to attract them to Christianity based on a promise to promote their ritual status through spiritual intercession.[178] However, in the long run, they could not secure a permanent conversion partly because the missionaries were too few and partly because these clans turned to other religious specialists and patronage networks who offered local elites a quicker and easier way to translate their military power into ritual honors.

A parallel process, however, worked to undermine the Jesuit global conversion project as it was envisaged by Xavier and later by Jesuits in Madurai when Christianity became associated with individual missionary "heroes" resembling typical Tamil power divinities. In other words, it became a personalized institution depending on the religious preceptor or guru, such as João de Brito (1647–93), or Xavier. According to the individual missionary's charisma, the network of followers either expanded or contracted. Upon the death of such a divine figure, his disciples often splintered away, establishing their personalized sects or groups. In this way, individual converts, usually with only scant knowledge of Christian theology or liturgy, spread into various regions and,

178 On Kaḷḷars and Maravas, see Susan Bayly, *Caste, Society and Politics in India from the Eighteenth Century to the Modern Age* (Cambridge: Cambridge University Press, 2001), 31, 61.

FIGURE 6 A Jesuit penitent in Madurai. Aquarelle. Source: manuscript confusingly mislabeled *Usages du Royaume de Siam: Cartes, plans et vues en 1688* [peinture], 1688–1700, Bibliothèque nationale de France, https://gallica.bnf.fr/ark:/12148/btv1b55007288r/f87.item

with varying success, established their own—more or less independent from Jesuit missions—devotional, *bhakti* sects.

Some Christian *bhakti* communities survived into the nineteenth century and were incorporated into new Catholic and Protestant proselytism movements that swept the South Indian countryside.[179] The typical attire—from head to feet—of a Jesuit missionary in South India is represented in figure 6.

Brito, a Portuguese Jesuit of aristocratic lineage, born in Lisbon in 1647, was a *paṇṭāracāmi* missionary among the Marava and Agamudayar (Akamuṭaiyār, அகமுடையார்) of the Ramnad region.[180] The adherence to Christianity for

179 Léon Besse, S.J., *La mission du Maduré: Historiques de ses Pangous* (Trichinopoly: Impr. de la Mission catholique, 1914); Domenico Ferroli, S.J., *The Jesuits in Malabar*, 2 vols. (Bangalore: King and Co., the National Press, 1939–51).

180 João de Brito (or Britto in English) was until the age of nine a playmate at the court of the future Portuguese king Pedro II (1648–1706, r.1683–1706). In 1662, he joined the Jesuit novitiate and subsequently studied at the Jesuit colleges of Évora and Coimbra. He left for Goa in 1673, where he completed the study of theology. A year later, he joined the Madurai

these warrior pastoralist groups in the second half of the seventeenth century may have had more to do with local political realignments than Christian illumination and fervor. However, the fact is that the "poligars" or *pāḷaiyakkārars* who wanted to shake off the authority of the Tanjore and Madurai Nayaka rulers and fought other poligars who were like them, found Christian saints and missionary teaching attractive as ideological props in their efforts to establish a political and spiritual basis for their rule.[181] The Sethupathi rulers of Ramnad proclaimed themselves patrons of the banyan tree shrine dedicated to St. James at Suranam (Sivagangai district), not because they had Christian illumination but because they perceived it as a special repository of power.[182] The site was considered an integral part of the sacred landscape that coincided with their political sovereignty. In such an agonistic political climate, Brito became all too closely associated with the traditional powerful deity of blood with supernatural and demonic qualities. Accommodating to his converts' expectations, Brito was playing the role of a Christian guru, renaming himself Aruḷāṉantar (the Graceful Joy). He was considered as powerful as Xavier, who was credited with stopping an army of Badaga (Telugu) soldiers when they attacked his Parava Christians in the mid-sixteenth century. The problem was that stopping violence is itself a violent gesture and can backfire. Antonio Criminali (1520–49), a Jesuit missionary among the Paravas, was martyred precisely in the act of protecting his Christians.[183]

Brito was identified as a dynamic hero with healing powers and became associated with one faction of the warring Marava poligars, that of the raja of Siruvaḷḷi (சிறுவள்ளி), whom he converted. The other clan chieftain had no other solution but to eliminate him in an appropriate blood-spilling way after all other solutions were disregarded. In 1686, Raghunatha Deva Kilavan Sethupathi, the first king of the Ramnad or "Maravar" kingdom (r.1671–1710), ordered Brito to leave his territory. However, the missionary returned in 1693 and was immediately killed at a place where the shrine subsequently grew into

mission as a *paṇṭāracāmi* (a non-Brahman penitent). Margherita Trento, "Martyrdom, Witnessing, and Social Lineages in the Tamil Country (Seventeenth and Eighteenth Centuries)," *Annales HSS* (English ed.) (2023): 1–35, doi: 10.1017/ahsse.2022.26 (accessed September 3, 2024).

181 V. Vriddhagirisan, *The Nayaks of Tanjore* (Annamalinagar: Annamalai University, 1942).

182 David Mosse, "Caste, Christianity, and Hinduism: A Study of Social Organisation and Religion in Rural Ramnad" (DPhil diss., Oxford University, 1984), 57; Bayly, *Saints, Goddesses, and Kings*, 395.

183 Županov, *Missionary Tropics*, 147–71. A stunning, dark oil painting portraying Xavier stopping the Badaga army is in the Museu de S. Roque/Santa Casa da Misericordia de Lisboa. See Vítor Serão, "Quadros da vida de São Francisco Xavier," *Oceanos* 12 (1992): 56–69.

a considerable pilgrimage place. Local lore and hagiographies tell a story of exceptional butchery and blood-spilling. The sand in the area became soaked with Brito's blood, according to the folk narratives, and is today distributed as a relic next to the old church in Ōriyūr (ஓரியூர்). Brito lost his Portuguese attributes for the Tamil Christians and became a hero saint, a grounded cult figure, and a Christian tutelary guru.[184]

4.5 *Tamil "Fringe" Christianity*

Without fully understanding the process of social and cultural migration they were involved in and partly flipped in motion, the Jesuit missionaries in the Tamil hinterland, the south Tirunelveli palmyra country, witnessed a mass movement of conversion to Christianity among the lowest castes as a mixed blessing. The low-status artisan and laboring groups such as Shanars (toddy tappers and jaggery producers) and Paraiyars ("untouchables") migrated from the Tamil core zones, subjected earlier to Chola and Pandyan royal dynasties, to new Christian centers established by either Jesuits or more often locally grown Christian charismatic gurus.[185] Vaṭakkaṉkuḷam, situated on the trans-Ghat trade route, became a booming Christian town.[186] Susan Bayly argues that the "modernization" argument does not apply to this eighteenth-century Christian conversion spree in Tamil Nadu since the converts were not opting out of the Hindu social order. On the contrary, their status ("honors") was fabricated by the hierarchical South Indian regional polities. They were transforming themselves into "high" castes by emulating traditional, pure, high-caste lifestyles.[187] Self-ascription took time and communal effort, and Jesuit missionaries provided skills and resources for local social mobilization, albeit not always for the right reasons. Most notably, they promoted one particular "caste" they took to be already "noble" (honorable) and sufficiently pure to become priests of all other low castes. Tamil Veḷḷāḷars (வெள்ளாளர்), who were a loose grouping of different people, some vegetarian, others carnivores, some associated with temple service, some small traders and landholders, were enthroned by the Jesuits as the highest non-Brahman, *sat*-Shudra (pure-Shudra), Christian caste. From the Veḷḷāḷa ranks, often carrying the patronym Piḷḷai, the Jesuits appointed catechists, teachers, and confessors for all Christians.

---

184 Brito was beatified in 1853 and canonized by Pius XI (1857–1939, r.1922–39) in 1947.

185 In 1720, Jesuits converted three thousand Shanars.

186 In 1713, the Jesuits estimated there were four thousand people in Vaṭakkaṉkuḷam. Bayly, *Saints, Goddesses, and Kings*, 407.

187 Bayly uses the term Sanskritization, which has been questioned in recent years. Bayly, *Saints, Goddesses, and Kings*, 408.

The establishment of the Vaṭakkaṉkuḷam church is mainly attributed to Citamparam Piḷḷai (1685–1757), renamed Gnanaprakasam (Ñaṉappirakācam) Piḷḷai after baptism, whose family migrated from Viṭṭalāpuram close to Paḷaiyaṅkoṭṭai (Palayamkottai) and whose ancestors served as *paṇṭāram* temple priests.[188] In the Jesuit accommodationist mindset, the way to build a thriving Christian community was to identify natural leaders and nobility and endow them with extraordinary powers over other lower-caste Christians. The Jesuits could not imagine an egalitarian Christian society at that point for two reasons: (1) they were competing with a hierarchically organized Hindu society, insisting on purity and pollution in all social contacts; (2) for the early modern Christian missionaries, spiritual equality did not mean social equality.

The problem of social and caste inequality, which the Jesuits considered a normal state of affairs in India, created conditions for later violent confrontations between low and high Christian castes. Two different models of sanctity clashed in the long run: the one closer to Tamil *bhakti* cults, and the other church-sponsored Christian "Piḷḷaimār" ritual supremacy, related to an aristocratic accommodationist framework.[189] In the early modern period, the European Jesuits were never numerous, totaling only a few dozen per mission in the best of times, and understood that the missionary and pastoral burden could not be carried out successfully only by the "foreigners." However, they doubted the capacity of the "native" priests to replace them. The prejudice of color and culture had been one of the problems in the Indian mission ever since Valignano defined Indians as incapable of transmitting Christian message. In the seventeenth century, a new generation of Indian priests, none of them admitted to the Society of Jesus, was coming of age and fighting for their place in the Catholic Church hierarchy, primarily in Goa, which was converted in the early sixteenth century.[190]

The case of Tēvacakāyam Piḷḷai (1712–52), a prominent South Indian martyr canonized in 2022, was somewhat different.[191] He was a Nayar warrior, called Nīlakaṇṭa Piḷḷai before conversion, born to a relatively prosperous landholding

188 Bayly, *Saints, Goddesses, and Kings*, 410. On the genealogies of Gnanapragasam's (Ñāṉappirakācam) family and other dynasties of catechists in the region, see Margherita Trento, *Writing Tamil Catholicism: Literature, Persuasion, and Devotion in the Eighteenth Century* (Leiden: Brill, 2022), 282–87.

189 The name Piḷḷai (or honorably Piḷḷaimār) means "a royal child," and it was used by various "noble" or aspiring castes in Kerala and Tamil Nadu in the early modern period.

190 Ângela Barreto Xavier, "Languages of Difference in the Portuguese Empire: The Spread of 'Caste' in the Indian World," *Anuario colombiano de historia social y de la cultura* 43, no. 2 (2016): 89–119.

191 Devasahayam Pillai, in common English transcription, was canonized on May 15, 2022.

family in southern Travancore near Kaṉṉiyākumari.[192] The Jesuits equated the noble status of Nayars in Kerala with that of Veḷḷāḷars in the Tamil country. Nīlakaṇṭa was, therefore, a perfect candidate for Christian leadership and sanctification. He received Christian instruction from a Flemish Catholic mercenary, Eustace de Lannoy (1715–77), employed by the Travancore king, Marthanda Varma (1706–58, r.1729–58). After conversion to Christianity in 1745, he changed his name to Tēvacakāyam (Beloved of God) and, according to local lore, received baptism from Ñaṉappirakācam Piḷḷai in Vaṭakkaṉkuḷam, who reclaimed Tēvacakāyam Piḷḷai's turban and sword as relics for the Vaṭakkaṉkuḷam church.[193] The connection to the saintly personality increased the prestige of the Ñaṉappirakācam catechist lineage, which, from father to son, continued to provide ecclesiastical services in Vaṭakkaṉkuḷam. Although the Jesuits tried to act as the patrons of the cult, local Christian actors took over, not without mutual rivalry, and modeled him into a grounded Tamil Christian saint. Regional oral lore continues to retell and celebrate the story of his life and martyrdom, and many different places are associated with the memory of his torture and the miraculous events he set in motion. For example, at the Muṭṭiṭicaṉ Paṟai, meaning the rocks from which water gushed forth, Tēvacakāyam, suffering horrible pain and thirst, rested his elbow (*muṭṭu*), and a fountain appeared that pilgrims still visit today. The hill where he was shot dead at Āralvāymoḻi (Aralvaimozhi), from which his dead body rolled down, is also a sacred place visited by the devotees.[194]

4.6 *Mysore Mission*

In the Mysore mission, Jesuits appear to have taken very seriously the mid-eighteenth-century directive to engage in proselytizing and pastoral work among the Paraiyars (*paṟaiyār*). Angelo de Franceschi (d. *c.*1750–53), stationed in Karumattampaṭṭi, wrote a letter in 1747 confirming that the Goan provincial had sent three missionaries for the Paraiyars, and they were envied by "ours," he claimed. However, he also suggested that the mission may not survive: "Very many Christians of the Mysore Christians are much afraid that with time, the Gentiles will come to know that the Paria missionaries are noble and familiar

192 Christian Masillamani Agur, *Church History of Travancore* (New Delhi: Asian Educational Services, 1990 [1903]), 280–82.

193 Trento, *Writing Tamil Catholicism*, 59.

194 J. Rosario Narchison, "Towards a Historiography of Martyr Devasahayam," in *India's Christian Heritage*, ed. O. [Oberland] L. Snaitang and George Menachery (Bangalore: CHAI, 2011), 135–45.

with the high born, that is to say, they belong to the Society, and thus the mission may finally be destroyed."[195]

The Mysore mission was one of the most difficult Jesuit missions, comparable to the Marava mission, where Jesuits had to juggle political actors, both Hindu and Muslim, as best as they could without ever being able to rely on the Estado da Índia's military intervention or help. The mission was inaugurated in 1647 by Leonardo Cinnami (1609–76), whose thirst for mission was nourished in Naples by the exemplary martyrdom of his college friend Marcello Mastrilli (1603–37) in 1637 in Japan. He excelled in literary pursuits and wrote and published Mastrilli's biography.[196]

The mission was first established in the region inland and south of Goa, mostly called Canará, which also designated the Kannada language, not to be confounded with the Konkani, called in Portuguese *lingoa canarim*. The first Jesuits were sent to Basrur, Honavar, and Mangalore in the sixteenth century, while in the seventeenth century the mission progressed farther inland toward the "Messur [Mysore]" kingdom, with the capital Seringapatam (Srirangapatna), where Cinnami spent most of his life and ultimately died. Inspired by Xavier's and Mastrilli's enthusiasm for martyrdom, and most importantly by the missionary work in Madurai, Cinnami insisted, after arriving at the mission, on dressing as a *sannyāsī*, traveling inland to the Mysore kingdom, and trying to convert Brahmans. He first traveled to Sathyamangalam, traversing the Ghat mountains, to meet the Jesuits in the Madurai missiona and get instructions and advice on accommodation.[197] According to missionary reports, he lived up to the role of the *sannyāsī* missionary model: walking long distances barefoot, being vegetarian, and engaging in theological discussions with whoever cared to listen. Simão Martinez (dates unknown), in his 1662 letter, attributed

195 Ferroli, *Jesuits in Malabar*, 2:455. Letter from August 12, 1747; Anthoni Muthu Mahimai Dass, "Jesuit Letters and Mysore History Annual Letters and Relations of Mysore Mission as Source for the Secular History of the Kingdom of Mysore from the Year 1648 till 1704" (PhD diss., Pontificia Università Gregoriana, 2020). Franceschi is also credited with literary work in Tamil. See E.R. [Édouard René] Hambye, *History of Christianity in India, Eighteenth Century* (Bangalore: Christian History Association of India, 1997), 3:193.

196 Leonardo Cinnami, *Vita e morte del Padre Marcello Francesco Mastrilli della Compagnia di Giesu: Composta dal Padre Leonardo Cinami della medesima Compagnia* (Viterbo: Mariano Diotallevi, 1645).

197 The Madurai and Mysore missions were juridically two independent missions, because the Madurai mission belonged to the Jesuit Malabar province, whereas the Mysore mission was under the Jesuit Goan province. Mahimai Das, "Jesuit Letters and Mysore History Annual Letters," 253.

to Cinnami miraculous healings, demon exorcism, premonition, and similar divine gifts.[198]

Cinnami also continued his literary activity. He wrote missionary reports, the first of which was "Istoria del Canara" (History of the Canara), which another Italian Jesuit, procurator of the province, Giovanni Maracci (1603–54), brought to Rome from Goa in 1648, among other documents.[199] Years later, he wrote a treatise on the Mysore mission.[200] He was the first to employ the Kannada language for missionary purposes, although not all manuscripts are extant.[201] Maracci wrote that Cinnami also composed a grammar (of Kannada) and a dictionary.[202]

198 Simão Martinez, *Lettera annua della missione di Mayssur (1664–1666)*, via II, ARSI, Goa 45 I, fol. 164.

199 Josef Wicki, "Kanara und die dortige Jesuitenmission 1646, 1648 in der Darsterllung des P. Leonardo Cinnamo S.I. Honävar Anfang 1648, in Addition to 'Istoria del Canara regno dell'India orientale nelle prov. Goana della Compagnia di Gesù,' scritta dal padre L. Cinnamo superiore di quella nuova missione (ms. A.R.S.I., Goa 34, II, ff. 308–372)," *Sonderbruck aus Portugiesiche Forschungen: Erste Reihe; Aufsätze zur Portugiesischen Kulturgeschichte* 16 (1980): 261–345. Maracci also brought *Breve ragguaglio sopra le missioni della Compagnia di Giesù della provincia goana nell'Indie Orientali: Appresentato all'Eminentissima Congregatione de Propaganda Fide dal Padre Giovanni Marracci, della medesima Comp[agni]a, procurator della detta provincia in Aprile dell'anno 1649*. ARSI, Goa 34, fols. 377r–385v. In the French printed version, he put together reports on the provinces of Malabar and Japan, as well as the vice-province of China, *Relation de ce qui s'est passé dans les Indes Orientales en ses trois provinces de Goa, de Malabar, du Iapon, de la Chine, & autres païs nouvellement descouverts: Par les peres de la Compagnie de Iesus; Présentée a la Sacreé Congregation de la Propagation de la Foy, Par le P. Iean Maracci procureur de la province de Goa, au mois d'Auril 1649; A Paris, chez Sebastien Cramoisy, imprimeur ordinaire du roy, & de la reyne regente; Et Gabriel Cramoisy; Ruë S. Iacques aux Cicognes. M. DC. LI.; Avec privilege du roy*. Most of the documents that pertain to the Mysore mission are found in ARSI in the two volumes classified as Goa 45 I and Goa 45 II.

200 Leonardo Cinnami, "Breve relatione della nuova missione del regno di Messur et altri contigui regni autore p. L. Cinnamo (or Cinnami), anno 1651," Goana historia: Mayssur; 1648–69, MS ARSI Goa 45, I, fols. 47–83. Leonardo Cinnami, "Breve relação de nova missão do reino de Messur no Canara," n.d., ARSI, Goa 34 II, fols. 264–89. See also Leonardo Cinnami, *Lettera annua della missione di Mayssur (1663)*, via IV, ARSI, Goa 45a, fol. 1, 40.

201 Mariagrazia Russo, "O pioneirismo na gramaticografia portuguesa de cunho italiano," *Lingue linguaggi* 57 (2023): 113–27. She claims that Cinnami wrote a Portuguese grammar in the context of the mission as well. Only the titles of the manuscripts survive: (1) *Cathechismum copiosissimum mysteriorum principalium nostrae fidei cum brevis compendio eiusdem catechismi*; (2) *Vitas sanctorum in eandem linguam a se conversas*; (3) *Apologia pro mysteriis nostra fidei cum confutatione sectarum, et superstitionum Gentilium regni Messurensis*. Russo, "O pioneirismo," 116. Wicki, "Kanara," 265.

202 Wicki, "Kanara," 265.

The missionaries also provided detailed descriptions and accounts of historical events, some of which they witnessed themselves, in the kingdom of Mysore. Cinnami wrote that the kingdom was positioned at an altitude of around eleven, twelve, and thirteen degrees, surrounded by the kingdom of Bijapur in the north, Kozhikode in the south, Kannur and Belur in the west, and the kingdom of Madurai in the east.[203] By 1666, the missionaries had recorded the growth of the Mysore kingdom—in the north until the kingdom of Ikkeri and Kaveripattanam (conquered by Bijapur), in the east and the south, it extended until the kingdoms of Omalur and Anthiyur—as well as military actions undertaken by the king Narasaraja Wodeyar (1615–59).[204]

Jesuit reports were a form of strategic knowledge, although the Portuguese were unable to capitalize on this information given their diminished army and growing disengagement from territorial expansion. On the other hand, a larger European audience also required the information, excited to know more about foreign fauna and flora, kings, kingdoms, curiosities, and romantic stories of Christian progress.

5 French Jesuit Mission

From the early seventeenth century, Jesuit missionaries in India ceased being sent exclusively by the Portuguese Padroado. The ever-growing problem of jurisdiction between the Portuguese crown, the Roman Propaganda Fide, and the French king's patronage of missions continued into the eighteenth century and was not resolved by the Jesuits until the suppression of the Society of Jesus. The map attributed to Jean Venant Bouchet (1655–1732) shows the geographical ambitions and knowledge of the Jesuit missionary agents (see fig. 7).

The geography of the South Indian missions, officially subdivided by the Padroado into the Malabar province from 1605 and thus separated from Goa, was highly complicated. Initially, in the 16th and early 17th century, the Portuguese Padroado was only able to administer ecclesiastical institutions relatively easily and without much "accommodation" within the territories under the military or administrative control of the Estado da Índia, such as Kochi on the Malabar Coast and, to a lesser degree, São Tomé de Meliapor on the Coromandel Coast. In all other places, from the St. Thomas Christian churches

203 Leonardo Cinnami, [Relation of Mysore Mission, 1649], ARSI, Goa 34 II, fol. 264. Mahimai Das, *Jesuit Letters and Mysore History*, 163.

204 Mahimai Das, *Jesuit Letters and Mysore History*, 163, 171. Mysore is spelled variously in the sources. Today it is called Mysuru.

FIGURE 7 Map entitled “Carte des missions des pères de Compagnie de Jésus dans les Indes orientales,” before 1719, Source: manuscript confusingly mislabeled *Usages du Royaume de Siam: Cartes, plans et vues en 1688* [peinture], 1688–1700, Bibliothèque nationale de France, BNf, Pet. fol. Od 55, view 87, https://gallica.bnf.fr/ark:/12148/btv1b55007288r/f87.%20%20Ms

in Kerala’s hinterland to missions in Mysore and in the Tamil country, proselytism, conversion, and pastoral care were improvised according to the local needs and political imperatives. The interior of Tamil Nadu was politically fragmented, with small Hindu and Muslim kingdoms competing and waging wars on each other, accompanied by ecological disasters such as droughts, epidemics, and famines.[205] In the late seventeenth and early eighteenth century, there were five prominent political actors: the Nayakas of Madurai–Tiruchirappalli, the Carnatic province under the nawab of the Nizam of Hyderabad, the Marava kingdom in Pudukkottai under the Sethupathi, and the Maratha kingdom of

205 Famines affected Marava country in 1709, 1712, 1713, 1716–19, and 1730. They extended to the Carnatic territory in 1735–36 and to the wider Puducherry in 1737–38 and 1747. Smallpox epidemics hit the region twelve times between 1710 and 1750. Adrian Launay, *Histoire des missions de l’Inde, Pondichéry, Maïssour, Coïmbatour*, 5 vols. (Paris: Ancienne Maison Charles Douliol, 1898), 1:xxv, xxxviii, 130–32. Hambye, *History of Christianity in India*, 3:117.

Thanjavur. With their mercantile and colonial interests, the Europeans were also divided and in a state of permanent predatory tug-of-war. From the mid-seventeenth century, the Dutch occupied the Portuguese territories on the Malabar Coast, forcing Jesuit missionaries to move their churches and residences inland under the protection of the local Christians and kings.

To add confusion to trouble, the Dutch permitted the Discalced Carmelite Vicars Apostolic, supported by the papacy and the Propaganda Fide, to set up mission stations in their territories around Kochi.[206] The rivalry between Catholic religious orders simmered and was easily instrumentalized by various historical actors who profited from missionary division. Moreover, a common denominator—"Malabar missions"—refers in the contemporary documents and early historiography to Jesuit missions throughout the eighteenth century in the regions of today's Karnataka and Tamil Nadu states, in the regions of Gingee, Kanara, Mysore, Travancore, Madurai, Marava, Thanjavur, and spreading northward to Golkonda. Puducherry, a French settlement south of São Tomé de Melipor (today called Mylapore, a suburb of Chennai), became the headquarters of the French empire in India and the French ecclesiastical and missionary establishment, including French Jesuit missionaries.

When the French Jesuits arrived in India, dreaming of joining the already famous Madurai mission, they were both welcomed by the Padroado missionaries and treated with suspicion by the Goan church authorities. A volatile political situation consolidated Catholic missionary spirit and political acumen as they tried to pacify and "seduce" local chieftains for the Greater Glory of God and even allowed for sporadic cooperation with the Protestants, mostly German Lutherans from Halle, who settled in the enclave of Tranquebar on the Coromandel Coast, south of Puducherry.[207]

French Jesuits in India are associated with the Carnatic mission, under the patronage of the French king and the Propaganda Fide and with the administrative center in Puducherry.[208] Some early Jesuit missionaries, such as Pierre Martin (1665–1716), arrived individually or were part of the ill-fated mission to

206 The permission was initially granted to the Italian Discalced Carmelite Matteo di San Giuseppe (alias Pietro Foglia [1612–91]) to administer the church in Chethiah, today in Ernakulam. See Ines G. Županov, "Amateur Naturalist and 'Professional' Orientalist: Paulinus a S. Bartholomaeo in Kerala and Rome (18th–19th c.)," *Revista de cultura/Review of Culture* 20 (2006): 77–101.

207 Andreas Gross, Y. Vincent Kumaradoss, and Heike Liebau, eds., *Halle and the Beginning of Protestant Christianity in India* (Halle: Verlag der Franckeschen Stiftungen zu Halle, 2006).

208 In the late seventeenth and early eighteenth century, the mushrooming of small Christian enclaves forced the provincials of the Jesuit Malabar province to delimit south Mysore missions from the Madurai mission and to assign some of the eastern territories, close

Siam that left them "stranded" in Puducherry in 1688.[209] The first batch of missionaries learned their "trade" in the Madurai mission and applied the accommodation method to their new Mission du Carnate. Guy Tachard (1651–1712), one of the "mathématiciens du roi" sent to Siam who ended up in Puducherry and died in Chandannagar (Chandernagore), was the first superior of the French mission. He continued to travel five times between France and India to establish official relations between the king of Siam and the king of France and forge an alliance against the Dutch. In Puducherry, the first three missionaries, Pierre Mauduit (1664–1711), Jean Baptiste de la Fontaine (1669–1718), and Jean Venant Bouchet, invested their energy in the Carnatic mission and were joined by others such as Martin, who also spent ten years in the Madurai mission. According to Jesuit historian Léon Besse (1853–after 1910), there were never more than six missionaries in the French mission, with the total amounting to one hundred for the entire eighteenth century.[210]

Nevertheless, the French mission in India was probably the most well-publicized and known Jesuit mission in India and the Christian world in the eighteenth century. There were two reasons for its notoriety and fame: first, the mission came into being simultaneously with the publication of the *LEC*, and many of the authors were members of the Indian mission; second, the mission was also the theater of the Malabar rites controversy that had simmered before without as yet being named as such but became an ecclesiastical public controversy in Puducherry during and after the visit (1703–4) of the Papal legate and patriarch of Antioch, Charles-Thomas Maillard de Tournon (1668–1710). The same prelate disappointed Jesuit missionaries in Puducherry by issuing his decree *Inter graviores* (June 23, 1704) and therefore condemning the use of Malabar rites in the missions—or the so-called accommodation strategy. He was accused of taking the side of the Capuchins, most notably François–Marie de Tours (d.1709), who went to Rome in 1702 to denounce Jesuit "theft" of the Capuchins' right to proselytize in the French settlement. Capuchins in Puducherry resented the Jesuit conversion monopoly and opposed their

to Puducherry, to the Jesuit missionaries sent by France in 1703 (Hambye, *History of Christianity in India*, 3:160).

209 Pierre Martin's journey to the mission is published in the first *LEC* volume. Pierre Martin to P. De Villette, Balassor (Bengal), January 30, 1699, *LEC* (1703), 1:1–29.

210 See Léon Besse, "Liste alphabetique des missionnaires du Carnatic de la Compagnie de Jésus au XVIIIe siecle," *Revue historique de l'Inde française* 2 (1918): 175–242; Gérard Colas, "Curiosité, science et interaction pédagogique: La mission française jésuite et la mission piétiste de Halle en Inde du sud au XVIIIe siècle," *Etudes epistémè; Revue de litérature et de civilization (XVIe–XVIIIe siècles)* 26 (2014): 1–14, https://doi.org/10.4000/episteme.335 (accessed September 19, 2024).

accommodation method. Tournon subsequently angered the Jesuits in Macau with his hard and forbidding line toward the Chinese rites and mysteriously died in prison.[211]

5.1 *The Malabar Rites Controversy*

For Indian neophytes, Tournon drew up a list of practices that the Jesuit missionaries allowed their Christian converts to perform after baptism and that they henceforward had to renounce: some marriage and baptism customs, the use of ashes to draw symbols or smear them above the eyes, reading "heathen" books, ritual baths, forbidding women to take sacraments during their period, and not providing viaticum to those who were dying in the huts of the untouchables or Paraiyars. The point behind all these practices was to preserve the purity of caste distinctions and hence avoid intervening in the society's pre-Christian hierarchical order. In the Jesuit experience in South India, forbidding the hierarchical order would have arrested and destroyed all missionary efforts at conversion and proselytizing. However, even the final papal bull *Omnium sollicitudinum* (September 12, 1744), which prohibited Malabar rites, left intact certain practices that were conceded to the missionaries in Madurai in the bull *Romanae Sedis Antistes* (January 31, 1623). The Christians were allowed to have *kuṭumi* (the tuft of hair, in the manner of Brahmans), wear *pūṇūl* (the sacred thread like the Brahmans), smear sandal ashes on the forehead, and take daily baths. According to Paolo Aranha, the Malabar rites were primarily Christianized Hindu *saṃskāras* or life-cycle ceremonies.[212]

The most prominent Jesuit and the superior of the mission during the Malabar rites controversy was Bouchet, who personally attended to Tournon and later accused him of inventing conversations with him.[213] He also spent

211 Since Tournon, upon arrival in Macau, abolished the use of "Chinese rites" and annulled the "accommodation" strategy, the Jesuits considered him a direct menace. Imprisoned, he died after allegedly being poisoned by the Jesuits. See also, *Epistola Franciscus Maria Turonensis cappuccinus ad Prop. Fide de ritibus malabaricis*, in V S.O., St. St. QQ 1-h., Archivio della Congregazione per la Dottrina della Fede, Rome. Tours published his *Mémoire* in Liege in 1704, entitled *Questioni proposte alla Sacra Congregazione di Propaganda Fide*. See Sabina Pavone, "Jesuits and Oriental Rites in the Documents of the Roman Inquisition," in Županov and Fabre, *Rites Controversies in the Early Modern World*, 165–89, here 172.

212 Paolo Aranha, "The Social and Physical Spaces of the Malabar Rites Controversy," in *Space and Conversion in Global Perspective*, ed. Giuseppe Marcocci et al. (Leiden: Brill, 2015), 214–34. The question of Jesuit discrimination against untouchables in the new Madurai mission has been studied by Alphonse Manickam, "Les jésuites et l'intouchabilité au Tamil Nadu: Études historiques et anthropologiques sur des approches longtemps différées" (PhD diss., École Pratique des Hautes Études, Paris, 2001), 252.

213 Ferroli, *Jesuits in Malabar*, 2:432.

forty years in the Tamil Nadu, Andhra Pradesh, and Karnataka missions, had been a spiritual advisor to Brito, and had founded the churches in Āvūr and Takkolam (Tarkolam).[214] He chose to be a *paṇṭāracāmi* missionary, and his Tamil name was Periya Cañcīvinātar, or Great Master of Spiritual Healing. Like most French Jesuits, he was an indefatigable missionary, traveler, thinker, and writer. Like Tachard, who defended the mission to Siam, Bouchet traveled to Rome in 1706, accompanied by the Jesuit Francisco Laínez (1656–1715), to defend the Carnatic mission and its accommodationist practices against Tournon's decrees. Laínez brought with him, or wrote on the boat while he travelled to Europe, a treatise, *Defensio indicarum missionum* (Defense of Indian missions), and presented it to the authorities, who treated it with disdain.[215] The treatise also extolled Jesuit travails in their mission territories stretching from Madurai and the Carnatic and Mysore regions, where they cared for 220,000 Christians. Laínez claimed to have baptized twenty thousand people during his twenty years of missionary service.[216] In 1708, Laínez was appointed bishop of Mylapore; he died in 1715 as he visited Bandel in Bengal. On the other hand, Bouchet stayed on until he received a "vivae vocis" confirmation from Cardinal Carlo Agostino Fabroni (1651–1727) that the pope allowed the Jesuits in India to keep all customs except those "detrimental to God's glory and the salvation of the souls."[217]

In 1715, another Jesuit from Puducherry arrived in Rome with yet another document witnessing the reasonableness of allowing the accommodation in the Indian mission. He presented the pope with the signed oaths of fifteen catechists from Madurai and forty-three from other missions, justifying the permitted "rites." Since Pierre Martin, the messenger, died before he could acquire any decisions from the papal curia, another Jesuit missionary, Broglia Antonio Brandolini (1677–1747), traveled to Rome with another witness account signed by fifteen pagan Brahmans and eleven catechists, and printed his treatise *Giustificazione del praticato sin' ora da' religiosi della Compagnia*

214 Francis X. Clooney, *Fr. Bouchet's India: An 18th-Century Jesuit's Encounter with Hinduism* (Chennai: Satya Nilayam Publications, 2005), 1.

215 The text is difficult to find and kept disappearing. See Aranha, "Social and Physical Spaces."

216 In 1703, there were only nine missionaries in Madurai, but Laínez baptized 7,700 catechumens in a single year. Ferroli, *Jesuits in Malabar*, 2:434. The Jesuits suspected that Laínez had been poisoned by their adversaries during his visit to Bandel.

217 Ferroli, *Jesuits in Malabar*, 2:434. The Capuchins in Puducherry treated the "viva voce" declaration of the cardinal as pure invention. The Capuchin party was supported by a Jesuit, Claude de Visdelou (1656–1737), who was appointed bishop by the papal legate Tournon in China and came back to Puducherry hurling accusations against the Jesuits. The Chinese rites controversy thus became connected with the Malabar rites controversy.

di Gesú, nelle missioni del Madurey, Mayssur, e Carnate (Justification of what has been practiced up until now by the religious of the Society of Jesus in the missions of Madurai, Mysore, and Carnatic).[218] The arguments for and against Tournon's decrees and for and against the Jesuit method of accommodating Christianity to "pagan" customs, rites, and imagination fill thousands of pages. Initially, during the seventeenth century, inaugurated by Nobili's and Matteo Ricci's (1552–1610) method in Madurai and China and supported entirely by Valignano, the controversy mainly concerned the Portuguese Padroado. The papacy and the Propaganda Fide sided with Jesuits, who advocated what appeared to be an openness to the cultures of others and provided arguments from the "ancient" church when Christianity had not been legalized in the Roman empire and the Christians had to dissemble their faith. The church was young and vulnerable, the arguments were made, and Nicodemism was a survival strategy. However, the Hieronymite archbishop of Goa, Cristóvão de Sá e Lisboa (*c.*1568–1622), who was an adamant opponent of "accommodation", convened a theological consultation in Goa in February 1619 to publicly denounce the Jesuit method.[219] For the occasion, Nobili wrote his erudite treatise on accommodation, *Narratio fundamentorum* (Narrative of the foundations), and persuaded some Goan theologians, such as the Jesuit visitor André Palmeiro (1569–1635), that the method of accommodation was the only valid strategy in Madurai.[220] Palmeiro wrote from Kochi to Nuno Mascarenhas (1552–1637), Jesuit assistant for Portugal, approving the method but was perplexed by the disrespect to the Portuguese:

> We should not mind that they dress like Brahmans and other similar things that shock some, because by thus doing they will attract them [the Brahmans]; nor if they say that they are Brahmans of the king of Spain or lords of Europe, for in all this they speak the truth, all of which may help them in their purpose. However, to deny that they are Portuguese and refuse to treat with them, even if it could be tolerated by some

218 Broglia Antonio Brandolini, *Giustificazione del praticato sin' ora da' religiosi della Compagnia di Gesú, nelle missioni del Madurey, Mayssur, e Carnate* (Rome: Stamperia della Rev. Camera Apost., 1724).

219 Županov, *Disputed Mission*, 90, 237.

220 In Nobili's obituary of 1656, António de Proença wrote that *Narratio* was written for the Goan Conference; see Županov, *Disputed Mission*, 90. See also Liam Matthew Brockey, *The Visitor: André Palmeiro and the Jesuits in Asia* (Cambridge, MA: Belknap Press of Harvard University Press, 2014).

> amphibology, such an opinion or rather dissimulation cannot be maintained or perpetuated.[221]

The archbishop was not convinced by any of it. Condemning and denouncing Jesuit "noble" pretensions, he wrote that Nobili

> makes himself a living idol, like those despisers of the world who are called *sannyasis*, among whom P. Roberto places himself, to be adored and venerated by all; not like St. Peter and St. John whom the Jews wanted to adore, but like an idol, to which a homage of adoration is rendered, which is not due to it, but to God alone.[222]

Nobili's staunch supporter and patron, in addition to Laerzio, the provincial of the Malabar province, was Ros, who had earlier been forced to devise ways to attract and keep St. Thomas Christians faithful to the Catholic Church by using similar accommodationist strategies. Nevertheless, the opinions were divided. Even among the Jesuits, there was no consensus. The controversy started with Fernandes Trancoso, Nobili's partner in Madurai, who denounced him to the Inquisition and the Goan authorities and even wrote a treatise.[223]

Although the archbishop censured Nobili in Goa, the inquisitor general of Portugal, Fernão Martins de Mascarenhas (1548–1628) approved Nobili's arguments in his *Resolutio questionis de permittendo Brachmanibus Indiae Orientalis lineas, coromineum, et caeteras ceremonias quibus ante suam ipsorum conversionem utuntur* (Resolution of the question related to allowing the Brahmans of Eastern India to use the thread, the tuft of hair, and other ceremonies that they used before their conversion), signed by him and six other theologians in Lisbon on April 18, 1621.[224] He was impressed with Nobili's historical argument that the ancients considered Brahmans equivalent to the wise men of Egypt and Persia, while idolatry had seeped into their teaching through the "ignorance of the succeeding generations."[225] After Lisbon, Rome gave its approval in the bull *Romanae Sedis Antistes*, issued by Pope Gregory XV (1554–1623,

221 Palmeiro to Mascarenhas, Kochi, December 20, 1620, ARSI, Goa 18, fol. 2508. Županov, *Disputed Mission*, 95.

222 Cristóvão de Sá e Lisboa to Muzio Vitelleschi, Goa, February 15, 1620, ARSI, Goa 18, fols. 7–8.

223 Županov, *Disputed Mission*, 95.

224 Županov, *Disputed Mission*, 96.

225 Županov, *Disputed Mission*, 96. *Resolutio questionis de permitiendo Brachmanibus*, Archivo Storico della Congregazione "de Propaganda Fide," Rome, Miscellaneae, varie (1631–54), fols. 107–53.

r.1621–23) on January 31, 1623, which offered a lukewarm *placet* with the proviso "until the matter can be resolved and forever established."[226]

In the eighteenth-century controversy in which French Jesuits were center stage, supporters of the Portuguese Padroado participated more as onlookers than participants since the debate did not concern them directly. The French Jesuit Carnatic mission was not under their patronage. The attack on the Jesuits was orchestrated by other (French) religious orders, all of whom had a grudge against the Jesuits and their vertiginous success in the missions worldwide.

The partisan Jesuit historian Domenico Ferroli (1887–1970) brushes off as ignorant the critique of Fr. Luigi Maria Lucino (1665–1745), which was published in 1729 in Rome as a response to Brandolini's *Giustificazione*. Nevertheless, Lucino's bulky text proves that even a Roman theologian who had never traveled had at his disposal a vast amount of information feeding his comparative and historical perspective.[227] He correctly identified that at the heart of accommodation was the question of caste. This word, coming from the early sixteenth-century Portuguese description of the social system encountered in India, had by the eighteenth century become an important concept of "Indian" difference. Lucino clearly states that all "peoples of Oriental India" are divided into two "factions [*fazioni*]": nobles (*nobili*) and despicables (*ignobili*):

> The first contains various tribes, that they call castes, and they are of the "Bramani," who practice sciences, and they take care of the cult of religion, of Xutres [*Kshatriya*], who are in charge of political government, and of Ray, who are employed to command and as soldiers. The other faction is a mix of various other castes of vile birth that are generally called Pareas.[228]

According to Lucino, these striking divisions were intolerable in Christian theology because they did not distinguish between people based on their wealth or cleanliness but on originating (or not) from Brahma's head or feet. He concluded that those who believe in caste should not be accepted into the Christian fold.[229]

The answer to Lucino came again from Brandolini with an explanation and appeal to Christian charity toward "weak" Indian converts. He claimed that

226 Županov, *Disputed Mission*, 97.

227 [Broglia Antonio Brandolini], *Risposta alle accuse date al praticato sin'ora* [...] *parte seconda* (Cologne, 1729).

228 Luigi Maria Lucino, *Esame, e difesa del decreto pubblicato in Pudisceri* [Puducherry] *da monsignor Carlo Tommaso di Tournon*, 2nd ed. (Rome: Nella Stamperia Vaticana, 1729), 266–67.

229 Ferroli, *Jesuits in Malabar*, 2:440.

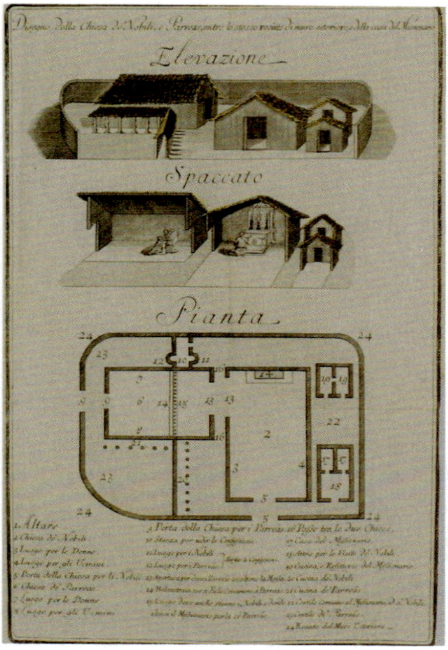

FIGURE 8
Drawing of the church for the nobles and the pariahs within the same exterior walls, and the missionary residence. *Disegno della Chiesa de' Nobili, e Parreas, entro lo stesso recinto di muro esteriore, e della casa del missionario.* Source: anonymous [Broglia Antonio Brandolini], *Risposta alle Accuse date al praticato sin'ora* [...] *parte seconda* (Cologne, 1729), 600–1

allowing caste was a temporary measure to preserve the social and moral integrity of the new Christians and help Paraiyars shed their dirty habits.[230] After a series of papal decisions, each as uncertain and contested by the Jesuits as by their "internal" enemies—a growing group of disgruntled missionaries sent to India by other religious orders—Benedict XIV (1675–1758, r.1740–58) issued the bull *Omnium sollicitudinum*. He confirmed all earlier bulls but added a special provision for the Paraiyar Christians, who were to be administered sacraments, especially the extreme unction in their houses. The segmentary and hierarchical distinctions observed in the Madurai, Mysore, and Carnatic missions amounted to instituting a special kind of missionary who could minister solely to the Paraiyars. The Paraiyar clause immediately became controversial. The enemies within and outside the church decried the sanctification of the "division" among the Christian community. According to Aranha, the depiction of the Jesuit church "divided" by caste—noble castes separated by wall from the low castes—in a "multi-view orthographic projection of a typical church in the Madurai mission," which Jesuit procurator Brandolini sent to the Roman Congregation of the Holy Office in 1725 and subsequently published in the anonymous (!) *Risposta alle accuse* (Response to accusations [1729]) (see fig. 8),

230 Ferroli, *Jesuits in Malabar*, 2:442.

shows "how the sacramental discrimination of the *paṛaiyār* was located at the crossroads between a specific European hierarchical culture and the dynamics of social conflict that characterized early modern South India."[231]

The most famous enemy of the French Jesuits in India and promoter of the condemnation of the Malabar rites was a person with many names. Initially a Capuchin friar in Puducherry between 1737 and 1740 under the name of (Père) Norbert de Bar-Le-Duc (1703–69), he later sported other names (Abbé Jacques Platel, Pierre Parisot, and Pierre Curel) upon his return to Europe, where he reportedly lobbied against Jesuits and published books of which the one published in July 1744 was dedicated to Benedict XIV, just a few months before the pope promulgated *Omnium sollicitudinum*.[232] He spent the rest of his life on the run in different European countries, persecuted by pro-Jesuit parties and protected by their enemies, and even managed to provoke tension between Lisbon and Rome when he argued against Brito's beatification process, insisting that the Jesuit missionary practiced Malabar rites and that his death did not qualify as martyrdom.[233]

When the superior general of the Society of Jesus, Franz Retz (1673–1750, in office 1730–50), suggested that some missionaries should specialize exclusively in Paraiyar ministry, Gaston-Laurent Coeurdoux (1691–1779), superior of the Carnatic mission in 1746, reported that all the missionaries desired precisely that lowest-status ministry.[234] The proof of obedience to the pope was publicized because it camouflaged half a century of the Jesuits' nail and teeth fight against Tournon's decision.

---

231 Aranha, "Social and Physical Spaces," 215–16.

232 In Puducherry, Norbert became friends with the Jesuit Claude de Visdelou (1656–1737), who supported Tournon's case in China and had to flee Macau for Puducherry where he lived from 1709 until death. Norbert wrote and published the funeral oration in Visdelou's honor. Norbert de Bar-Le-Duc, *Mémoires historiques présentés au souverain pontif Benoit XIV sur les missions des Indes orienales, où l'on fait voir que les Pères Capucins missionnaires ont eu reason de se séparer de communion des révérends pères missionnaires jésuites qui on refusé de se soumettre au décret de Monsieur le Cardinal de Tournon, légat du Saint Siege, contre les Rites Malabare*, 2 vols. (Lucca, 1744). For his biography, see L.-J. Husson, "Le P. Norbert de Bar-le-duc, Capucin (Pierre Curel Parisot, dit l'abbé Platel)," *Études franciscaines: Mélange d'histoire et de doctrine* 49 (1937): 632–49; 50 (1938): 63–77, 220–39; 51 (1939): 55–75.

233 Paolo Aranha, "Les meilleures causes embarrassent les juges, si elles manquent de bonnes preuves: Père Norbert's Militant Historiography on the Malabar Rites Controversy," in *Europäische Geschichtskulturen um 1700 zwischen Gelehrsamkeit, Politik und Konfession*, ed. Thomas Wallnig et al. (Berlin: De Gruyter, 2012), 239–70.

234 Ferroli, *Jesuits in Malabar*, 2:452–53.

6 Knowledge

By the mid-eighteenth century, Jesuit missionary networks girdled the globe, but so did the complaints about the order's clandestine dealings, dissimulation, disobedience, atheism, and, in general, an excess of knowledge about everything.[235] Jesuits were global and local, polyglot actors, peddling information and objects from one end of the earth to another and writing letters, treatises, and histories of their success in the most elaborate propagandist style and in as many languages as they mastered. They were also seen as quarrelsome, doggedly defending their opinions, such as those that fueled the controversies over the Malabar and Chinese rites, and many others. They were teachers of the world, having set up the most successful schools that educated most of their intellectual enemies. Finally, their close relationship with the Iberian empire proved to be the nail on which they were "hanged" and sacrificed after the 1750s. The tragic Jesuit finale in the eighteenth century begs the question: Why and how can knowledge be so toxic and self-destructive for an enterprise self-professedly guided by humility, poverty, and obedience? The most obvious reason is that it increasingly became associated with symbolic or real power, and the Society of Jesus did not have the means to sustain and control the effort at centralization in the age of rising, aggressively imperialist nation-states. Jesuits excelled in various fields of knowledge and arts and recorded their results: linguistics, ethnography, botany, pharmacology, medicine, geography, astronomy, mathematics, and various practical techniques (textile dies, growing coconuts), church art, and architecture.

6.1 *Linguistic Enterprise*

The early steps taken, and the roots of the Jesuits' power, were in linguistic knowledge and mobility. Mission was a gigantic and global Jesuit enterprise closely connected with pedagogy and literary production. Loyola's *Spiritual Exercises* stimulated a mandatory "self-cultivation," which strengthened the missionary's interior self and helped him with decision-making in unknown situations, but it also opened the space for the encounter with alterity.

235 Athanasius Kircher (1602–80) was called the man who knew everything; see Paula Findlen, ed., *Athanasius Kircher: The Last Man Who Knew Everything* (New York: Routledge, 2004). See also Francis X. Clooney, *Western Jesuit Scholars in India: Tracing Their Paths, Reassessing Their Goals* (Leiden: Brill, 2020).

Xavier, the first overseas missionary who never truly learned any Indian languages, communicated with whatever he had at hand.[236] His body was the first tool available, hence his premature death due to exhaustion and illness. The second was language. In Goa, in 1542, he wrote that he spoke in a mixture of local and Portuguese idioms with the recent converts, but on the Fishery Coast he identified the language as Malavar. In the territories under the Estado da Índia, Portuguese became a *lingua franca*, although it succumbed immediately to the process of creolization or "barbarization" that the famous intellectual João de Barros (1496–1570) identified in his *Grammática* (1539–40).[237]

Henriques, the Jesuit who replaced Xavier—who was determined to travel farther east—in the mission on the Fishery Coast in 1547 was the first European grammarian of Tamil and author of the *Arte Malavar* (The Malabar grammar). He wrote that

> he had a sort of a grammar [*arte*] to learn it [Tamil] because just as in Latin we learn conjugations, I made an effort to learn this language, [and] I conjugated the verbs; and to arrange [*allar*] preterits, futures, infinitive, subjunctive, etc., cost me great work; also to learn accusative, genitive, dative, and other cases; and as well to learn what comes first, the verb or a number or a pronoun, etc.[238]

Moreover, he insisted that one must know Latin to learn Tamil from his *Arte*. He was enthusiastic about learning and composing grammars of other missionary languages such as Malayalam, Konkani, and Telugu, and even Japanese, Ethiopian (or Prester John), and Chinese.[239]

His missionary experience preceded and perhaps had been discussed at the Council of Trent (1545–63), which declared all languages a gift of God and an appropriate worship medium. Subsequently, the five provincial councils of Goa repeated that preaching and confession should be performed "in the languages of the country."[240] In his long career tending to the converted

---

236 André Retif, S.J., "Missionnaire et savants dans le domaine linguistique," *Studia missionalia* 7 (1953): 394–413.

237 João de Barros, *Grammatica da lingua portuguesa* (Lisbon: Apud Lodouicum Rotorigiu[m], Typographum, 1540).

238 *DI*, 1:285–86.

239 *DI*, 5:688; *DI*, 7:375, 442.

240 "And because such preaching will be so much more fruitful, the better the preachers know the language of those to whom they preach [...]"; Joaquim Heliodoro da Cunha Rivara, *Archivo portugues oriental*, fasc. 4 (Madras: Asian Educational Service, 1992 [Nova Goa: Imprensa Nacional, 1862]), 10.

Parava fishermen, he wrote and printed two catechisms, as well as a *Confession Manual* and a *Life of Saints*. The mission was a complete success, and it became the Tamil language school for the missionaries destined for inland missions in Madurai, Marava country, and the Carnatic mission.

Valignano, who acted as the visitor and later as the provincial, was a significant figure who wholeheartedly supported Japan's and China's "linguistic conquest" but not India's. He was attracted to the "*gente branca* [white people]" of the Far East who were "intelligent" enough to receive the glad tidings by way of reason and through speech, without coercion, unlike "black" Indians. Nevertheless, Jesuit missionaries in the frontier missions had no choice but to invest in local linguistic idioms since they were always a tiny minority among the Christians who remained a small minority among the vast multireligious and multilingual population on the Indian subcontinent.

Even in Goa, where the core area, the so-called Old Conquests, had been aggressively Christianized, and the Portuguese language had initially been imposed in churches, the need for instruction in the local Konkani inspired an English Jesuit, Thomas Stephens (1549–1619), to write *Arte da lingoa Canarim* (The grammar of the Canarim [Konkani] language), printed posthumously in Rachol College in 1640 for the use of future pastors and missionaries.[241] According to the tradition, the grammar was published in Latin script because no "indigenous" fonts were available. A nuanced reason is probably that Konkani was a spoken language of the people and considered by the church authorities as a sort of atavism, doomed to disappear. Of course, it did not, and it flourished through Jesuit use. However, the Jesuits discovered early on that another literary language, Marathi, had a prestige they wanted to give to Christian topics and pastoral literature. Written in eleven thousand stanzas in lyrical verse form, Stephens's *Krista purana* (The story of Jesus) is a mix of Konkani and Marathi, a language with a longer literary tradition.[242] A comment he wrote on

241 Thomas Stephens, *Arte da lingoa Canarim composta pelo Padre Thomaz Estevão da Companhia de IESUS & acrecentada pello Padre Diogo Ribeiro da mesma Cõpanhia e nouemente reuista & emendada por outros quarto Padres da mesma Companhia* (Rachol: Collegio de S. Ignacio, 1640). For other Konkani grammars, see Mario Saldanha, "História de gramática concani," *Bulletin of the School of Oriental Studies* 8, nos. 2–3 (1936): 715–35, and Joaquim Heliodoro da Cunha Rivara, *Ensaio histórico da lingua concani* (Nova Goa: Imprensa Nacional, 1858).

242 Thomas Stephens, *Discurso sobre a vinda do Jesu-Christo Nosso Salvador ao mundo, dividido em dous tratados, pelo Padre Thomaz Estevão, Ingrez, da Companhia de Jesu: Impresso em Rachol com licencia da Santa Inquisição, e ordinario no Collegio de Todos os Santos da Companhia de Jesu anno 1616*, 1st ed. (Rachol, Goa, 1616 [in Roman script]); Annie Rachel Royson, "Audacious Retellings: Multilingualism and Translation in Jnāneswari and Kristapurāṇa," *Translation Studies* 14, no. 2 (2021): 150–66, doi:

the similarity between local languages with Greek and Latin in a letter to his brother in 1583 was probably the first linguistic insight into what would much later be called the theory of an Indo-European language family, attributed to William Jones (1746–94).[243] It is possible that, without mentioning it explicitly, he was referring to Sanskrit, which he also knew and admired.[244]

The Jesuits' elitist conception of culture—as attested by the method of accommodation—commanded the choice of language. As they learned about the local cultures, they tried to identify political and intellectual "nobility," for which they relied on local go-betweens who were always socially and culturally biased.

Just as Stephens employed Marathi to signal the high status of the life of the Christian God, Nobili felt compelled to rewrite the Tamil Christian idiom differently. He rejected Henriques's expressions and translations because they were intended for the Parava pearl-fishing folk on the periphery of the classical Tamil literary world that Nobili identified with Madurai Brahmans. Nobili's Tamil texts, catechisms, and treatises, such as *Ñaṉōpatēcam* (Spiritual teaching), *Āttuma Nirṇayam* (Determination of the soul), and *Tūsaṇattikkāram* (Refutation of blasphemies), were composed in a highly Sanskritized Tamil, an invention of his own.[245] The Jesuit believed that the words he was uttering (and putting on paper) had to correspond to his external *sannyāsī* performance. He publicly stated that he was a Brahman or a learned man from Rome and Kshatriya by birth since he belonged to a Roman aristocratic family. What his interlocutors thought about this is unclear, but he was tweaking his

---

10.1080/14781700.2021.1899980 (accessed September 3, 2024). See also Royson, *Texts, Traditions, and Sacredness: Cultural Translation in Kristapurāṇa* (London: Routledge, 2022); Pär Eliasson, "Towards a New Language: Christology in Early Modern Marathi, Konkani, and Hindustani" (PhD diss., Uppsala University, 2022).

243 *DI*, 12:825. See Thomas R. Trautmann, *Aryans and British India* (New Delhi: Vistaar Publication, 1997), 2.

244 It was a Florentine humanist and merchant in Goa, Filippo Sassetti (1540–88), who wrote about Sanskrit as an Indian language of sciences a few years later and remarked that it was similar to Greek and Roman. It is highly unlikely that Sassetti, who arrived in Goa in 1583 and mostly lived there, and Stephens arrived at this conclusion independently of each other. Stephens resided in Goa between 1579 and his death in 1619. Rosane Rocher, "The Knowledge of Sanskrit in Europe," in *History of the Language Sciences/Geschichte der Sprachwissenschaften*, ed. Sylvain Auroux et al. (Berlin: Walter de Gruyter, 2000), 1156–63, here 1156.

245 Tattuva Potakar, *Āttuma Nirṇayam*, ed. Saverimuttu Rajamanickam (Tuttukuṭi: Tamiḻ Ilakkiyak kaḻakam, 1967); S. Rajamanickam, ed., *Cesunātar Carittiram* (Tuttukuṭi: Tamiḻ, Ilakkiyak kaḻakam 1964); Rajamanickam, ed., *Ñaṉōpatēcam; 26 Piracaṅkaṅkaḷ* (Tuttukuṭi: Tamiḻ Ilakkiyak kaḻakam, 1963); Rajamanickam, ed., *Tūsaṇattikkāram* (Tuttukuṭi: Tamiḻ Ilakkiyak kaḻakam, 1964).

persona to fit local expectations. Accommodation became a Jesuit program of self-fashioning to fit local models of sanctity, priesthood, and literary practices. As the Jesuit Giuseppe Beschi (1670–1747) explained in his Tamil work a century later:

> Because teaching the scriptures (*vētam*) is one among the six occupations prescribed for men of high birth, i.e., Brahmans, they are called *vētiyar*. However, as this name is derived from the occupation, it would be correct to call *vētiyar* anyone who performs that occupation, irrespective of the class into which they were born. Therefore, the *gurus* (i.e., missionaries) who teach the Veda and the catechists sent to preach the insights of the *guru*'s Veda should be called *vētiyar*.[246]

However, Nobili may have based his *sannyāsī* model on an erroneous or prejudiced ethnography provided by his Brahman informants. The *paṇṭāram* (a Śaiva priest for the lower castes) Jesuit missionary model, introduced later by Baltasar da Costa (1610–73), corresponded better to the actual political structure to which the top local elites—such as the Nayakas, the Telugu warriors of Śudra caste—belonged. The Nayakas' kingly authority and scripts of power, and their ideal of personhood, marginalized Brahmans as nothing but ritualist servants and, at times, political advisors.[247] The Brahmanical ideology of purity was not an unbreakable rule, as the Jesuits in Madurai believed at the beginning of their mission. Costa's *paṇṭāram* costume was thus introduced precisely to counter influential non-Brahman religious antagonists in the Nayaka political context. It was especially important for the mission among the Paraiyars, who were emerging as the largest communities of converts.

Costa, like most Jesuits who engaged in the pastoral care of the fledgling Christian communities, composed a language manual for future missionaries, not theological treatises to attract the learned Brahmans.[248] His Portuguese–Tamil dictionary was printed in Ambalakkadavu (Ambalakkad) in 1680, and his

---

246 Trento, *Writing Tamil Catholicism*, 100.

247 Ananya Chakravarty, "The Many Faces of Baltasar da Costa: *Imitatio* and *Accommodatio* in the Seventeenth-Century Madurai Mission," *Etnográfica* 18, no. 1 (2014): 135–58; Narayana Rao, David Shulman, and Sanjay Subrahmanyam, *Symbols of Substance: Court and State in the Nayaka Period Tamil Nadu* (New Delhi: Oxford University Press, 1993).

248 Anand Amaladass, S.J., and Francis X. Clooney, S.J., *Preaching Wisdom to the Wise: Three Treatises by Roberto de Nobili, S.J., Missionary and Scholar in 17th-Century India* (St. Louis, MO: Institute of Jesuit Sources, 2000). See also Soosai Arokiasamy, S.J., *Dharma, Hindu, and Christian, according to Roberto de Nobili: Analysis of Its Meaning and Its Use in Hinduism and Christianity* (Rome: Editrice Pontificia Università Gregoriana, 1986).

grammar of the Tamil language, *Arte Tamul*, of which five copies exist, had been appropriated by other religious actors.[249] Discalced Carmelites used one, and another was the basis for Barholomäus Ziegenbalg's (1683–1719) *Grammatica Damulica* (Tamil grammar).[250] Jesuits rarely signed ancillary manuals such as grammars, dictionaries, and stories meant as language exercises. This is why fragments of Portuguese–Tamil and Tamil–Portuguese dictionaries or shorter vocabularies available in European and Indian archives are difficult to date and attribute.[251] It is possible that all the missionaries kept adding words to their vocabularies as they learned them. As another Jesuit in the Tamil country, Antão de Proença (1625–66), explained in the introduction to his bulky Tamil–Portuguese dictionary published posthumously in Ambalakkadavu in 1679, he used vocabularies that existed in manuscripts and was lucky to inherit at least one from the Jesuit Ignacio Bruno (1576–1659), who worked in South India and Jaffna.[252] He also included words from Jesuit Tamil writers such as Manuel Martins (1597–1665) as well as from the books of the "natives [*naturaes*]."

Proença addressed the central accommodation issue, the hierarchical structuration of society, and language:

> Regarding the purity and dignity of the words (*pureza e alteza de palavras*), I well understand that it would be better to include both high and low, pure and corrupt, following the usage of the various classes of people, so as thus to meet better the range of the language with a particular

249 One of the manuscripts is in Central Library, Panjim, MS M34. Cristina Muru, *The Linguistic and Historical Contribution of the* Arte Tamulica *by Baltasar da Costa S.J. (c.1610–1673)* (Vila Real: Centro de Estudos em Letras, Universidade de Trás-os-Montes e Alto Douro, 2022), i.

250 Daniel Jeyaraj, trans. and ed., *Tamil Language for Europeans: Ziegenbalg's* Grammatica damulica *1716* (Wiesbaden: Harrassowitz Verlag, 2010); Hephzibah Israel, *Religious Transactions in Colonial South India: Language, Translation, and the Making of a Protestant Identity* (New York: Palgrave MacMillan, 2011); Will Sweetman, "Reading Jesuit Readings of Hinduism," *Jesuit Historiography Online*, ed. Robert A. Maryks (Leiden: Brill, 2019), https://referenceworks.brill.com/display/entries/JHO/COM-217891.xml (accessed September 3, 2024); Sweetman, "Bartholomaus Ziegenbalg, the Tranquebar Mission, and 'The Roman Horror,'" in *Halle and the Beginning of Protestant Christianity in India*, ed. Andreas Gross, Y. Vincent Kumaradoss, and Heike Liebau (Halle: Verlag der Franckeschen Stiftungen zu Halle, 2006), 2:797–811.

251 Muru, *Linguistic and Historical Contribution*, 19.

252 Xavier S. Thani Nayagam, "Antão de Proença's Tamil–Portuguese Dictionary, 1679," *Tamil Culture* 6 (1964): 117–132; Thani Nayagam, *Antão de Proença's Tamil–Portuguese Dictionary A.D. 1679* (Kuala Lumpur: Department of Indian Studies, 1966).

> indication of words used by humble and rural people and those current on the Coast and the Kingdom of Jaffnapatam.[253]

However, he continued, he did not have time for that and mainly included those from the kingdom of Madurai. He also excluded poetic words because "they are useless for a practical purpose or the prose, and the Tamil poets have their vocabularies," but included Sanskritic words "spoken by the Brahmans, whose language is more elevated."[254] Another Jesuit grammarian Baltasar da Costa quoted with admiration was Gaspar de Aguilar (1588–?), who wrote an *Arte* recently found in Philippus Baldaeus's (1632–1672) handwritten copy.[255] He was dismissed from the Society of Jesus in 1639 for unruly behavior and was thus easy prey for borrowing without acknowledgment.

Beschi, also called Vīramāmunivar, left an extraordinary and rich literary opus in Latin and Tamil that contains three grammars. This Italian Jesuit and Tamil poet understood the diglossia inherent in Tamil expressions and consequently wrote two grammars of "high" and "low" dialects in Latin. Both texts were highjacked by Lutherans in Tranquebar and subsequently printed by the British.[256] He also wrote a Tamil poetical grammar, *To<u>nn</u>ūlviḷakkam* (The illumination of the classics), which blends Tamil literary culture with Latin and Italian humanism as a foundation for the composition of Tamil Christian (epic) poetry.[257]

For each language and its literary tradition, if there was one, the Jesuits were required to fashion a particular combination of Latin (Portuguese) and local eloquence. However, they also tapped unsystematically into Indian grammatical traditions or grammaticography, unlike Jesuit missionary grammarians in the Americas, who often transcribed oral languages and calqued

---

253 Thani Nayagam, *Antão de Proença's Tamil–Portuguese Dictionary*, 12–13. He did include words from Henriques's *Flos sanctorum* and Bruno's vocabulary.

254 Thani Nayagam, *Antão de Proença's Tamil–Portuguese Dictionary*, 13.

255 Gaspar de Aguilar, *Arte Tamul sive institvtio grammatica linguae Malabaricae* (1659), MS cod. Orient 283, Staats- und Universitäts Biblioteck Hamburg Carl von Ossietzky. See Cristina Muru, "Gaspar de Aguilar: A Banished Genius," in Amaladass and Županov, *Intercultural Encounter*, 353–89.

256 Costanzo Giuseppe Beschi [Vīramāmu<u>n</u>ivar], S.J., *A Grammar of the High Dialect of the Tamil Language, Termed Shen-Tamil*, trans. Guy Babington (Madras: College Press, 1822); Costanzo Giuseppe Beschi [Vīramāmu<u>n</u>ivar], S.J., *A Grammar of the Common Dialect of the Tamil Language Called Koṭuntami<u>l</u>, Composed for the Use of the Missionaries of the Society of Jesus*, trans. George William Mahon (Madras: Christian Knowledge Society's Press, 1848).

257 Vīramāmu<u>n</u>ivar [Costanzo Giuseppe Beschi], *To<u>nn</u>ūlviḷakkam* (1730); Trento, *Writing Tamil Catholicism*, 159.

their grammar on the Latin model.[258] Henriques, who used Latin grammar and Barros's Portuguese grammar to identify the declensions and conjugations, also employed the Tamil grammatical distinction between rational and irrational classes of nouns. Interestingly, Aguilar did not follow Henriques but used Sanskrit terms to define different cases and Tamil grammatical terms when he described the orthography and morphology of nouns and verbs.[259]

As a rule, until Beschi, grammatical manuals taught how to speak and write good Tamil prose. Beschi, however, singlehandedly challenged this trend—although he also wrote polemic prose, mostly against Tranquebar Protestants—by fashioning himself into a Tamil poet-scholar, a *pulavar*, and his major text into didactic versified epic, *Tēmpāvaṇi* (The unfading ornament).[260] He also tried his hand at composing Christian *ammāṉai*, a locally popular and oral ballad genre, such as the *Kittēriyammāḷ ammāṉai*, the life of the Portuguese saint Quiteria (*fl.* second century), and humoristic folk stories.[261] Beschi, under his alias Vīramāmuṉivar, wrote a fourfold Tamil–Tamil dictionary.[262] He was not simply teaching European Jesuits to speak Tamil but taught them and Tamil Christians to appreciate poetic Tamil.

Jesuit grammatical and lexicographical work both preceded and accompanied literary and poetic compositions. The French Jesuit Noël de Bourzés (1673–1735) wrote French–Tamil and Tamil–French dictionaries, while Charles de Montalembert (1682–1743), who found himself administering the French "factory" of Chandannagar in Bengal after the death of company employee d'Hardencourt, is also reputed for his poetry in Tamil in honor of St. Thomas

---

258 Otto Zwartjes, *Portuguese Missionary Grammars in Asia, Africa, and Brazil, 1550–1800* (Amsterdam: John Benjamins, 2011), 27. On "grammatography," see Toon van Hall and Christophe Viele, "Introduction of the *Editio princeps* of J.E. Hanxleden's *Grammatica Grandonica*," in *The Sanskrit Grammar of Johann Ernst Hanxleden S.J. (1681–1732)*, ed. Toon van Hal and Christophe Vielle, with a photographical reproduction of the original manuscript by Jean-Claude Muller (Potsdam: Universitätsverlag Potsdam, 2013).

259 Muru, "Father Gaspar de Aguilar," 365.

260 Francis X. Clooney, S.J., *Saint Joseph in South India: Poetry, Mission, and Theology in Costanzo Gioseffo Beschi's Tēmpāvaṇi* (Vienna: De Nobili Research Library, 2022). The title can be interpreted in two ways as *The Unfading Ornament* or *The Bouquet of Sweet Song*.

261 Ammāṉai is a type of Tamil poetry presented in the form of questions and answers. The title means "The Poem of St. Quiteria." Trento, *Writing Tamil Catholicism*, 35. *Paramārtta kuruviṉ katai* (The story of the guru Paramārtta) is a collection of short stories about a stupid Brahman guru and his even more stupid disciples, available today as graphic comic books.

262 Vīramāmuṉivar [Costanzo Giuseppe Beschi], *Caturakarāti: Iḥtu vīramāmuṉivar ceyta caturakarāti* (n.p.: Ceṉṉaiccaṅkattil accuppatittatu, 1825).

the Apostle and St. Francis Xavier.[263] Jean Venant Bouchet (1655–1732), the founder of Āvūr parish, was a prolific writer in Tamil, as was Carlo Michele Bertoldi (1662–1740) and Giacomo Tommaso de' Rossi (1721–74). They were known locally as Ñāṉacañcīvinātaṉ, Ñāṉappirakācacuvāmi, and Ciṉṉa Cavēriyar.

Although the *sannyāsī* missionary model disappeared because it proved impossible and expensive to maintain, the Jesuit interest in Sanskrit remained. Even Beschi, with his *pulavar* persona based on the Tamil literary model, considered Sanskrit important for a "few things."[264] He also learned that Sanskrit provided genres and blueprints for Tamil literary expression. His *Tēmpāvaṇi*, retelling the life of St. Joseph, is a long narrative poem written in a *peruṅkāppiyam* (long poem) genre, which was introduced relatively late in Tamil from the Sanskrit genre of *mahākāvya*: "Ethical instruction (*upatēcam*) was inherent to the *kāppiyam* genre both in Tamil and Sanskrit."[265] His prose handbook for catechists, *Vētiyaroḻukkam* (Discipline for the catechists), was used by generations of Protestant missionaries. Just as Nobili tried to combine Tamil and Sanskrit in his catechetical texts, Johann Ernst Hanxleden (1681–1732), known in Kerala as Arnos Padiri, focused in his studies and writings on both Malayalam and Sanskrit.[266] Paulinus a Sancto Bartholomaeo (1748–1806), a Discalced Carmelite missionary of Croatian origin, who arrived more than forty years after Hanxleden's death, is credited with preserving and bringing many of Hanxleden's writings to Rome. Manuscripts of his grammars and dictionaries of Malayalam and Sanskrit are still available in different European libraries. He is also known to have copied and annotated Sanskrit grammatical texts such as *Siddharūpa* (The correct form), *Vyākaraṇa* (Explanation), and a Sanskrit dictionary, *Amarakoṣa*, which came to be known under the name of

263 H. Castonnet des Fosses, "Le R.P. Charles de Montalembert, missionnaire aux Indes au XVIIIe siècle," *Annales de l'Extrême Orient et de l'Afrique* 8 (Paris: Challamel Ainé, July 1885–June 1886): 321–36, https://www.google.co.in/books/edition/Annales_de_l_Extr%C3%AAme_Orient_et_de_l_Afr/9hlAAQAAMAAJ?hl=en&gbpv=1 (accessed September 19, 2024); Danna Agmon, *Colonial Affair: Commerce, Conversion, and Scandal in French India* (Ithaca, NY: Cornell University Press, 2017), 209. Kanchana Mukhopadhyay, "Bengal," South Asia, Bibliothèque nationale de France, https://heritage.bnf.fr/france-southasia/en/bengal-article#_ftn4 (accessed September 19, 2024).

264 Trento, *Writing Tamil Catholicism*, 199.

265 Trento, *Writing Tamil Catholicism*, 220–21.

266 Christopher Vielle, "Devotional Christianity and Pre-Indology in Early Eighteenth-Century Kerala: Johann Ernst Hanxleden, S.J., Alias Arnos Padiri, Scholar and Poet," in *Transposition and Transformation, Controversy and Discovery: On the Christian Encounter with the Religions of Eighteenth- and Nineteenth-Century India*, ed. Karin Preisendanz and Johanna Buss (Vienna: Samlung De Nobili, 2021), 1–48.

its author as *Amarasinha*. Most of these texts collected by Hanxleden were published and commented on in Latin by Paulinus in late eighteenth- and early nineteenth-century Rome.[267] Even the manuscript of the *Grammatica Grandonica* (The Sanskrit Grammar) written in Hanxleden's hand bears the notation of Paulinus and at least two archivists. Interestingly, Hanxleden used Latin as the metalanguage of his Sanskrit grammar and Portuguese for his treatises on Malayalam.[268] Based on Hanxleden's copies and annotations, Paulinus was able to publish in Rome the first two printed Sanskrit grammars: *Sidharùbam seu grammatica Samscrdamica* (The correct form or the Sanskrit grammar [1790]) and *Vyàcarana seu locupletissima Samscrdamicae linguae institutio* (The explanation, or the richest institution of the Sanskrit language [1804]).[269]

Stephens was the first Jesuit interested in Sanskrit, but he left no traces of his learning. However, in addition to Hanxleden, the most important Jesuit Sanskritist was Heinrich Roth (1620–68), who served as a missionary at the Mughal court in Agra. There were quite a few French Jesuits who learned Sanskrit, such as Martin, Mauduit, Gilbert Ducros (1692–1730), Memmius René Gargam (1686–1754), Jean-François Pons (1698–1753), and Jean Calmette (1692–1740).[270]

267 Paulinus a Sancto Bartholomaeo, *Amarasinha, sectio prima de caelo ex tribus codicibus indicis manuscriptis* (Rome: Apud Antonium Fulgonium, 1798); Van Hall and Viele, "Introduction," 7.

268 Van Hall and Viele, "Introduction," 8.

269 Carmela Mastrangelo, "History and Pedagogy of Sanskrit Grammar through the works of Western Missionaries: Johann Ernst Hanxleden and Paulinus a Sancto Bartholomaeo," *Indologica Taurinensia* 41–42 (2016): 83–98; Ines G. Županov, "Orientalist Museum: Roman Missionary Collections and Prints (Eighteenth Century)," in *Ancient to Modern: Religion, Power, and Community*, ed. Ishita Banerjee-Dube and Saurabh Dube (New Delhi: Oxford University Press, 2009), 207–35; Ludo Rocher, *Paulinus a S. Bartholomaeo: Dissertation on the Sanskrit Languages*, Studies in the History of Linguistics 12 (Amsterdam: Benjamins, 1977).

270 Memmius René Gargam (1686–1754) was the scribe and probably co-author with Pons of the Telugu–Sanskrit–French dictionary sent to France in 1730. Jean Calmette (1692–1740) claimed to have written verses in Sanskrit in 1737. See Gérard Colas, "Les traditions sanskritistes de la mission du Carnate entre oubli et réinvention," in *Le sanctuaire dévoilé: Antoine-Léonard de Chézy et les débuts des études sanskrites en Europe, 1800–1850*, ed. Jérôme Petit and Pascale Rabault-Feuerhahn (Paris: Bibliothèque nationale de France, 2019), 17–38. Also, Gérard Colas and Usha Colas-Chauhan, "*Une pensée en morceaux*: Two Works from the Carnatic Mission; A Refutation of Metempsychosis in Sanskrit and a Collection of Sermons in Telugu," in Amaladass and Županov, *Intercultural Encounter*, 62–87. On Calmette's Sanskrit translations, see Anand Amaladass, s.j., and Richard Fox Young, *The Indian Christiad: A Concise Anthology of Didactic and Devotional Literature in Early Church Sanskrit* (Anand: Gujarat Sahitya Prakash, 1995).

Pons's survey of Sanskrit literature was published in 1743 in the *LEC*.[271] Pons also composed a Sanskrit grammar in Latin with Sanskrit words in Bengali script since he resided in Chandernagore until 1732 and worked with Bengali Sanskrit pundits. He seems to have been initiated in two different ancient Indian grammatical models: *Saṃkṣiptasāra* by Kramadīśvara (*fl.* late thirteenth century), a follower of Pāṇini's (*fl.* between fourth and seventh century BCE) grammar, and *Mugdhabodha*, by Bopadeva (*fl.* early thirteenth century), using a different metalanguage than Pāṇini.[272] Incidentally, Roth, whose pundits were in Benares, followed yet another school of Sanskrit grammarians (the Sārasvata). While studying grammar, Pons was naturally initiated into Indian systems of Scholastic philosophy, including logic.[273]

Before moving to Puducherry in 1733, Pons started sending from Bengal Sanskrit manuscripts to Paris for the Parisian Bibliothèque du Roi, at the time under the helm of Abbé Jean-Paul Bignon (1662–1747). In 1718, Bignon had asked missionaries to send him curious manuscripts, and more than 160 volumes arrived in Paris, becoming a prestigious core collection of "Indien" manuscripts of the Bibliothèque national de France.[274] Pons continued to work on Sanskrit in Puducherry and in the French Carnatic mission, where Telugu Brahman scholars, versed in the Pāṇinian tradition, provided their expertise. In addition to Pons's grammar, an annex in Telugu and Roman script was sent to Paris in 1772 by another Jesuit, Gaston–Laurent Coeurdoux. Although Abraham Hyacinthe Anquetil–Duperron (1731–1805), a famous early

271 Pons to Jean-Baptiste du Halde, *LEC*, ed. Louis-Aimé Martin (Paris: Desrez, 1849), 2:642–48.

272 André Couture, review article, "Pierre-Sylvain Filliozat, À l'origine des études sanscrites: La Grammatica Sanscritica de Jean-François Pons S.J. Étude, édition et traduction; Paris, Éditions de Boccard (coll. 'Mémoires de l'Académie des Inscriptions et Belles-Lettres,' 56), 2020, 296 p.," *Laval théologique et philosophique* 77, no. 2 (2020): 324–26, https://doi.org/10.7202/1090564ar (accessed September 19, 2024).

273 Filliozat, *À l'origine des études sanskrites*; Arnulf Camps, "The Sanskrit Grammar and Manuscripts of Father Heinrich Roth, S.J. (1620–1668): Introduction; The History of his Sanskrit Manuscripts," in *Studies in Asian Mission History 1956–1998* (Leiden: Brill, 2000), 84–104; Pierre-Sylvain Filliozat, "L'approche scientifique du sanscrit et de la pensée indienne par Heinrich Roth, S.J. au XVIIe siècle," in *L'œuvre scientifique des missionnaires en Asie*, ed. Pierre-Sylvain Filliozat and Jean Leclant (Paris: Académie des Inscriptions et Belles-Lettres, 2012), 17–30. For the Jesuits in the Mughal mission, see Alexandre Coello de la Rosa and João Vicente Melo, *The Jesuit Encounters with Islam in the Asia-Pacific* (Leiden: Brill, 2023), 38; Gérard Colas and Usha Colas-Chauhan, "An 18th-Century Jesuit 'Refutation of Metempsychosis' in Sanskrit," *Religions* 8, no. 9 (2017): 192, doi: 10.3390/rel8090192 (accessed September 3, 2024).

274 Gérard Colas, "Les manuscrits envoyés de l'Inde par les jésuites français entre 1729 et 1734," in *Scribes et manuscits du Moyen-Orient*, ed. François Déroche and Francis Richard (Paris: Bibliothèque nationale de France, 1997), 246–62.

French Orientalist, tried to publish it, the text remained in manuscript form. It was, however, used by the first students of Sanskrit in Paris.[275] Coeurdoux's rich and varied opus of writings—linguistic, ethnological, botanical, and astronomical—met a tortured destiny of being plagiarized, misunderstood, and treated with indifference until the twentieth century.[276] Although he made a number of important linguistic insights, his elucidations were part of a dogmatic Christian paradigm. He thus provided an important account of connections between Sanskrit, Latin, and Greek, only to conclude that they resulted from the post-Babel dispersion.[277]

6.2 *"Ethnographic" Production*

Jesuit "ethnographic" sensibility when encountering overseas cultures was closely and primarily connected to their proselytizing goals, unlike the contemporaneous interest of the travelers and merchants who noticed commercial items, curiosities, female bodies, and similar "secular" objects.[278] Although Jesuits also indulged European audiences with "edifying" and "curious" narratives, enshrined in the title of the famous eighteenth-century French Jesuit collection printed in Paris, the focus on religious experiences runs through all ethnographic-like texts. Most of the early Jesuit ethnographic fragments tried to distinguish the religious appurtenance of the encountered peoples: Were they Muslim, Gentile, or Christian—*mouros, gentios, cristãos*? Minute descriptions of gods and rituals (ceremonies) offered to them were added to the evolving classification grid. The description aimed to identify non-Christian "errors" and extirpate, destroy, or correct them. New descriptive categories emerged as they acquired more specialized knowledge in the missions outside the Portuguese colonial territories. Some of them, like "casta," were Portuguese epistemic tools to distinguish and hierarchize non-Christian social groups; others were indigenous self-appellations such as "Bramenes," "Nayres," "Chatins," and many others followed. The distinctions were based alternatively on perceived civility, social hierarchy, skin color, and purity of blood. The extent to which the Portuguese

275 Rocher, "Knowledge of Sanskrit in Europe," 1158; Urs App, *The Birth of Orientalism* (Philadelphia: University of Pennsylvania Press, 2010), 363–430; Stéphane van Damme, "Capitalizing Manuscripts, Confronting Empires: Anquetil-Duperron and the Economy of Oriental Knowledge in the Context of the Seven Years' War," in *Negotiating Knowledge in Early Modern Empires*, ed. László Kontler et al. (New York: Palgrave Macmillan, 2014), 109–28.

276 See Murr, *L'inde philosophique entre Bossuet et Voltaire*.

277 Rocher, "Knowledge of Sanskrit in Europe," 1158.

278 Joan Pau Rubiés, *Travel and Ethnology in the Renaissance South India through European Eyes, 1250–1625* (Cambridge: Cambridge University Press, 2000).

"caste" label refurbished the Indian sense of self-perception is still debated today.[279] According to Sumit Guha, "the Iberian idea of bounded, normatively endogamous groups based on biological (of 'blood') descent" had been "added to the chaotic mix of social categories in southern Asia in the 16th century."[280] The Jesuits' unintentional contribution to the contemporary debates over the nature of Hinduism—as a source of the ideology of Hindu *varna* (color) classification often confounded with caste—is evident in their insistence on clearly defining the distinction between "religious" and "political." Nobili and Fernandes Trancoso sharpened their arguments as they fought each other in the first decades of the seventeenth-century Madurai mission. Although they "used" the same locally learned literati, Nobili's Brahmanically inflected point of view made him conceive of Indian civility as based on "political" customs. He also admired certain "theological schools"—as opposed to others that were "worshippers of idols"—that showed traces of monotheistic revelation. Missionaries, according to Nobili, had to work through the Sanskrit theological text to discern "indifferent" or non-religious cultural material presumed to be the acceptable object for inclusion into Christianity. All one had to do, according to the Jesuit Scholastic theories, was to change the object's interior purpose (*intentio*). The theological analysis in his Latin treatises, awash with nominalism reminiscent of Pierre Abélard (*c.*1079–1142), revealed that almost all the indifferent things (*ex natura sua indifferentes*) were transformable through the act of volition.[281] He concluded that Indians have "one civil way of life (*civilem cultum*)" but "many religions (*religionem vero multiplicem*)."[282] The method of accommodation was advised to preserve "civility" and divert erroneous intentions from the "religious sects." Moreover, he maintained that a person can change religious sect (by becoming Christian, for example) but not their caste (*strips*). This precocious ethnographic insight into a caste system, based on the Brahmanical view of Indian society, fed anthropological theories of the twentieth century, most directly that of Dumont.[283]

279 Xavier, "Languages of Difference in the Portuguese Empire," 89–119.

280 Sumit Guha, *Beyond Caste: Identity and Power in South Asia, Past and Present* (Leiden: Brill, 2013), 24–25.

281 Robert de Nobili, *L'apôtre des Brahmes: Premiere apologie, 1610*, trans. and annotated "Responsio" by Pierre Dahmen (Paris: Editions Spes, 1931), 96.

282 *Roberto de Nobili on Adaptation*, ed. Saverimuttu Rajamanickam, S.J., trans. of *Narratio fundamentorum* (Palayamkottai: De Nobili Research Institute, 1971), 112–13. *Religio* in this period had a meaning of "religious sect" or "religious order," not a unified religious system. Ines G. Županov, "*Antiquissima Christianità*: Indian Religion or Idolatry? (17th–18th c.)," *Journal of Early Modern History* 24 (2020): 471–98.

283 Dumont, *Homo hierarchicus*.

Fernandes Trancoso questioned the Italian Jesuit ethnographic description and definition of Indian society as "civility" while he saw it as nothing but the "machine of Brahmanism (*máquina do Bramanismo*)."[284] According to him, Brahmanism was a quintessential paganism. His label—Brahman*ism*—subsequently had a long historical afterlife.

The first steps toward accommodation, however, based on the distinction between political and religious rites and customs, were taken, interestingly, in a "Christian" missionary context by Ros, a famous Jesuit writer in Syriac and Malayalam and Nobili's early patron and supporter. It was his ethnographic insight that St. Thomas Christians resisted "reforming" their liturgy and customs to fit Portuguese Catholic ecclesiastical norms for fear of losing prestige and high caste status.[285] As a Jesuit historian in Goa put it in the early eighteenth century:

> These oriental nations are inordinately passionate about their customs. The efforts to impose our [customs] on these nations as if they are the commandments of God or as the precepts of the church is tantamount to making the yoke of the Gospel very heavy to them and to add difficulties in the conversion of the pagans.[286]

Jesuit ethnography in India is often embedded in texts refuting religious "errors" of the pagan and Christian societies the Jesuits encountered. Both Nobili and Fernandes Trancoso were engaged in a battle of proofs and testimonies. Fernandes Trancoso, in particular, provided a detailed description of the life-cycle ceremonies performed by the Brahmans, while Nobili focused on providing a classificatory list of primary sects and sectarian divisions. Around the same time, Giacomo Fenicio (1558–1632) and Diogo Gonçalves, Jesuit missionaries in Kerala, wrote similar treatises describing life-cycle ceremonies, accounts of "pagan" gods and mythologies surrounding their birth and deeds, descriptions of geographical territory and local political arrangements.[287]

---

284 Županov, *Disputed Mission*, 35.

285 Mecherry, *Testing Ground for Jesuits*, chapter 5, 351–438.

286 Francisco de Sousa, *Oriente conquistado*, 2:72; Antony Mecherry, S.J., "*On the Errors of the East Syrians* (by Francisco Ros, S.J., 1586): An Introduction with English Translation of a Latin–Syriac Treatise from Early Modern Malabar," *AHSI* 91, fasc. 181-I (2022): 187–222.

287 Jacobo Fenicio, *Livro da seita dos indios orientais*, ed. Jarl Charpentier (Uppsala: Alqvist & Wiksells Boktryckeri-A-B, 1933). The *Livro da Seita dos Indios Orientais* was completed in 1609 and was to serve as a handbook of "paganism" for the missionaries. Giacomo (or Jacome, Jacobo) Fenicio, alias Arthunkal Veluthachan, also wrote a report on the tribal Toda in the Nilgiri Mountains. Anthony R. Walker, *Between Tradition and Modernity*

According to his "temperament," each saw and recorded what he considered curious and strategic information. Fenicio, who developed descriptions and qualifications of power-filled Indian divine figures, carefully painting a background against which he would ultimately propose (or impose) his psychological definition of a Hindu person as a sexually high-strung being without a proper sense of ethical or theological direction, who reveled in extremes.[288] Compared with today's descriptions of Hindu mythology, his assessment sometimes resonates with the conclusions proposed by Sanskritists such as Wendy Doniger. She contends that the Hindu mentality does not function through compromises but tends to exaggerate polarities, "including potentially dangerous excesses."[289]

On the other hand, Diogo Gonçalves wrote both as a missionary and a Portuguese spy. He provided strategic information on, for example, the exact location of temples, the quantity of precious materials kept in the precincts, and the feasibility of an attack by Portuguese soldiers, to which he actively exhorted his compatriots. The temple of Chimindirão (Suchīndram), dedicated to Śiva and located between Kōttār and Kanniyākumāri, is, according to Gonçalves, built "in the flatland, a league away from the beach from where the Portuguese, if they so desire, can attack since it is the best place on the Cape (Comorin) to disembark."[290]

Leading up to and after the beginning of the Malabar rites quarrel, a series of documents and manuscripts in addition to those by Fernandes Trancoso, Gonçalves, and Fenicio were focused on "gentile errors": Manuel Barradas's (1572–1646), *Livro da Seita dos Indios Orientaes principalmente dos Malavares* (The sect of the East Indians, mostly Malabars [1609])[291] and *Breve relação das*

and Other Essays on the Toda of South India (New Delhi: B. R. Publishing Corporation, 1998), 101.

288 *Stricto sensu*, according to the Jesuit description of, and prescription for, human subjectivity, personhood would not be an appropriate word at all for "Hindu" and "pagan" human beings because the field of "personal" action and choice was too restricted. For an interesting view of the history and historiography of individualism in the Renaissance, see John Martin, "Inventing Sincerity, Refashioning Prudence: The Discovery of the Individual in Renaissance Europe," *American Historical Review* 102, no. 5 (December 1997): 1309–42. A collection of articles dealing with Indian subjectivity was published in *Cahiers Confrontation* 13 (Spring 1985). Unfortunately, editorial misrepresentation of issues and authors made the project irrelevant.

289 Wendy Doniger O'Flaherty, *Asceticism and Eroticism in the Mythology of Śiva* (Oxford: Oxford University Press, 1973) (my citation is from the French edition, *Śiva: Érotique et ascétique* [Paris: Gallimard, 1993], 110).

290 Gonçalves, *Historia*, 83.

291 Biblioteca Pública de Évora (Portugal), Manizola, cod. 29–2.

escrituras dos gentios da India oriental e dos seus costumes (A short account of the writings of the Gentiles of the East Indies and their customs [n.d.]),[292] and Brito's *Breve noticia dos erros que tem os Gentios do Concão na India* (A short account of the errors of the Gentiles of the Konkan in India [n.d.]).[293] Brito's text had been appropriated by European authors, even including staunch anti-Jesuit authors such as the Venetian adventurer Niccolò Manucci (1638–1717) and Huguenot physician Charles Gabriel Dellon (1649–*c.*1710). Manucci, close to the Capuchins in Puducherry and thus an enemy of the Jesuits, incorporated Brito's text into the account of his travels, albeit excluding the passages in defense of the Jesuit method of accommodation. Dellon's translated version of Brito's treatises omitted the discussion on Hinduism.[294] Another version was included in the eighteenth-century bestseller on religious ethnography *Cérémonies et coutumes religieuses de tous les peuples du monde* (Religious ceremonies and customs of all the people in the world [1723]), assembled by Jean-Frédéric Bernard (1683–1744) and Bernard Picart (1673–1733).[295]

Another Jesuit in Kerala, Francisco Garcia (1580–1659), who served as an archbishop of St. Thomas Christians who were on the verge of rebelling against Portuguese priests throughout his tenure, translated popular Portuguese

292 In *Collecção de notícias para a história e geografia das nações ultramarinas*, vol. 1, no. 1 (Lisbon: Academia das Ciências de Lisboa, 1812), Panduronga Pissurlencar attributed this treatise to Fernão de Queirós: "Um Hindu, autor desconhecido de duas publicações portuguesas," separata of the *Memórias* (Classe de Letras) (Lisbon: Academia de Ciências de Lisboa, 1959), 7:129–32.

293 Biblioteca de Ajuda (BA), *Miscelânea Ultramarina*—século XVII, cod. 51–VII–27, fols. 81v–116r. See Theodor Zachariae, "Über die 'Breve noticia dos erros que tem os Gentios do Concão da India,'" *Nachrichten von der Königlichen Gesellschaft der Wissenschaften zu Göttingen, Philologisch-historische Klasse aus dem Jahre 1918* (Berlin: Weidmannsche Buchhandlung, 1918), 1–34.

294 Ricardo Nuno de Jesus Ventura, "Conversão e conversabilidade: Discursos da missão e do gentio na documentação do Padroado Português do Oriente (séculos XVI e XVII)" (PhD diss., Lisbon University, 2011); Joan Pau Rubiés, "From Christian Apologetics to Deism: Libertine Readings of Hinduism, 1600–1730," in *God in the Enlightenment*, ed. William J.J. Bulman and Robert G. Ingram (Oxford: Oxford University Press, 2016), 107–35, here 115. By 1700, the manuscript circulated in a French translation possibly composed by Jean Venant Bouchet, with the title "Relation des erreurs qui se trouvent dans la religion des gentils Malabars de la coste de Coromandel dans l'Inde." According to Rubiés, Bouchet was responding to antiquarian debate in Europe. Joan Pau Rubiés, "From Antiquarianism to Philosophical History: India, China, and the World; History of Religion in European Thought (1600–1770)," in *Antiquarianism and Intellectual Life in Early Modern Europe and China, 1500–1800*, ed. Peter N. Miller and François Louis (Ann Arbor: University of Michigan Press, 2012), 313–67.

295 Sweetman, "Reading Jesuit Readings of Hinduism," 6.

stories from Malayalam into Portuguese. Catholics were particularly quick to appropriate narratives with ethical and pious messages. His translation of the life of an exemplary Indian king, Vikramaditya, and King Hariścandra's ordeal remained in the manuscript until the twentieth century.[296] These texts were found in myriad recensions and oral literature in Sanskrit and vernacular Indian languages. They belong to a genre of "mirrors for princes." David Gordon White has called Hariścandra the "Job of medieval India."[297] The life of Hariścandra is part of the Purāṇic tradition (historical narrative), while Vikramaditya is a famous king figure in Indian folklore and stories (*katha*) written in Sanskrit and Prākrits. Garcia showed his manuscript text with translations of Indian "histories" to the Discalced Carmelite Vincenzo Maria di Santa Caterina da Siena (1626–79) in the mid-seventeenth century. Vincenzo included their summaries in his travelogue, but the Jesuit text was not published until the twentieth century.[298]

Polemical Jesuit texts in Indian languages, in prose and versified, have not yet been adequately studied and are still awaiting accurate editions and translations. Jesuit and pious editors in the twentieth century mostly decided misguidedly to cut out polemical sections to signal contemporary respect for ecumenism and tolerance.[299] Many of them languish in manuscripts and archives inaccessible until recently, which is still true with archives in India. Beschi's *Vētaviḷakkam* (Illustration of the scriptures), a robust polemic in Tamil

296 A manuscript of the Hariścandra story in Marathi, attributed to Vishnu Das Nama, in Roman transcription from the Jesuit college in Rachol and dated to the first part of the seventeenth century, may have been the source of Garcia's translation. The text is in the Biblioteca Pública de Braga, codex 773, fols. 71–101. On Vishnu Das Nama, see Christian Lee Novetzke, *Religion and Public Memory: A Cultural History of Saint Namdev in India* (New York: Columbia University Press, 2008); [Dom Garcia, S.J.], *O homen de trinta e duas perfeições e outras histórias* (*Ms. Opp. NN.192 do Arq. Rom. S.J.*), ed. Josef Wicki, S.J. (Lisbon: Agencia Geral do Ultramar, 1958). *Mārkandeyapurāna*, cantos 7 to 9 is where the story of Hariścandra is told; versions exist from the medieval period in Sanskrit and regional languages. The ur-story is present in a different shape in the Vedic literature, in *Aitareya Brahmana* (7.13–18). David Shulman, *The Hungry God: Hindu Tales of Filicide and Devotion* (Chicago: University of Chicago Press, 1993).

297 David Gordon White, *Myths of the Dog-Man* (Chicago: University of Chicago Press, 1991), 84.

298 Xavier and Županov, *Catholic Orientalism*, 299.

299 Fenicio's *Seita* in Portuguese underwent the same editorial cuts. The most learned and industrious Jesuit historians of the twentieth century, Josef Wicki and Georg Schurhammer (1882–1971), thankfully remained faithful to accepted historical methods. Anand Amaladass and Richard Fox Young openly professed the principle of omission in an otherwise important book—Amaladass and Young, *Indian Christiad*—dealing with Christian literature in Sanskrit.

against the Tranquebar missionaries, enjoyed many editions and responses from the Protestants. Some Jesuit polemical and didactic texts fell into the "wrong" hands and were used for purposes directly opposed to the initial intention. Such is the case of *Ezourvedam*, a text that Voltaire (1694–1778) mistook for a translation into French of ancient Indian deist philosophy.[300] It was probably no more than a French Jesuit notebook with Sanskrit translations for preaching and catechesis. In 1763, Louis-Laurent de Féderbe, Chevalier Maudave (1725–77), commander of a French fortress in Karikal, gave a copy to Voltaire. Modern research suggests that the work was initially written in French, possibly by the Jesuit Antoine Mosac (1704–79), and was meant to be translated into South Indian vernaculars. The authorship is uncertain. It is believed that Nobili and Calmette may have inspired the composition of the Sanskrit texts preserved in the Puducherry mission and mistaken as translations of the original Vedas.[301] The best-studied appropriation of Jesuit ethnographic-cum-didactic writings is the case of Coeurdoux, whose 1777 treatise—*Moeurs et coutumes des Indiens* (Mores and customs of the Indians)—a classic of early ethnography, was plagiarized by both Nicolas-Jacques Desvaulx (1745–1817), who published it in France in 1777, and by Abbé Jean-Antoine Dubois (1765–1848), director of the MEP.[302]

6.3 *Natural History*

Although medicine and botany were not taught in Jesuit colleges, Jesuits who were global travelers were expected to give an account of the social and natural world and their health in their correspondence. The state of Jesuit bodies was important information since the administration of missionary networks depended on the careful distribution of able-bodied men. Only healthy members, with few exceptions, were sent overseas.[303] Just as education was a criti-

300 Ezourvedam's title is made to resemble the title of Jesus Veda (Iesuvedam).

301 See Ludo Rocher, *Ezourvedam: A French Veda of the Eighteenth Century* (Amsterdam: John Benjamins, 1984), 20.

302 Sylvia Murr, "L'Indologie du père Coeurdoux, apologétique et scientificité," in *L'Inde philosophique entre Bossuet et Voltaire*, 2 vols. (Paris: École française d'Extrême-Orient, 1987). Jean-Antoine Dubois was a member of the MEP who had inherited many materials from the Jesuits upon the dissolution of their order, and he published them in his book in addition to Coeurdoux's text. Dubois sold his text to be translated in English for the then-huge sum of £800, and his book became an authoritative British ethnography: Abbé J.A. Dubois, *Description of the Character, Manners, and Customs of the People of India, and of Their Institutions, Religious and Civil* (London: Longman, Hurst, Rees, Orme, and Brown, Paternoster-Row, 1817).

303 One exception is the famous Jesuit moral theologian, Francisco Rodrigues (*c.*1515–73), who was sent to Goa. Research on his writings as legal theologian has recently been

cal Jesuit task in Europe, natural history and, especially, medical knowledge imposed themselves in the missions. Already in 1546, a Hospital of the Poor Natives was established in Goa by the Jesuits, and by the end of the sixteenth century they became the most cherished administrators of the Goan Royal Hospital.[304] Pedro Afonso (*c.*1528/30–78), a temporal coadjutor in the Society of Jesus, started his career as a surgeon in 1560 in the Hospital of the Poor Natives, "attached" to the Jesuit College of Saint Paul. Unable to become an ordained priest, he described his medical profession as another "fishery of the souls (*pescaria das almas*)."[305] However, within Jesuit missionary ranks, curing the body was of lesser importance than curing the soul.[306] Jesuits were even more famous for their pharmacies in Goa, Macau, and all major capitals of the Portuguese empire. Ever curious about indigenous healing techniques and medicines, they combined and peddled recipes and techniques worldwide, thus acquiring a massive field of experimentation. By the end of the seventeenth century, they had acquired a monopoly over sales of pharmaceutical products in specific areas such as the Philippines.[307] Many Jesuit pharmacological products were strategic secrets.[308] A Florentine Jesuit, Gaspar Antonio (*fl.* mid-seventeenth century), a temporal coadjutor just like Afonso a hundred years earlier, made a name for himself in the pharmacological world for his

---

taken up by historians. See Rômulo da Silva Ehalt, "Casuística nos Trópicos: A pragmática teológico-moral de Francisco Rodrigues na Ásia portuguesa (séculos XVI e XVII)," *Revista de história da sociedade e da cultura* 19 (2019): 399–418.

304 João Manuel Pacheco Figueiredo, "Goa dourada nos séculos XVI e XVII: O hospital dos pobres do padre Paulo Camerete, esboco de sua reconstituição histórica," *Studia* 25 (1968): 117–46; Xavier and Županov, *Catholic Orientalism*, 100.

305 Ines G. Županov, "Curar o corpo, sarara alma: A missão médica jesuíta na Índia do século XVI (Curing the Body, Healing the Soul: The Jesuit Medical Mission in Sixteenth-Century India)," *Oriente* (Revista quadrimestral da Fundação Oriente) 11 (2005): 3–19. Pedro Afonso to the members in Europe, Goa, December 1, 1560. *DI*, 4:749.

306 See the case of Giovanni Battista de Loffreda; Županov, *Missionary Tropics*, chapter 6, 195–231.

307 Ostwald Sales Colín has shown that in 1635, two pharmacists from Mexico, Cristóbal Flores and Urban Martínez, were awarded an *asiento* (a licensed monopoly) from the viceroyalty over the provision of medicines for the Philippines. Ostwald Sales Colín, "Las actividades médicas en las Filipinas durante la primera mitad del siglo XVII," *Perspectivas latinoamericanas* 2 (2005): 167–86. Šebestián Kroupa, "*Ex epistulis Philippinensibus*: Georg Joseph Kamel, S.J. (1661–1706) and His Correspondence Network," *Centaurus* 57 (2005): 229–59; Kroupa, "Georg Joseph Kamel (1661–1706): A Jesuit Pharmacist at the Frontiers of Colonial Empires" (PhD diss., University of Cambridge, 2019).

308 Jorge M. dos Santos Alves, "A pedra-bezoar: Realidade e mito em torno de um antídoto (séculos XVI e XVII)," in *Mirabilia asiatica: Produtos raros no comércio marítimo*, ed. Jorge M. dos Santos Alves, Claude Guillot, and Roderich Ptak (Wiesbaden: Harrasowitz Verlag, 2003), 121–34.

Goan *pedra cordial*, as efficacious as *bezoar stone*, that is, not at all, except for its psychological effect on the trusting patients.

On the other hand, Jesuit bioprospecting succeeded in identifying active medicinal substances in relatively common plants and commercializing fruits and vegetables. A substance called "fever bark" or "Jesuit bark" or quinine (Cinchona species) found in Peru cured the Chinese emperor Kangxi (1654–1722, r.1661–1722), while the discovery and use of coconut trees became a significant source of revenue for the Jesuits in Goa. An anonymous seventeenth-century Jesuit manual on selecting, planting, and tending coconut palm trees—*Arte palmarica*—is an exemplary treatise on agronomy and the cultivation of coconut trees.[309]

Jesuit writers were generally very versatile—some were able to write equally knowledgeably about Indian ethnography and botany and astronomy. The art of astronomical observation and recording stellar events was a task of Jesuit astronomers wherever they were. Between August and November, the three comets that appeared in 1618 were sighted by many, including Wenceslaus Pantaleon Kirwitzer (1588–1626) in Goa and Antonio Rubino (1578–1643) in Kochi.[310]

The self-effacing, true polymath of the French mission, Gaston-Laurent Coeurdoux, stands out among the French Jesuits. After Gervais Papin (1656–1712) in Bengal, who wrote about different arts and techniques, medicine in particular, and Calmette, who also learned Sanskrit, wrote on astronomy, and was the first to use the word *ayurveda* (in 1732) in his description of the local medical systems, Coeurdoux was one of the most industrious and prolific Jesuit writers on natural sciences.[311] He wrote about everything, including Indian mordant-based textile printing and dyeing, and contributed to discussions in Paris among the chemists in the Royal Academy of Sciences (Académie royale des sciences).[312] In 1738, he sent grains of medicinal plants

309 Xavier and Županov, *Catholic Orientalism*, 105.

310 R. [Ramesh] C. Kapoor, "Nur ud-di Jahangir and Father Kirwitzer: The Independent Discovery of the Great Comets of November 1618 and the First Astronomical Use of the Telescope in India," *Journal of Astronomical History and Heritage* 19, no. 3 (2016): 264–97.

311 Arion Roşu, "Les missionnaire dans l'histoire des science et des technique indienne (I): Un inédit jésuite sur la phytothérapie indienne au XVIIIe siècle," *Journal of European Ayurvedic Society* 3 (1993): 174–228.

312 Cotton was very difficult to dye, and the knowledge of "mordants" bonding the color was considered an industrial secret. George Bryan Souza, "The French Connection: Indian Cottons, Their Early Modern Technology and Diffusion," in *How India Clothed the World: The World of South Asian Textiles, 1500–1850*, ed. Giorgio Riello and Tirthankar Roy (Leiden: Brill, 2009), 347–63.

to be planted or studied in Europe with the name list and short description.[313] Responding to the "Enlightenment" ideas in Paris, he wrote in 1742 in a letter on Indian textile coloring that the Jesuits could acquire "knowledge[s], which communicated to Europe, would contribute perhaps to the progress of sciences and the perfection of arts."[314]

Jesuit knowledge collected in India is an impressive catalogue of fragments of Indian Sanskrit and vernacular texts encompassing various disciplines and *in situ* observations and measurements.[315] Not all were as sedentary as Coeurdoux, but the result was the same. Tachard left accurate astronomic observations in his travel diaries—he traveled three times between Europe and India. He also collected Sanskrit astronomical texts—one of which he presented to Louis XIV (1638–1715, r.1643–1715) in 1687—containing rules for the computation of longitudes of the sun and the moon.[316] Measuring longitudes, latitudes, and magnetic declinations through astronomical observation was commissioned by Gian-Domenico Cassini (1625–1712), the director of the Paris Observatory in the 1670s. Jean-Baptiste Colbert (1619–83) personally sent Jesuits overseas to do the required measurements.[317] Colbert also employed the Jesuits in China to study astronomy, and they were in close touch—as much as the postal service allowed—with their French colleagues. Antoine Goubil (1689–1759), whose research on traditional Chinese astronomy influenced French astronomer and mathematician Pierre Simon Laplace (1749–1827), exchanged letters with Claude Stanislas Boudier (1687–1757) in India, who famously traveled from Chandannagar to Jaipur at the invitation of Maharaja Sawai Jai Singh II (1688–1743), the Kachwaha Rajput ruler and the Mughal-appointed governor of Agra and Malwa (in 1719). The Jesuit mission in Jaipur was primarily a "scientific mission" that started sometime before 1740 with Anthony Gabelsberger

313 Roşu, "Les missionnaires dans l'histoire des sciences et des techniques indiennes," 196. Roşu, "Les missionnaires dans l'histoire des sciences et des techniques indiennes," 189; *LEC* (Paris, 1743), 26:173. On the fabrication and priming of textiles, see *LEC* (Paris, 1722), 15:392.

314 Roşu, "Les missionnaires dans l'histoire des sciences et des techniques indiennes," 196, 189. See the letter by Turpin in 1718 from Puducherry, *LEC* (Paris, 1722), 15:393–404.

315 Of ninety-eight Jesuits in the French missions, not all were savants and researchers.

316 Dhruv Raina, "Betwixt Jesuit and Enlightenment Historiography: Jean Sylvain Bailly's History of Indian Astronomy," *Revue d'histoire des mathématiques* 9 (2003): 253–306.

317 Dhruv Raina, "French Jesuit Scientists in India: Historical Astronomy in the Discourse on India, 1670–1770," *Economic and Political Weekly* (January 30, 1990): 30–38; Raina, "The French Jesuit Manuscripts on Indian Astronomy: The Narratology and Mystery Surrounding a Late Seventeenth–Early Eighteenth Century Project," in *Looking at It from Asia: The Processes That Shaped the Sources of History of Science*, ed. Florence Bretelle-Establet (New York: Springer, 2010), 115–39.

FIGURE 9 Jay Prakash, Jantar Mantar (Astronomical Observatory), Jaipur, India
PHOTO: AUTHOR, 2024

(1703–41) and Andreas Strobl (1703–58), who contributed to the maharaja's project of constructing (from 1727) his new town of Jaipur based on auspicious astrological rules, underscored by astronomical measurements.[318] Astrology was associated with kingship and divinity in Hindu and Muslim traditions.[319] During the same period, the maharaja constructed astronomical observatories in Jaipur, Delhi, Benares, Mathura, and Ujjain. The best-preserved compound with astronomical instruments is in Jaipur (see fig. 9).

318 Dhruv Raina, "Becoming All Things to All: French Jesuit Scientists and the Construction of the Antiquity of the Sciences of India," in *L'Inde des Lumières*, ed. Marie Fourcade and Ines G. Županov, Purushārtha 31 (Paris: Éditions de l'École des hautes études en sciences sociales, 2013), 335–57, doi: https://doi.org/10.4000/books.editionsehess.22722 (accessed September 3, 2024).

319 Gauvin A. Bailey, "A Portuguese Doctor at the Maharaja of Jaipur's Court," *South Asian Studies* 11, no. 1 (1995): 51–62; Dhruv Raina, "Circulation and Cosmopolitanism in 18th-Century Jaipur: The Workshop of *Jyotishis*, *Nujumi*, and Jesuit Astronomers," ed. Corinne Lefevre, Ines G. Županov, and Jorge Flores, Purusārtha 33 (Paris: Éditions de l'École des Hautes Études en Sciences Sociales, 2015): 307–30.

Although Jai Singh II's astronomy was initially derived from Indian sources, "his contact with modern astronomy commenced in 1724, when he began working on the Jantar Mantar in Delhi and initiated a discussion with *Danayan-i-Firang* ('learned men from the West')."[320] In 1734, he invited French Jesuit astronomers Boudier and Pons to Jaipur, his capital. Although the Jesuits' stay was short—despite traveling one thousand miles from Chandannagar—they nevertheless made copious measurements of the latitudes and longitudes of about sixty Indian towns and observed two eclipses in 1734.[321]

If Jesuit measurements were correct, their interpretation of Sanskrit and the vernacular treatises they procured from local astronomers/astrologers was tweaked to fit their and their European audience's eighteenth-century cultural and epistemic expectations and imperatives. One of them was to locate human history in the antediluvian timeline and chronology, contradicted by Chinese and Indian sources, especially concerning the universal deluge. The dispersion of the nations and the deluge had to be fixed to combat deist critics such as Voltaire, who claimed that it never occurred and that all religions shared a universal core. Moreover, the philosopher also insisted that Brahmans and Chinese were "more reasonable," a claim he derived paradoxically from Jesuit missionary reports.

Coeurdoux's interest in astronomy had a lot to do with his effort at accommodating ancient people, Indian and Chinese, within Christian chronology. His antediluvian hypothesis also included "geography" since he claimed that ancient people lived close to the fiftieth parallel, and thus, Brahmans were descendants of the northern people who arrived in India via Mount Caucasus.[322] Coeurdoux claimed that the North, associated with the cold climate, was thus the cradle of intelligent people who invented sciences and that they eventually migrated southward. Coeurdoux's proposition confirmed the Aryan hypothesis, which was made famous by Jones and British Orientalists. Most of the climate and linguistic theories of Aryan migration had their early precursors in Jesuit missionary speculations. Contemporary Indian society and religion were considered degenerated and disfigured compared to their early

---

320 Dhruv Raina, "'Come, let us ascend to the heavens': The Jantar Mantar at Jaipur and the Politics of Scientific Architecture," in Mochizuki and Županov, *Palimpsests of Religious Encounter in Asia*; S.A. Khan Ghori, "The Impact of Modern European Astronomy on Raja Jai Singh," *Indian Journal of History of Science* 15, no. 1 (1980): 50–57.

321 Raina, "French Jesuit Scientists," 33. See Boudier's observations and measurements during the journey between Chandannagar, Delhi, and Jaipur, *LEC* (Toulouse: Noel-Etienne Sens, 1810), 15:269–91.

322 Murr, *L'inde philosophique entre Bossuet et Voltaire*, 2:177.

luminous beginnings. While the Enlightenment theories privileged European progress through stages, from barbarism to "light," Coeurdoux imagined that the fall of Indians to ignorance and idolatry was due to Brahmans who forgot "knowledge" to make themselves into "gods on earth."[323]

Jesuit research and conclusions streamed into European "sciences" on a capillary level, although a backlash provoked by the Society's "enemies" covered some of their theories with a thick layer of dust. Less controversial was Jesuit cartography and geographical knowledge. Geographical knowledge stimulated the emergence of a prominent school of geography in France by the end of the seventeenth century.[324] Already in the last decade of the sixteenth century, a Catalan Jesuit, Antoni de Montserrat (*c.*1536–1600) attached to his *Mongolicae legationis commentarius* (Commentary on the embassy to the Mughal court) "a path-breaking map of India, which combined Montserrat's latitude calculations with other sources."[325] Two centuries later, Joseph Tiefenthaler (1710–85), who was first sent to join Jesuit astronomers in Jaipur, settled in Agra after 1743 upon Jai Singh Sawai's death. In 1747, he moved to Narwar, where he died in 1765. He left the most detailed and precise maps of the places he visited in North India and calculated their geographical positions (see fig. 10).[326]

Anquetil-Duperron made Tiefenthaler's work known in Europe and Johann Bernoulli (1744–1807) in Berlin.[327] In 1759, Tiefenthaler wrote to Anquetil-Duperron:

> Next to the salvation of souls and their conquest for God, nothing has afforded me greater pleasure than studying the geographical positions of places [...]. I have spared no trouble and undergone great hardships to

323 Murr, *L'inde philosophique entre Bossuet et Voltaire*, 2:81.

324 François de Dainville, *La geographie des humanistes* (Paris: Beauchesne, 1940), 113–14, 167, 205–321. See also Catherine Bousquet-Bressolier, ed., *Francois de Dainville S.J. (1909–1971) pionnier de l'histoire de la cartographie et de l'education* (Paris: École des chartes, 2004).

325 João Vicente Melo, ed., *The Writings of Antoni de Montserrat at the Mughal Court*, trans. Lena Wahlgren-Smith (Leiden: Brill, 2023), xvii.

326 Michaël Sievernich, "Geographical Mapping of India in the 18th Century: The Contribution of the German Jesuit Joseph Tief[f]enthaler (1710–85)," in Amaladass and Županov, *Intercultural Encounter*, 290–320.

327 See Abraham Hyacinthe Anquetil-Duperron, *Recherches hist. et géogr. sur l'Inde* (1786), and *Carte général du cours du Gange et du Gagra dressée par les cartes particuliéres du P. Tieffenthaler* (Paris, 1784). Johann Bernoulli (1744–1807) eventually published this manuscript along with many other memoirs between 1784 and 1789. His work was also used by the English geographer James Rennell (1742–1830), who became known in the nineteenth century as the "Father of Indian Geography." Restif-Filliozat, "Jesuit Contribution," 83.

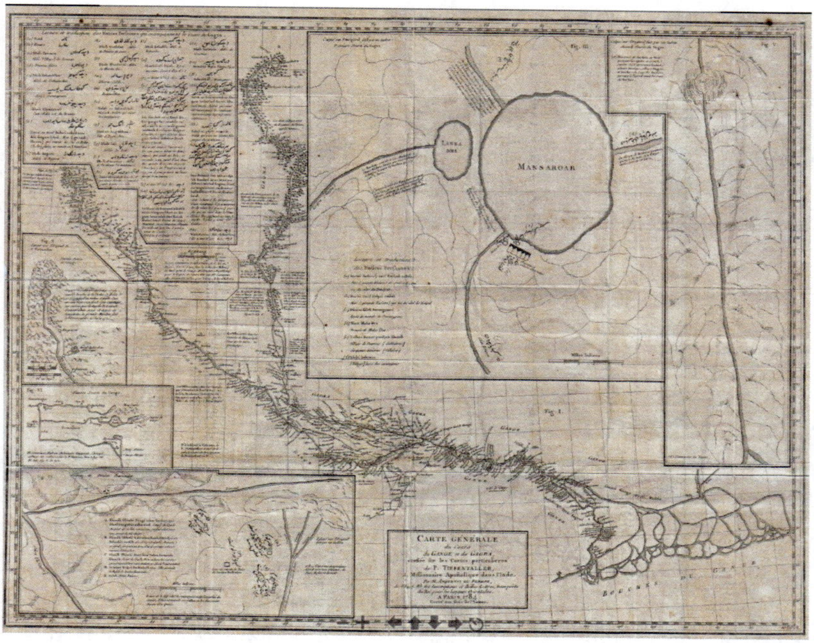

FIGURE 10 Joseph Tiefenthaler and Abraham Hyacinthe Anquetil-Duperron's 1784 map of the Ganges and Ghaghara (Karnali) river system, public domain, https://upload.wikimedia.org/wikipedia/commons/d/db/1784_Tiefenthaler_Map_of_the_Ganges_and_Ghaghara_Rivers%2C_India_-_Geographicus_-_Ganges-teifentaller-1784.jpg

> disclose nature's mysteries, thereby acquiring a greater knowledge of the Creator to fix my mind on heavenly things.[328]

The knowledge of the French Jesuit geographers—Bouchet, Louis-Noël de Bourzes (1673–1735), Claude Moriset (1667–1742), Boudier, and Coeurdoux—fared better in the face of the Enlightenment backlash because of the tradition of publishing letters and treatises in the *LEC*. In addition, they corresponded with the institutions and individuals in Europe, dependent on Jesuit fieldwork.[329]

---

328 Severin Noti, "Joseph Tieffenthaler, a Forgotten Geographer of India," *East and West* 5, nos. 51–54 (1906): 142–54. Tiefenthaler's map shows that he had access to local cartography.

329 The map attributed to Bouchet in the French *LEC* and in the German printed edition (Joseph Stöcklein, *Allerhand so Lehr- als Geist-reiche Brief* [...] [Augsburg: Philipp Martin, 1726]) was probably originally drawn by Bourzes, Moriset, and Hyacintho Serra

If maps were strategic tools for the Jesuits and the European colonizers in waiting, there is evidence they were also diplomatic gifts to local rulers who may have enjoyed them as curiosities rather than useful documents. Perhaps Antonio Rubino presented a map inscribed with Telugu names to the king of Vijayanagara in 1606.[330] In 1700, Bouchet gave the king of Madurai a globe with Tamil captions.[331]

7 Suppression and Return

In 1773, Pope Clement XIV (1705–74, r.1769–74) suppressed the Society of Jesus, which was accused of being too involved with local political structures, taking wrong sides in quarrels that raged in European intellectual and political circles, and getting rich despite the vow of poverty.[332] When the Jesuits were expelled from India, Indian Christian communities such as the Paravas continued to thrive, attached to its particular Catholic worship, to its corporate (or caste) ceremonies and rituals, and its churches and their leaders. However, the Indian hierarchical Christianization project, as conceived by Nobili, encompassing all social layers from the Brahmans on top to Paraiyars at the bottom, failed to materialize.

The Jesuits' ability to find local and rooted symbolic expression for the new religious sensibility and sociability was at the root of missionary success or failure of conversion. Those rituals and ceremonies that fostered community, kinship, and hierarchical organization of "honors" (*mariyatai*) served as vehicles

(1662–1712); see Restif-Filliozat, "Jesuit Contribution," 76n18. Bourzes informed Souciet that he was surprised to see his map published in the 1724 edition of the *LEC*. See Étienne Souciet, *Observations mathématiques, astronomiques, géographiques, chronologiques et physiques, tirées des anciens livres chinois, ou faites nouvellement aux Indes et à la Chine, par les Pères de la Compagnie de Jésus* (Paris: Rollin, 1729–32), 180–81.

330 Joan-Pau Rubiés, "The Jesuit Discovery of Hinduism: Antonio Rubino's Account of the History and Religion of Vijayanagara (1608)," *Archiv für Religionsgeschichte* 3, no. 1 (2001): 210–56, here 219.

331 Danna Agmon, "Conflicts in the Context of Conversion: French Jesuits and Tamil Religious Intermediaries in Madurai," in Amaladass and Županov, *Intercultural Encounter*, 179–98.

332 After the suppression, other religious orders took over Jesuit missions and institutions. In French India, Jesuit missions and parishes were taken over by the Capuchins, the Portuguese bishop of Mylapore, and the MEP. However, unlike in Goa and other places in the Portuguese rump empire, from which the Jesuits were sent to Portugal in chains, the remaining Jesuits in Puducherry stayed on and joined the MEP. Stephen Neill, *A History of Christianity in India, 1707–1858* (London: Cambridge University Press, 1985), 129.

for the implantation of Christianity. In a Durkheimian sense, only those communities of believers who found a way to worship themselves in Christian rituals adhered enthusiastically to a new religion.

The geographical, economic, social, and cultural context in which specific communities were converted was more propitious to "religious migration" than others. The decision to convert to Christianity was often a pragmatic, political decision, but the subsequent religious fervor and piety resulted from interaction and adjustment between a new lifestyle, new economic patterns, corporate identity, and religious innovation. On the surface, Indian Christians adopted a global religion. However, Christianity became essential and indispensable for the collective ordering of experience by becoming a microscopic, traditional, local, caste-based, ritual, and social framework.

India's pre-colonial model of creative and resilient pluralism frustrated, nevertheless, all efforts of globalizing Catholicism despite its remarkable adaptability to change. Nobili's universalist dream, based partly on his Brahmanical bias and his belief in "textual" Hinduism, had to be replaced by strategies similar to those of the indigenous *bhakti* movements and to the Parava type of caste-forming model of conversion. Nevertheless, the globalizing project was never abandoned; it was only deferred for when, as the missionaries had hoped, the political situation was to become more propitious for their enterprise.

Jesuit missionaries' experience of religious pluralism in India and their utopian project of globalization seeped a century later into the British colonial and administrative imagination. Popular Hinduism, that is, a tightly knit community-based ritual practice, was devalued as ancestral demon- or hero-worship, no religion at all, but a superstition, while textual Hinduism, as expounded to the British by the Brahman literati, gained respect and became the "true" representation of the Indian religious spirit. This inherent ambiguity in interpretating the "essence" of Hindu religious belief and practice was left as a legacy to the Indian religious reformers and nationalist intellectuals and leaders whose reformulations of Hinduism, based on the model of Christianity, as a global Indian religion, never corresponded on the whole to the local, "traditional," "village," and "microcosmic" religious and cultural realities.

The Society of Jesus was reinstated in 1814, an unprecedented event in the Catholic Church. Jesuit missionaries recruited in France had a chance to reclaim and redefine their order's missionary legacy in India. On October 24, 1837, four French Jesuits arrived in Puducherry after a prolonged and tedious journey from Toulouse. The moment was triumphant for Joseph Bertrand (1801–84), Louis Garnier (1805–43), Louis du Ranquet (1806–43), and Alexander Martin (1799–1840), who came to reclaim the Madurai mission and its history.

"Animated by the same spirit" as those who had come before, they tried to connect the golden, if martyred past with the present and future.[333] In the nineteenth century, the Jesuits labored to pick up the pieces and reanimate the former mission territories through pastoral and historiographical work. One of the tasks was also to create history and memory of the evangelical past by writing and publishing apologetic and hagiographic accounts and collections of primary sources.[334] And to make them available, and to teach them to the world. In the long run, the Jesuits became the most important Indian educators. Mostly Indian Jesuits currently run "118 primary and middle schools, 155 high schools, 50 university colleges, 22 technical institutes, and 15 business administration institutes with 11,225 teachers, educating 324,538 students from different religious, linguistic, and socioeconomic groups."[335] Since in the new democratic India, foreign missionaries were forbidden, and even conversion to Christianity was frowned upon by the Indian authorities, Jesuits had no other solution but to recruit Indian Christians to become full members of the Society of Jesus. The question asked by Pedro Luís Bramane in 1559—who remained the only Indian Jesuit recruit until 1773—of why he was the only native Jesuit in India can finally be shelved away in the archives of discrimination that European colonialism disseminated worldwide.[336] Today, Indian Jesuits are the third largest national contingent after those from the United States and Spain.

333 Joseph Bertrand to a Jesuit, February 27, 1838, FMd150, Archives des Jésuites de France in Vanves, where most of the documentation from the new Madurai mission is available. See Henria Aton, "Walking, Mapping, Knowing: Indianization and Survival in the Jesuit New Madura Mission (1837–1890)" (PhD diss., McGill University, 2016).

334 Joseph Bertrand, *Mission du Maduré*, d'après des documents inédits, 4 vols. (Paris: Paris, Librairie de Poussielgue-Rusand, 1847).

335 St. Mary's High School and Inter College, "Jesuit Contribution to Nation Building in India," n.d., https://saintmaryschoolsimdega.com/jesuits-in-india/ (accessed September 3, 2024). About four thousand Jesuits—mostly Indians—are now working in eighteen provinces/regions in India.

336 However, the question of (Indian) Jesuit discrimination against untouchables in the premodern and contemporary Madurai mission remains an issue and has been studied by Alphonse Manickam, "Les jésuites et l'intouchabilité au Tamil Nadu," 252.

Bibliography

Primary Sources (Prints)

Albuquerque, Afonso de. *Cartas*. Edited by Raymundo Antonio de Bulhão Pato and Henrique Lopes de Mendonça. Vol. 1. Lisbon: Typ. da Academia real das sciencias de Lisboa, 1884.

Alvares, Francisco. *Verdadeira informação sobre a terra do Preste João da Indias*. 2 Vols. Lisbon: Alfa, 1989 [1540].

Amaladass, Anand, S.J., and Francis X. Clooney, S.J. *Preaching Wisdom to the Wise: Three Treatises by Roberto de Nobili, S.J., Missionary and Scholar in 17th-Century India*. St. Louis, MO: Institute of Jesuit Sources, 2000.

Amaladass, Anand, S.J., and Richard Fox Young. *The Indian Christiad: A Concise Anthology of Didactic and Devotional Literature in Early Church Sanskrit*. Anand: Gujarat Sahitya Prakash, 1995.

Anonymous [Broglia Antonio Brandolini]. *Risposta alle Accuse date al praticato sin'ora [...] parte seconda*. Cologne, 1729.

Anquetil-Duperron, Abraham Hyacinthe. *Carte général du cours du Gange et du Gagra dressée par les cartes particuliéres du P. Tieffenthaler*. Paris: n.p., 1784.

Anquetil-Duperron, Abraham Hyacinthe. *Recherches hist. et géogr. sur l'Inde*. N.p., 1786.

App, Urs. *The Birth of Orientalism*. Philadelphia: University of Pennsylvania Press, 2010.

Baião, António. *A Inquisição de Goa*. Lisbon: Academia das Sciencias de Lisboa, 1945.

Bar-Le-Duc, Norbert de. *Mémoires historiques présentés au souverain pontif Benoit XIV sur les missions des Indes orienales, où l'on fait voir que les Pères Capucins missionnaires ont eu raison de se séparer de communion des révérends pères missionnaires jésuites qui on refusé de se soumettre au décret de Monsieur le Cardinal de Tournon, légat du Saint Siege, contre les Rites Malabare*. 2 Vols. Lucca, 1744.

Barros, João de. *Grammatica da lingua portuguesa*. Lisbon: Apud Lodouicum Rotorigiu[m], Typographum, 1540.

Bertrand, Joseph. *Mission du Maduré. D'après des documents inédits*. 4 Vols. Paris: Librairie de Poussielgue-Rusand, 1847.

Beschi, Costanzo Giuseppe [Vīramāmuṉivar]. *Caturakarāti: Iḥtu vīramāmuṉivar ceyta caturakarāti*. N.p.: Ceṉṉaiccaṅkattil accuppatittatu, 1825.

Beschi, Costanzo Giuseppe [Vīramāmuṉivar]. *A Grammar of the Common Dialect of the Tamil Language Called Koṭuntamiḻ, Composed for the Use of the Missionaries of the Society of Jesus*. Translated by George William Mahon. Madras: Christian Knowledge Society's Press, 1848.

Beschi, Costanzo Giuseppe [Vīramāmuṉivar]. *A Grammar of the High Dialect of the Tamil Language, Termed Shen-Tamil*. Translated by Guy Babington. Madras: College Press, 1822.

Beschi, Costanzo Giuseppe [Vīramāmuṉivar]. *Toṉṉūlviḷakkam*. N.p., 1730.

Broglia, Antonio Brandolini. *Giustificazione del praticato sin' ora da' religiosi della Compagnia di Gesú, nelle missioni del Madurey, Mayssur, e Carnate*. Rome: Stamperia della Rev. Camera Apost., 1724.

Cérémonies et coutumes religieuses de tous les peuples du monde representées par des figures dessinées de la main de Bernard Picard: Avec une explication historique, & quelques dissertations curieuses. 7 Vols. Amsterdam: J.F. Bernard, 1723–37.

Cinnami, Leonardo. *Vita e morte del Padre Marcello Francesco Mastrilli della Compagnia di Giesu: Composta dal Padre Leonardo Cinami della medesima Compagnia*. Viterbo: Mariano Diotallevi, 1645.

Collecção de notícias para a história e geografia das nações ultramarinas. Vol. 1. No. 1. Lisbon: Academia das Ciências de Lisboa, 1812.

Croze, Mathurin Veyssière de la. *Histoire du Christianisme des Indes*. La Haye: Chez Freres Vaillant, & N. Prevost, 1724.

Dahmen, Pierre, S.J., ed. *Robert de Nobili, l'apôtre des Brahmes: Première apologie, 1610*. Paris: Edition Spes, 1931.

Dalgado, Sebastião Rodolfo. *Glossário Luso-Asiático*. Coimbra: Inprensa da Universidade, 1919.

Dellon, Charles. *The History of the Inquisition as It Is Exercised at Goa*. London: Printed for James Knapton, at the Queen's Head in St. Paul's Church-yard, 1688.

Dubois, Abbé J.A. *Description of the Character, Manners, and Customs of the People of India, and of Their Institutions, Religious and Civil*. London: Longman, Hurst, Rees, Orme, and Brown, Paternoster-Row, 1817.

Fenicio, Jacobo. *Livro da seita dos indios orientais*. Edited by Jarl Charpentier. Uppsala: Alqvist and Wiksells Boktryckeri-A-B, 1933.

Garcia, Francisco. *O homem das trinta e duas perfeições et outras histórias (Ms. Opp. NN. 192 do Arq. Rom. S. J.: Escritos da literatura indiana por Francisco Garcia S.J.* Edited and annotated by Josef Wicki, S.J. Lisbon: Agencia Gerl do Ultramar, 1958.

Gonçalves, Diogo. *História do Malavar*. Edited by Josef Wicki. Münster: Aschendorffische Verlagsbuchhandlung, 1955.

Gonçalves, Sebastião. *Primeira parte da história dos religiosos da Companhia de Jesus e do que fizeram com a divina graça na conversão dos infieis a nossa sancta fee catholica nos reynos e provincias da India Oriental* [1614]. Edited by Josef Wicki. 3 Vols. Coimbra: Atlantida, 1957–62.

Gouvea, António de. *Jornada do Arcebispo de Goa Dom Frey Aleixo de Menezes* [...]. Coimbra: Diego Gomez Loureyro, 1606.

Gouvea, António de. "Synodo diocesano da igreja e bispado de Angamale dos antigos cristãos de Sam Thome [...]." In *Jornada do Arcebispo de Goa Dom Frey Aleixo de Menezes* [...]. Coimbra: Diego Gomez Loureyro, 1606.

Guerreiro, Fernão. *Relacam annual das cousas que fizeram os padres da Companhia de Jesus, nas partes da India Oriental, & em alguas outras da conquista deste Reyno*. 5 Parts. Lisbon: Pedro Crasbeeck, 1611; Modern edition: *Relacão anual das coisas que fizeram os padres da Companhia de Jesus nas sua missões*. Edited by Artur Viegas. 3 Vols. Coimbra: Imprensa da Universidade, 1930–31, 1942.

Hausherr, Irénée, ed. *De erroribus nestorianorum qui in hac India Orientali versantur, auctore P. Francisco Roz, S.J.* Orientalia Christiana 11:1. No. 40. Rome: Pont. Institutum Orientalium Studiorum 1929.

Henriques, Henrique, S.J. *Doctrina Christam* [*Kirīcittiyāṉi vaṇakkam*]. Cochim [Kochi]: Collegio de Madre de Deos, 1579.

Henriques, Henrique, S.J. *Flos sanctorum*. Edited by S. Rajamanickam. Thoothukudi: n.p., 1967 [Punnayakāyal, 1586].

Jarric, Pierre du. *Histoire des choses plus memorables advenues tant ez Indes Orientales, que autres païs de la descouverte des Portugais*. 3 Vols. Bordeaux: Simon Millanges, 1610–14.

Jeyaraj, Daniel. *Tamil Language for Europeans: Ziegenbalg's* Grammatica Damulica *1716*. Translated from Latin and Tamil. Annotated and commented on by Daniel Jeyaray. Wiesbaden: Harrassowitz Verlag, 2010.

Jordão, Levy Maria, and João Augusto da Graça Barreto, eds. *Bullarium patronatus Portugalliae regum in ecclesiis Africae, Asiae atque Oceaniae*. 5 Vols. Lisbon: Ex Typographia nationali, 1868–79.

Lettres édifiantes et curieuses. 34 Vols. Paris, 1702–76.

Lobo, Jerónimo. *The* Itinerario *of Jerónimo Lobo*. Translated by Donald M. Lockhart, edited by M. Gonçalves da Costa, with an introduction and notes by Charles Fraser Beckingham. London: Hakluyt Society, 1984.

Lockman, John. *Travels of the Jesuits*. 2 Vols. London: John Noon, 1743. Facsimile ed. Vol. 1. New Delhi: Asian Educational Services, 1995.

Lucena, João de. *Historia de vida do padre Francisco de Xavier*. Lisbon: Pedro Crasbeck, 1600.

Lucino, Luigi Maria. *Esame, e difesa del decreto pubblicato in Pudisceri da monsignor Carlo Tommaso di Tournon*. 2nd ed. Rome: Nella Stamperia Vaticana, 1729.

Maffei, Giovanni Pietro. *Historiarum Indicarum libri XVI*. Florence: Apud Philippum Iunctam, 1588.

Maldonado, Jean-Baptiste de. *Illustre certamen R.P. Joannis de Britto e Societatis Jesu Lusitani, in odium fidei à Regulo Maravâ trucidati, quartâ die Februarij 1693*. Antwerp: Apud Petrum Jouret, in plateâ dictâ de Melck-Marckt, sub signo trium Monachorum, 1697.

Mecherry, Antony, S.J. "*On the Errors of the East Syrians* (by Francisco Ros, S.J., 1586): An Introduction with English Translation of a Latin–Syriac Treatise from Early Modern Malabar." *AHSI* 91, fasc. 181 (2022-I): 187–222.

Melo, João Vicente, ed. *The Writings of Antoni de Montserrat at the Mughal Court*. Translated from Latin by Lena Wahlgren-Smith. Leiden: Brill, 2023.

Murr, Sylvia. "*L'Indologie du père Coeurdoux*: Apologétique et scientificité." In *L'Inde philosophique entre Bossuet et Voltaire*. Vol. 1. Paris: École française d'Extrême-Orient, 1987.

Nobili, Roberto (Tattuva Potakar). *Āttuma Nirṇayam*. Edited by S. Rajamanickam. Tuttukuṭi: Tamil̲ Ilakkiyak kal̲akam, 1967.

Nobili, Roberto (Tattuva Potakar). *Cesunātar Carittiram*. Edited by S. Rajamanickam. Tuttukuṭi: Tamil̲ Ilakkiyak kal̲akam, 1964.

Nobili, Roberto (Tattuva Potakar). *Ñan̲ōpatēcam; 26 Piracaṅkaṅkaḷ*. Edited by S. Rajamanickam. Tuttukuṭi: Tamil̲ Ilakkiyak kal̲akam, 1963.

Nobili, Roberto (Tattuva Potakar). *Robert de Nobili, l'apotre des Brahmes: Premiere apologie, 1610*. Translated and annotated by Pierre Dahmen. Paris: Editions Spes, 1931.

Nobili, Roberto (Tattuva Potakar). *Tūsaṇat tikkāram*. Edited by S. Rajamanickam. Tuttukuṭi: Tamil̲ Ilakkiyak kal̲akam, 1964.

Nunes, M. da Costa. *Documentação para a história da Congregação do Oratório da Santa Cruz dos Milagres do Clero Natural do Goa*. Lisbon: Centro de Estudos Históricos Ultramarinos, 1966.

Páez, Pedro. *Pedro Páez's* History of Ethiopia, *1622*. Translated by Christopher J. Tribe, edited by Isabel Boavida, Hervé Pennec, and Manuel João Ramos. London: Ashgate for the Hakluyt Society, 2011.

Paulinus à Sancto Bartholomaeo. *Amarasinha: Sectio prima de caelo ex tribus codicibus Indicis*. Rome: Apud Antonium Fulgonium, 1798.

Payne, C.H. [Charles Herbert], trans. and ed. *Akbar and the Jesuits: An Account of the Jesuit Missions to the Court of Akbar by Father Pierre Du Jarric, S.J.* New York: Harper & Brothers, 1926.

Payne, C.H. [Charles Herbert], ed. and trans. *Jahangir and the Jesuits with an Account of the Travels of Benedict Goes and the Mission to Pegu*. London: George Routledge & Sons, 1930.

Pereira, Duarte Pacheco. *Esmeraldo de situ orbis*. Lisbon: Academia Portuguesa de História, 1988.

Propagation of the Gospel in the East: Being an Account of the Success of Two Danish Missionaries, Lately Sent to the East-Indies for the Conversion of the Heathens in Malabar. London: J. Downing, 1709.

Pyrard de Laval, François. *Voyages aux Indes orientales*. Paris: Louis Billaine, 1615.

Queirós, Fernão de. *Conquista temporal e espiritual de Ceylão*. Edited by Paul E. Pieris. Colombo: H.C. Cottle, 1916.

Queirós, Fernão de. *Historia da vida do veneravel irmaõ Pedro de Basto coadjutor temporal da Companhia de Jesus, e da variedade de sucessos que Deos ilhe manifestou*. Lisbon: Miguel Deslandes, 1689.

Queirós, Fernão de. *The Temporal and Spiritual Conquest of Ceylon*. Translated and edited by S.G. Perera. 3 Vols. New Delhi: Asian Educational Services, 1992 [Colombo, 1930].

Rajamanickam, Savarimuthu, S.J. *The First Oriental Scholar*. Tirunelveli: De Nobili Research Institute, 1972.

Rajamanickam, S. [Saverimuttu], ed. and trans. *Roberto de Nobili on Adaptation*. Palayamkottai: De Nobili Research Institute, 1971.

Rego, António da Silva, ed. *Documentacão para a história das missões portugues do Oriente*. 12 Vols. Lisbon: Agência Geral do Ultramar, 1947–58.

Rego, António da Silva. *História das missões*. Lisbon: Agência Geral das Colónias, Divisão de Publicações e Biblioteca, 1949.

Relation de ce qui s'est passé dans les Indes Orientales en ses trois provinces de Goa, de Malabar, du Iapon, de la Chine, & autres païs nouvellement descouverts: Par les peres de la Compagnie de Iesus; Présentée a la Sacreé Congregation de la Propagation de la Foy, par le P. Iean Maracci procureur de la province de Goa, au mois d'Auril 1649. Paris: Chez Sebastien Cramoisy, Imprimeur ordinaire du Roy, & de la Reyne Regente et Gabriel Cramoisy. Ruë S. Iacques aux Cicognes. M. DC. LI. Avec Privilege du Roy, 1649.

Rivara, Joaquim Heliodoro da Cunha. *Archivo portuguez oriental*. 6 Fasciculos in 10 Parts. Fasciculo 4 and 5. Part 1. New Delhi: Asian Educational Services, 1992.

Rocher, Ludo. *Ezourvedam: A French Veda of the Eighteenth Century*. Amsterdam: J. Benjamins, 1984.

Rocher, Ludo. *Paulinus a S. Bartholomaeo: Dissertation on the Sanskrit Languages*. Studies in the History of Linguistics 12. Amsterdam: Benjamins, 1977.

Saldanha, Mario. "História de gramática concani." *Bulletin of the School of Oriental Studies* 8, nos. 2–3 (1936): 715–35.

Schurhammer, Georg, S.J., and Josef Wicki, S.J., eds. *Epistolae S. Francisci Xaverii alliaque eius scripta*. Vol. 2. Rome: Apud Monumenta Historica Societatis Iesu, 1996.

Sodini, Carla. *I Medici e le Indie Orientali: Il diario di viaggio di Placido Ramponi emissario in India per conto di Cosimo III*. Florence: Leo Olschki Editore, 1996.

Souciet, Étienne, *Observations mathématiques, astronomiques, géographiques, chronologiques et physiques, tirées des anciens livres chinois, ou faites nouvellement aux Indes et à la Chine, par les pères de la Compagnie de Jésus*. Paris: Rollin, 1729–32.

Sousa, Francisco de. *Oriente conquistado a Jesus Christo pelos padres da Companhia de Jesus da província de Goa*. 2 Vols. Lisbon: Valentim da Costa Deslandes, 1710.

Stephens, Thomas. *Arte da lingoa Canarim composta pelo Padre Thomaz Estevão da Companhia de IESUS & acrecentada pello Padre Diogo Ribeiro da mesma Cõpanhia e nouemente reuista & emendada por outros quarto Padres da mesma Companhia*. Rachol: Collegio de S. Ignacio, 1640.

Stephens, Thomas. *Discurso sobre a vinda do Jesu-Christo Nosso Salvador ao mundo, dividido em dous tratados, pelo Padre Thomaz Estevão, Ingrez, da Companhia de Jesu: Impresso em Rachol com licencia da Santa Inquisicão, e Ordinario no Collegio de Todos os Santos da Companhia de Jesu anno 1616*. Rachol, Goa, 1616 [in Roman script].

Stöcklein, Joseph. *Allerhand so Lehr- als Geist-reiche Brief* [...]. Augsburg: Philipp Martin, 1726.

Thani Nayagam, Xavier S. *Antão de Proença's Tamil–Portuguese Dictionary* A.D. *1679*. Kuala Lumpur: Department of Indian Studies, 1966.

The Travels of Pietro della Valle in India. Vol. 1. Madras: Asian Educational Services, 1991 [London: Hakluyt Society, 1892].

Tursellinus, Horatius. *De vita Francisci Xaverii*. Rome: Ex typographia Aloysii Zannetti, 1596.

Tours, Francois-Marie de. *Questioni proposte alla Sacra Congregazione di Propaganda Fide*. Liège, 1704.

Trinidade, Paulo da, O.F.M. *Conquista espiritual do Oriente*. 3 Vols. Lisbon: Centro de Estudos Históricos Ultramarino, 1962–67.

The Sanskrit Grammar of Johann Ernst Hanxleden S.J. *(1681–1732)*, introduced and edited by Toon Van Hall and Christophe Vielle, with a photographic reproduction of the original manuscript by Jean-Claude Muller. Potsdam: Universitätsverlag Potsdam, 2013.

Wicki, Josef, S.J. ed. *O livro do "Pai dos Cristãos"*. Lisbon: Centro de Estudos históricos Ultramarinos, 1969.

Wicki, Josef, and John Gomes, eds., *Documenta Indica*. 18 Vols. Rome: Institutum Historicum Societatis Iesu, 1948–88.

Witte, Charles-Martial de. "Les bulles pontificales et l'expansion portugaise au XVe siècle." *Revue d'histoire ecclésiastique* 48 (1953): 683–718; 49 (1954): 438–61; 51 (1956): 413–53; 53 (1958): 5–46, 443–71.

Xavier, Francis. *Epistolae S. Francisci Xaverii*. Edited by Georg Schurhammer, S.J., and Josef Wicki, S.J. Vol. 1. Rome: Monumenta Historica Societatis Iesu, 1944.

Secondary Sources

Agmon, Danna. *Colonial Affair: Commerce, Conversion, and Scandal in French India*. Ithaca, NY: Cornell University Press, 2017.

Agmon, Danna. "Conflicts in the Context of Conversion: French Jesuits and Tamil Religious Intermediaries in Madurai." In *Intercultural Encounter and Jesuit Mission in India (16th–18th Centuries)*, edited by Anand Amaladass and Ines G. Županov, 179–98. Bangalore: Asian Trading Corporation, 2014.

Agur, Christian Masillamani. *Church History of Travancore*. New Delhi: Asian Educational Services, 1990 [1903].

Aiyar, R. Sathyanatha. *The History of the Nayaks of Madura*. Madras: University of Madras, 1980.

Albuquerque, Viriato António Caetano Brás de. "Congregação do Oratorio de S. Felippe Nery em Goa." *O Oriente Portuguez* 2 (1905): 310–26.

Almeida, Fortunato de. *História da igreja em Portugal*. 2nd ed. Vol. 2. Porto: Livraria Civilização, 1968.

Alves, Jorge M. dos Santos, "A pedra-bezoar: Realidade e mito em torno de um antídoto (séculos XVI e XVII)." In *Mirabilia asiatica: Produtos raros no comércio marítim*, edited by Jorge M. dos Santos Alves, Claude Guillot, and Roderich Ptak, 121–34. Wiesbaden: Harrasowitz Verlag, 2003.

Amaro, Ana Maria. "A famosa Pedra cordial de Goa ou de Gaspar Antonio." *Revista da cultura* (Macau) 19, no. 22 (1988–89): 87–108.

Ames, Glenn J. "Religious Life in the Colonial Trenches: The Role of the *pai dos Christãos* in Seventeenth-Century Portuguese India, c.1640–1683." *Portuguese Studies Review* 16, no. 2 (July 2008): 1–23.

Amiel, Charles. "Les archives de l'Inquisition portugaise: Regards et réflexions." *Arquivos do Centro cultural português* 14 (1979): 421–43.

Appadurai, Arjun. *Worship and Conflict under Colonial Rule: A South Indian Case*. Cambridge: Cambridge University Press, 1981.

Appadurai, Arjun, and Carol Appadurai Breckenridge. "The South Indian Temple: Authority, Honour, and Redistribution." *Contributions to Indian Sociology* 10, no. 2 (1976): 187–209.

Aranha, Paolo. "Les meilleures causes embarrassent les juges, si elles manquent de bonnes preuves: Père Norbert's Militant Historiography on the Malabar Rites Controversy." In *Europäische Geschichtskulturen um 1700 zwischen Gelehrsamkeit, Politik und Konfession*, edited by Thomas Wallnig, Thomas Stockinger, Ines Peper, and Patrick Fiska, 239–70. Berlin: De Gruyter, 2012.

Aranha, Paolo. "The Social and Physical Spaces of the Malabar Rites Controversy." In *Space and Conversion in Global Perspective*, edited by Giuseppe Marcocci, Wietse de Boer, Aliocha Maldavsky, and Ilaria Pavan, 214–34. Leiden: Brill, 2015.

Armenteros, Carolina. "The Enlightened Conservatism of the Malabar Missions: Gaston-Laurent Coeurdoux (1691–1779) and the Making of an Anthropological Classic." *Journal of Jesuit Studies* 6, no. 3 (2019): 439–66.

Arokiasamy, Soosai, S.J. *Dharma, Hindu, and Christian, according to Roberto de Nobili: Analysis of Its Meaning and Its Use in Hinduism and Christianity*. Rome: Editrice Pontificia Università Gregoriana, 1986.

Aton, Henria. "Walking, Mapping, Knowing: Indianization and Survival in the Jesuit New Madura Mission (1837–1890)." PhD diss., School of Religious Studies, McGill University, Montreal, August 2016.

Auroux, Sylvain, E.F.K. [Ernst Frideryk Konrad] Koerner, Hans-Josef Niederehe, and Kees Versteegh, eds. *History of the Language Sciences: An International Handbook on the Evolution of the Study of Language from the Beginnings to the Present*. Berlin: Walter de Gruyter, 2000.

Baião, António. *A Inquisição de Goa, tentativa de história da sua origem, estabelecimento, evolução e extinção*. 2 Vols. Lisbon: Academia Das Ciencias, 1930–45.

Bailey, Gauvin Alexander. *Art on the Jesuit Missions in Asia and Latin America, 1543–1773*. Toronto: University of Toronto Press, 1999.

Bailey, Gauvin Alexander. *The Jesuits and the Grand Mogul: Renaissance Art at the Imperial Court of India, 1580–1630*. Washington, DC: Freer Gallery of Art, Arthur M. Sackler Gallery, Smithsonian Institution, 1998.

Bailey, Gauvin Alexander. "A Portuguese Doctor at the Maharaja of Jaipur's Court." *South Asian Studies* 11, no. 1 (1995): 51–62.

Barbuda, Claudio Lagrange Monteiro de, ed. *Instrucções com que El-Rei D. José I mandou passar ao Estado da India, o governador e Capitão general e o Arcebispo Primaz do Oriente no anno de 1774*. Pangim: Na Typographia nacional, 1844.

Barreto, Luís Filipe. *Descobrimentos e Renascimento, formas de ser e pensar nos séculos XV e XVI*. 2nd ed. Lisbon: Imprenssa Nacional/Casa da Moeda, 1983.

Barroso, Maria do Sameiro. "The Goa Stone: Myths, Empiricism, and Insights on Chemistry." *Vesalius* 26, no. 1 (2020): 3–60.

Bayly, Susan. *Caste, Society, and Politics in India from the Eighteenth Century to the Modern Age*. Cambridge: Cambridge University Press, 2001.

Bayly, Susan. "A Christian Caste in Hindu Society: Religious Leadership and Social Conflict among the Paravas of Southern Tamilnadu." *Modern Asian Studies* 12, no. 2 (1981): 203–34.

Bayly, Susan. *Saints, Goddesses, and Kings: Muslims and Christians in South Indian Society 1700–1900*. Cambridge: Cambridge University Press, 1989.

Beaujard, Philippe. "L'Afrique de l'Est et les réseaux d'échanges océaniques entre les Ier et XVe siècles." *Afriques* [online] 6 (2015). https://journals.openedition.org/afriques/1996 (accessed September 19, 2024).

Benay, Erin. *Italy, by Way of India: Translating Art and Devotion in the Early Modern World*. Turnhout: Harvey Miller Publishers, 2021.

Besse, Léon. "Liste alphabetique des missionnaire du Carnatic de la Compagnie de Jésus au XVIIIe siecle." *Revue historique de l'Inde française* 2 (1918): 175–242.

Besse, Léon. *La mission du Maduré: Historiques de ses Pangous*. Trichinopoly: Impr. de la Mission catholique, 1914.

Biedermann, Zoltán. "'Was it a vision or a waking dream?' Exploring the Oneiric World of a Seventeenth-century Jesuit Visionary in Portuguese India." In *From the Supernatural to the Uncanny*, edited by Stephen M. Hart and Zoltán Biedermann, 43–70. Cambridge: Cambridge Scholars Publishing, 2017.

Blackburn, Stuart. *Print, Folklore, and Nationalism in Colonial South India*. New Delhi: Permanent Black, 2003.

Blankemeyer, Bradley T. "Conversos, Accommodation, and the Goan Inquisition: The First Five Decades of the Society of Jesus in India, between Theory and Practice." *AHSI* 91, fasc. 181 (2022-I): 82–119.

Bouchon, Geneviève. *Albuquerque: Le lion des mers d'Asie*. Paris: Editions Desjonquères, 1992.

Bouchon, Geneviève. "Premières expériences d'une société coloniale: Goa au XVIe siècle." In *Inde découverte, Inde retrouvée 1498–1630: Études d'histoire Indo-Portugaise*, 291–301. Lisbon: Commission Nationale pour les Commémorations des Découvertes Portugaises; Centre Culturel Calouste Gulbenkian, 1999.

Bousquet-Bressolier, Catherine, ed. *François de Dainville, S.J. (1909–1971), pionnier de l'histoire de la cartographie et de l'education*. Paris: Ecole des chartes, 2004.

Boxer, Charles R. *The Church Militant and Iberian Expansion, 1440–1770*. Baltimore: Johns Hopkins University Press, 1978.

Boxer, Charles R. *The Portuguese Seaborne Empire, 1425–1825*. London: Hutchinson, 1969.

Boxer, Charles R. *Race Relations in the Portuguese Colonial Empire*. Oxford: Oxford University Press, 1963.

Braga, Teófilo. *História da universidade de Coimbra nas suas relações com a instrucção publica Portuguesa*. Vol. 1. Lisbon: Na typ. do Academia real das sciencias, 1892.

Brockey, Liam. "A vinha do Senhor: The Portuguese Jesuits in China in the Seventeenth Century." *Portuguese Studies* 16 (2000): 125–47.

Brockey, Liam. *The Visitor: André Palmeiro and the Jesuits in Asia*. Cambridge, MA: Belknap Press of Harvard University Press, 2014.

Brown, Leslie W. *The Indian Christians of St. Thomas*. Cambridge: Cambridge University Press, 1982.

Camps, Arnulf. "The Sanskrit Grammar and Manuscripts of Father Heinrich Roth, S.J. (1620–1668): Introduction; The History of His Sanskrit Manuscripts." In *Studies in Asian Mission History 1956–1998*, 84–104. Leiden: Brill, 2000.

Caraman, Philip. *The Lost Empire: The Story of the Jesuits in Ethiopia*. London: Sidgwick & Jackson 1985.

Castonnet des Fosse, Henri. *R.P. Charles de Montalembert, missionnaire aux Indes au XVIIe siècle, extrait des annales de l'Estreme Orient et de l'Afrique*. Paris: Challamel Ainé, Libraire-Editeur, 5, rue Jacob, 5, 1886.

Certeau, Michel de. "La formalité des pratiques: Du système religieux à l'éthique des Lumières (XVIIe–XVIIIe s.)." In *L'écriture de l'histoire*, 152–214. Paris: Gallimard, 1975.

Certeau, Michel de. *The Writing of History*. New York: Columbia University Press, 1988.

Chakravarty, Ananya. "The Many Faces of Baltasar da Costa: *Imitatio* and *accommodatio* in the Seventeenth-Century Madurai Mission." *Etnográfica* 18, no. 1 (2014): 135–58.

Chandeigne, Michel. "Albuquerque, le conquérant." In *Goa 1510–1685: L'inde portugaise, apostolique et commerciale*, edited by Michel Chaindeigne, 19–39. Paris: Ed. Autrement, 1996.

Clooney, Francis X., S.J. *Fr. Bouchet's India: An 18th-Century Jesuit's Encounter with Hinduism*. Chennai: Satya Nilayam Publications, 2005.

Clooney, Francis X., S.J. *Saint Joseph in South India: Poetry, Mission, and Theology in Costanzo Gioseffo Beschi's Tēmpāvaṇi*. Vienna: De Nobili Research Library, 2022.

Clooney, Francis X., S.J. *Western Jesuit Scholars in India: Tracing Their Paths, Reassessing Their Goals*. Leiden: Brill, 2020.

Coates, Timothy J. *Degredados e órfãs: Colonizacão dirigida pela coroa no império português, 1550–1755*. Lisbon: Comissão nacional para as comemoracões dos descobrimentos portugueses, 1998.

Coello de la Rosa, Alexandre, and João Vicente Melo. *The Jesuit Encounters with Islam in the Asia-Pacific*. Leiden: Brill, 2023.

Cohen, Leonardo. *The Missionary Strategies of the Jesuits in Ethiopia, 1555–1632*. Wiesbaden: Harrassowitz Verlag, 2009.

Cohen, Leonardo. "Patience, Suffering, and Tolerance: The Experience of Defeat and Exile among the Jesuits of Ethiopia (1632–59)." *Journal of Jesuit Studies* 9, no. 1 (2022): 76–94.

Colas, Gérard. "Les manuscrits envoyés de l'Inde par les jésuites français entre 1729 et 1734." In *Scribes et manuscrits du Moyen-Orient*, edited by François Déroche and Francis Richard, 246–62. Paris: Bibliothèque nationale de France, 1997.

Colas, Gérard. "Les traditions sanskritistes de la mission du Carnate entre oubli et reinvention." In *Le sanctuaire dévoilé: Antoine-Léonard de Chézy et les débuts des études sanskrites en Europe, 1800–1850*, edited by Jérôme Petit and Pascale Rabault-Feuerhahn, 17–38. Paris: Bibliothèque nationale de France, 2019.

Colas, Gérard, and Usha Colas-Chauhan. "An 18th-Century Jesuit 'Refutation of Metempsychosis' in Sanskrit." *Religions* 8, no. 9 (2017): 192. DOI: 10.3390/rel8090192 (accessed September 19, 2024).

Colas, Gérard, and Usha Colas-Chauhan. "Une pensée en morceaux: Two Works from the Carnatic Mission; A Refutation of Metempsychosis in Sanskrit and a Collection of Sermons in Telugu." In *Intercultural Encounter and the Jesuit Mission in South Asia (16th–18th Centuries)*, edited by Anand Amaladass and Ines G. Županov, 62–87. Bangalore: Asian Trading Corporation, 2014.

Colín, Ostwald Sales. "Las actividades médicas en las Filipinas durante la primera mitad del siglo XVII." *Perspectivas latinoamericanas* 2 (2005): 167–86.

Correia-Afonso, John. *Jesuit Letters and Indian History: A Study of the Nature and Development of the Jesuit Letters from India (1542–1773) and Their Value for Indian Historiography*. Bombay: Indian Historical Research Institute, St. Xavier's College, 1955.

Costa, Cosme Jose. *Life and Achievements of Blessed Joseph Vaz*. Goa: Pilar Publications, 1996.

Costa, João Paulo Oliveira e. "Em torno da criação do bispado do Japão." In *O Japão e o Cristianismo no sèculo XVI: Ensaios de história luso-nipônica*, 129–57. Lisbon: Sociedade Histórica da Independência de Portugal, 1999.

Couture, André. "Pierre-Sylvain Filliozat, *À l'origine des études sanscrites: La Grammatica Sanscritica de Jean-François Pons S.J.* Étude, édition et traduction (coll. 'Mémoires de l'Académie des Inscriptions et Belles-Lettres,' 56) (Paris, Éditions de Boccard, 2020)." *Laval théologique et philosophique* 77, no. 2 (June 2021): 324–26.

Cruz, Maria Augusta Lima. "Exiles and Renegades in Early Sixteenth-Century Portuguese India." *Indian Economic and Social History Review* 23, no. 3 (1986): 263–88.

D'Costa, Anthony. *Christianisation of the Goa Island*. Bombay: Heras Institute, 1965.

Dainville, François de. *La geographie des humanistes*. Paris: Beauchesne, 1940.

Delumeau, Jean. *Christianisme entre Luther et Voltaire*. Paris: PUF, 1971.

Dirks, Nicholas B. *The Hollow Crown: Ethno-history of an Indian Kingdom*. Cambridge: Cambridge University Press, 1987.

Ditchfield, Simon. "Thinking with Jesuit Saints: The Canonization of Ignatius Loyola and Francis Xavier in Context." *Journal of Jesuit Studies* 9, no. 3 (2022): 327–37.

Dumont, Louis. *Homo hierarchicus*. Chicago: University of Chicago Press, 1970.

Dürr, Renate, and Ulrike Strasser. "Wissensgenerierung als emotionale Praktik: Ethnographisches Schreiben und emotionalisiertes Lesen in Joseph Stöckleins S.J. Neuem Welt-Bott." *Historische Anthropologie* 28 (2020): 354–78.

Duve, Thomas José Luis Egío, and Christiane Birr, eds. *The School of Salamanca: A Case of Global Knowledge Production*. Leiden: Brill, 2021.

Ehalt, Rômulo da Silva. "Casuística nos trópicos: A pragmática teológico-moral de Francisco Rodrigues na Ásia portuguesa (séculos XVI e XVII)." *Revista de história da sociedade e da cultura* 19 (2019): 399–418.

Eliasson, Pär. "Towards a New Language: Christology in Early Modern Marathi, Konkani, and Hindustani." PhD diss., Uppsala University, 2022.

Faria, Patricia Souza de. "O pai dos cristaos e as populacoes escravas em Goa: Zelo e controle dos cativos convertidos (séculos XVI e XVII)." *História* (São Paulo) 39 (2020): 1–30.

Ferroli, Domenico, S.J. *The Jesuits in Malabar*. 2 Vols. Bangalore: King and Co., the National Press, 1939–51.

Figueiredo, João Manuel Pacheco. "Goa dourada nos séculos XVI e XVII: O hospital dos pobres do padre Paulo Camerete, esboco de sua reconstituição histórica." *Studia* 25 (1968): 117–46.

Filliozat, Pierre-Sylvain. "L'approche scientifique du sanscrit et de la pensée indienne par Heinrich Roth, S.J. au XVIIe siècle." In *L'œuvre scientifique des missionnaires en*

Asie, edited by Pierre-Sylvain Filliozat and Jean Leclant, 17–30. Paris: Académie des Inscriptions et Belles-Lettres, 2012.

Filliozat, Pierre-Sylvain. *À l'origine des études sanskrites: La grammatica sanscritica de Jean-François Pons s.j.* Paris: Academie *des* Inscriptions *et* Belles Lettres, 2020.

Findlen, Paula, ed. *Athanasius Kircher: The Last Man Who Knew Everything*. New York: Routledge, 2004.

Flores, Jorge M. "'Cael Velho,' 'Calepatanão,' and 'Punicale': The Portuguese and the Tambraparni Ports in the Sixteenth Century." *Bulletin de l'Ecole française d'Extrême-Orient* 82 (1995): 9–26.

Franco, José Eduardo, and Célia Tavares. "New Christians, Converted Hindus, Jesuits, and the Inquisition." *Journal of Jesuit Studies* 8, no. 2 (2021): 195–213.

Friedrich, Markus. *The Jesuits: A History*. Princeton: Princeton University Press, 2023.

García-Gallo, Alonso. "Las bullas de Alejandro VI y el ordenamiento jurídico de la expansión portuguesa y castellana en Africa e Indias." In *Los orígines españoles de las instituciones americanas: Estudios de derecho indiano*, 461–830. Madrid: R. Academia de Jurisprudencia y Legislación, 1987.

Geertz, Clifford. *The Interpretation of Cultures*. New York: Basic Books, 1973.

Ghesquière, Theodore. *Mathieu de Castro, premier vicaire apostolique aux Indes*. Louvain: Revue de la Bibliotheque de l'histoire ecclesiastique (fasc. 20), 1937.

Ghori, S.A. Khan. "The Impact of Modern European Astronomy on Raja Jai Singh." *Indian Journal of History of Science* 15, no. 1 (1980): 50–57.

Gomes, Paulo Varela. *Whitewash, Red Stone: A History of Church Architecture in Goa*. New Delhi: Yoda Press, 2011.

Gracias, Fatima da Silva. *Health and Hygiene in Colonial Goa (1510–1961)*. New Delhi: Concept Publishing, 1994.

Guha, Sumit. *Beyond Caste, Identity, and Power in South Asia, Past and Present*. Leiden: Brill, 2013.

Habbi, Joseph. "Signification de l'union chaldeenne de Mar Sulaqa avec Rome en 1553." *L'Orient Syrien* 11 (1966): 117–21.

Hambye, E.R. [Édouard René]. *History of Christianity in India, Eighteenth Century*. Vol. 3. Bangalore: Christian History Association of India, 1997.

Hart, George L. *The Poems of Ancient Tamils*. Berkeley: University of California Press, 1975.

Hornell, James. *The Sacred Chank of India: A Monograph of the Indian Conch (Turbinella pyrum)*. Madras: Govt. Press, 1914.

Horton, Robin. "On the Rationality of Conversion: Part I." *Africa: Journal of the International African Institute* 45, no. 3 (1975): 219–35.

Houpert, James C. *A South Indian Mission: The Madura Catholic Mission from 1535–1935*. 2nd ed. Trichinopoly: St. Joseph Industrial School, 1937.

Husson, L.-J. "Le P. Norbert de Bar-le-duc, Capucin (Pierre Curel Parisot, dit l'abbé Platel)." *Études franciscaines: Mélange d'histoire et de doctrine* 49 (1937): 632–49; 50 (1938): 63–77, 220–39; 51 (1939): 55–75.

Israel, Hephzibah. *Religious Transactions in Colonial South India: Language, Translation, and the Making of a Protestant Identity*. New York: Palgrave MacMillan, 2011.

Kamen, Henry. *The Spanish Inquisition*. London: White Lion Publishers, 1965.

Kapoor, R. [Ramesh] C. "Nur ud-di Jahangir and Father Kirwitzer: The Independent Discovery of the Great Comets of November 1618 and the First Astronomical Use of the Telescope in India." *Journal of Astronomical History and Heritage* 19, no. 3 (2016): 264–97.

Keyes, Charles F. "Why the Thais Are Not Christians: Buddhist and Christian Conversion in Thailand." In *Conversion to Christianity*, edited by Robert W. Hefner, 259–84. Berkeley: University of California Press, 1993.

Koch, Ebba. "The Influence of the Jesuit Missions." In *The Phenomenon of "Foreign" in Oriental Art*, edited by Annette Hagedorn, 117–30. Wiesbaden: Reichert, 2006.

Kroupa, Šebestián. "*Ex epistulis Philippinensibus*: Georg Joseph Kamel, S.J. (1661–1706) and His Correspondence Network." *Centaurus* 57 (2005): 229–59.

Kroupa, Šebestián. "Georg Joseph Kamel (1661–1706): A Jesuit Pharmacist at the Frontiers of Colonial Empires." PhD diss., University of Cambridge, 2019.

Launay, Adrian. *Histoire des missions de l'Inde, Pondichéry, Maïssour, Coïmbatour*. Vol. 1. Paris: Ancienne Maison Charles Douliol, 1898.

Liebau, Heike. "Controlled Transparency: The Hallesche Berichte and Neue Hallesche Berichte between 1710 and 1848." In *Reporting Christian Missions in the Eighteenth Century: Communication, Culture of Knowledge, and Regular Publication in a Cross-confessional Perspective*, edited by Markus Friedrich and Alexander Schunka, 133–48. Wiesbaden: Harrassowitz Verlag, 2017.

Llinares, Armand. *Raymond Lulle, philosophe de l'action*. Paris: Presse Universitaire de France, 1963.

Mahimai Dass, Anthoni Muthu. "Jesuit Letters and Mysore History Annual Letters and Relations of Mysore Mission as Source for the Secular History of the Kingdom of Mysore from the Year 1648 till 1704." PhD diss., Pontificia Università Gregoriana, Rome, 2020.

Malekandathil, Pius. *Portuguese Cochin and the Maritime Trade of India, 1500–1663*. New Delhi: Manohar, 2001.

Manickam, Alphonse. "Les jésuites et l'intouchabilité au Tamil Nadu: Études historiques et anthropologiques sur des approches longtemps différées." PhD diss., École Pratique des Hautes Études, Paris, 2001.

Marcocci, Giuseppe. "Jesuit Missionaries and the Portuguese Inquisition in South Asia: A Controversial History (16th–18th Centuries)." In *Intercultural Encounter and the*

Jesuit Mission in South Asia (16th–18th Centuries), edited by Anand Amaladass and Ines G. Županov, 232–56. Bangalore: Asian Trading Corporation, 2014.

Marques, António Henrique de Oliveira. *History of Portugal: From Lusitania to Empire, Vol. 1*. New York: Columbia University Press, 1976.

Martin, John. "Inventing Sincerity, Refashioning Prudence: The Discovery of the Individual in Renaissance Europe." *American Historical Review* 102, no. 5 (December 1997): 1309–42.

Martins, José F. Ferreira. *História de Misericórdia de Goa*. 3 Vols. Nova Goa: Imprensa Nacional, 1910–1914.

Maryks, Robert A. *The Jesuit Order as a Synagogue of Jews: Jesuits of Jewish Ancestry and Purity-of-Blood Laws in the Early Society of Jesus*. Leiden: Brill, 2010.

Mastrangelo, Carmela. "History and Pedagogy of Sanskrit Grammar through the Works of Western Missionaries: Johann Ernst Hanxleden and Paulinus a Sancto Bartholomaeo." *Indologica Taurinensia* 41–42 (2016): 83–98.

Mecherry, Anthony, S.J. *Testing Ground for Jesuit Accommodation in Early Modern India: Francisco Ros, s.j. in Malabar (16th–17th Centuries)*. Rome: Institutum Historicum Societatis Iesu, 2019.

Meersman, Achilles. *The Ancient Franciscan Provinces in India 1500–1835*. Bangalore: Christian Literature Society, 1971.

Melo, Carlos M. de, s.j. *The Recruitment and Formation of the Native Clergy in India*. Lisbon: Agencia geral do Ultramar, 1955.

Mendiratta, Sidh Losa. "From Rome to Goa: The Question of the First Goan Church." In *Palimpsests of Religious Encounter in Asia, 1500–1800*, edited by Mia M. Mochizuki and Ines G. Županov. Leiden: Brill, in press.

Merrill, William L. "Conversion and Colonialism in Northern Mexico: The Tarahumara Response to the Jesuit Mission Program, 1601–1767." In *Conversion to Christianity*, edited by Robert W. Hefner, 129–65. Berkeley: University of California Press, 1993.

Metzler, Josef, o.m.i. *Sacrae Congregationis de Propaganda Fide Memoria Rerum: 350 Years in the Service of the Missions*, vol. 1/1, (*1522–1700*). Rome: Herder, 1972.

Milhou, Alain. "Découvertes et christianisation lointaine." In *Histoire du Christianisme: De la réforme à la Réformation (1450–1530)*, edited by Charles Pietri, Luce Pietri, André Vauchez, Marc Venard, and Jean-Marie Mayeur, 521–616. Paris: Desclée, 1994.

Mines, Mattison, and Vijayalakshmi Gourishankar. "Leadership and Individuality in South Asia: The Case of the South Indian Big-Man." *Journal of Asian Studies* 49, no. 4 (November 1990): 761–86.

Mosse, David. "*Caste, Christianity, and Hinduism: A Study of Social Organisation and Religion in Rural Ramnad.*" PhD diss., University of Oxford, 1984.

Mourelle, Noel Blanco. "Every Knowable Thing: The Art of Ramon Llull and the Construction of Knowledge." PhD diss., Columbia University, New York, 2017.

Mudenge, S.I.G. *A Political History of Munhumutapa, c.1400–1902*. Harare: Zimbabwe Publishing House, 1988.

Mundadan, Mathias, C.M.I. *History of Christianity in India: From the Beginning up to the Middle of the Sixteenth Century (up to 1542)*. Bangalore: Church History Association of India, 1989.

Murr, Sylvia. *L'Inde philosophique entre Bossuet et Voltaire: L'Indologie du père Coeurdoux*. 2 Vols. Paris: EFEO, 1987.

Muru, Cristina. "Gaspar de Aguilar: A Banished Genius." In *Intercultural Encounter and the Jesuit Mission in South Asia*, edited by Anand Amaladass and Ines G. Županov, 353–89. Bangalore: Asian Trading Corporation, 2014.

Muru, Cristina. *The Linguistic and Historical Contribution of the* Arte Tamulica *by Baltasar da Costa, S.J. (c.1610–1673)*. Vila Real: Centro de Estudos em Letras, Universidade de Trás-os-Montes e Alto Douro, 2022.

Narayana Rao, Velcheru, David Shulman, and Sanjay Subrahmanyam. *Symbols of Substance: Court and State in Nāyaka Period Tamil Nadu*. New Delhi: Oxford University Press, 1993.

Narchinson, J. Rosario. "Towards a Historiography of Martyr Devasahayam." In *India's Christian Heritage*, edited by O. [Oberland] L. Snaitang and George Menachery, 135–45. Bangalore: CHAI, 2011.

Natif, Mika. *Mughal Occidentalism: Artistic Encounters between Europe and Asia at the Courts of India, 1580–1630*. Leiden: Brill, 2018.

Neill, Stephen. *A History of Christianity in India, 1707–1858*. London: Cambridge University Press, 1985.

Nevett, Albert. *John De Britto and His Times*. Anand: Gujarat Sahitya Prakash, 1980.

Noti, Severin. "Joseph Tieffenthaler: A Forgotten Geographer of India." *East and West* 5, nos. 51–54 (1906): 142–54.

O'Flaherty, Wendy Doniger. *Asceticism and Eroticism in the Mythology of Siva*. Oxford: Oxford University Press, 1973.

O'Malley, John W., S.J. *The First Jesuits*. London: Harvard University Press, 1993.

Osswald, Maria Cristina. *Written in Stone: Jesuit Buildings in Goa and Their Artistic and Architectural Features*. Saligao: Goa 1556 and Golden Heart Emporium Book Shop, 2013.

Padipara, Placid J., C.M.I. *The Hierarchy of the Syro-Malabar Church*. Alleppey: Prakasam Publications, 1976.

Pagden, Anthony. *The Fall of Natural Man: The American Indian and the Origins of Comparative Anthropology*. Cambridge: Cambridge University Press, 1983.

Pavone, Sabina. "Jesuits and Oriental Rites in the Documents of the Roman Inquisition." In *The Rites Controversies in the Early Modern World*, edited by Ines G. Županov and Pierre-Antoine Fabre, 165–88. Leiden: Brill, 2018.

Pearson, Michael N. *Port Cities and Intruders: The Swahili Coast, India, and Portugal in the Early Modern Era*. Baltimore: Johns Hopkins University Press, 1998.

Pearson, Michael N. *The Portuguese in India*. Cambridge: Cambridge University Press, 1987.

Perczel, István. "Accommodationist Strategies on the Malabar Coast: Competition or Complementarity?" In *The Rites Controversies in the Early Modern World*, edited by Ines G. Županov and Pierre-Antoine Fabre, 191–232. Leiden: Brill, 2018.

Perczel, István. "Cosmopolitismes de la Mer d'Arabie: Les chrétiens de saint Thomas face à l'expansion Portugaise." In *Cosmopolitismes en Asie du Sud: Sources, intinéraires, langues (XVIe–XVIIIe siècle)*, edited by Corinne Lefèvre, Ines G. Županov, and Jorge Flores, 143–69. Collection Puruṣārtha 33. Paris: Éditions de l'École des hautes études en sciences sociales, 2015.

Perczel, István. "Syriac Christianity in India." In *The Syriac World*, edited by Daniel King, 653–97. London: Routledge, 2018.

Pereira, José. *Baroque Goa: The Architecture of Portuguese India*. New Delhi: Books and Books, 1995.

Pereira, José. *Churches of Goa*. New Delhi: Oxford University Press, 2001.

Perera, Simon Gregory, S.J. *Life of the Venerable Father Joseph Vaz*. Galle: Loyola House, 1953 [1943].

Pillei, Muttusami. "A Brief Sketch of the Life and Writings of Father C. J. Beschi, or Viramamunivar." *Madras Journal of Literature and Science* 11 (1840): 250–300.

Pissurlencar, Panduronga. "Um Hindu, autor desconhecido de duas publicações portuguesas." Separata of *Memórias* (Classe de Letras) 7 (Lisbon: Academia de Ciências de Lisboa, *1959*): 129–32.

Pothan, Sidney George. *The Syrian Christians of Kerala*. New York: Asia Pub. House, 1963.

Price, Pamela. *Kingship and Political Practice in Colonial India*. Cambridge: Cambridge University Press Cambridge, 1996.

Priolkar, Anant K. *The Goa Inquisition*. Bombay: Bombay University Press, 1961.

Puthur, Bosco, ed. *St. Thomas Christian and Nambudiris, Jews, and Sangam Literature: A Historical Appraisal*. Kochi: LRC Publications, 2003.

Raina, Dhruv. "Becoming All Things to All: French Jesuit Scientists and the Construction of the Antiquity of the Sciences of India." In *L'Inde des Lumières*, edited by Marie Fourcade and Ines G. Županov, 335–58. Collection Purushartha 31. Paris: Éditions de l'École des hautes études en sciences sociales, 2013. https://doi.org/10.4000/books.editionsehess.22722 (accessed September 21, 2024).

Raina, Dhruv. "Betwixt Jesuit and Enlightenment Historiography: Jean Sylvain Bailly's History of Indian Astronomy." *Revue d'histoire des mathématique* 9 (2003): 253–306.

Raina, Dhruv. "Circulation and Cosmopolitanism in 18th-Century Jaipur: The Workshop of *Jyotishis, Nujumi,* and Jesuit Astronomers." In *Cosmopolitismes en Asie du Sud: Sources, intinéraires, langues* (XVIe–XVIIIe *siècle*), edited by Corinne Lefèvre, Ines G. Županov, and Jorge Flores, 307–30. Collection Purushartha 33. Paris: Éditions de l'École des hautes études en sciences sociales, 2015.

Raina, Dhruv. "'Come, let us ascend to the heavens': The Jantar Mantar at Jaipur and the Politics of Scientific Architecture." In *Palimpsests of Religious Encounter in Asia, 1500–1800*, edited by Mia M. Mochizuki and Ines G. Županov. Leiden: Brill, in press.

Raina, Dhruv. "The French Jesuit Manuscripts on Indian Astronomy: The Narratology and Mystery Surrounding a Late Seventeenth–Early Eighteenth Century Project." In *Looking at It from Asia: The Processes That Shaped the Sources of History of Science*, ed. Florence Bretelle-Establet, 115–39. New York: Springer, 2010.

Raina, Dhruv. "French Jesuit Scientists in India: Historical Astronomy in the Discourse on India, 1670–1770." *Economic and Political Weekly* 34, no. 5 (January 30–February 5, 1990): 30–38.

Restif-Filliozat, Manonmani. "The Jesuit Contribution to the Geographical Knowledge of India in the Eighteenth Century." *Journal of Jesuit Studies* 6, no. 1 (2019): 71–84.

Retif, André, S.J. "Missionnaire et savants dans le domaine linguistique." *Studia missionalia* 7 (1953): 394–413.

Ribeiro, Lorhany Cordeiro. "Chronologia da Congregação do Oratório de Goa: Uma construçãode memória (século XVIII)." Paper presented at XXVII Simposto Nacional de Historia, Natal, July 22–26, 2023.

Rivara, Joaquim Heliodoro da Cunha. *Ensaio histórico da lingua concani.* Nova Goa: Imprensa Nacional, 1858.

Roche, Patrick A. *Fishermen of the Coromandel.* New Delhi: Manohar, 1984.

Rocher, Rosane. "The Knowledge of Sanskrit in Europe." In *History of the Language Sciences/Geschichte der Sprachwissenschaften*, edited by Sylvain Auroux, E.F.K. [Ernst Frideryk Konrad] Koerner, Hans-Josef Niederehe, and Kees Versteegh, 1156–63. Berlin: Walter De Gruyter, 2000.

Royson, Annie Rachel. *Texts, Traditions, and Sacredness: Cultural Translation in Kristapurāṇa.* London: Routledge, 2022.

Roufe, Gai. "The Reasons for a Murder: Local Cultural Conceptualizations of the Martyrdom of Gonçalo da Silveira in 1561." *Cahiers d'études africaines* 219 (2015): 467–87.

Rubiés, Joan Pau. "From Antiquarianism to Philosophical History: India, China, and the World; History of Religion in European Thought (1600–1770)." In *Antiquarianism and Intellectual Life in Early Modern Europe and China, 1500–1800*, edited by Peter N. Miller and François Louis, 313–67. Ann Arbor: University of Michigan Press, 2012.

Rubiés, Joan Pau. "From Christian Apologetics to Deism: Libertine Readings of Hinduism, 1600–1730." In *God in the Enlightenment*, edited by William J.J. Bulman and Robert G. Ingram, 107–35. Oxford: Oxford University Press, 2016.

Rubiés, Joan Pau. "The Jesuit Discovery of Hinduism: Antonio Rubino's Account of the History and Religion of Vijayanagara (1608)." *Archiv für Religionsgeschichte* 3, no. 1 (2001): 210–56.

Rubiés, Joan Pau. *Travel and Ethnology in Renaissance South India through European Eyes, 1250–1625*. Cambridge: Cambridge University Press, 2000.

Russell, Camilla. "Becoming 'Indians.'" *Renaissance and Reformation/Renaissance et Réforme* 43, no. 1 (Winter 2020): 9–50.

Russo, Mariagrazia. "O pioneirismo na gramaticografia portuguesa de cunho italiano." *Lingue linguaggi* 57 (2023): 113–27.

Sá, Isabel dos Guimarães. *Quando o rico se faz pobre: Misericordias, caridade e poder no imperio portugues, 1500–1800*. Lisbon: Comissão nacional para as comemoracões dos descobrimentos portugueses, 1997.

Saulière, Auguste, s.j. *Red Sand: A Life of St. John De Britto, s.j., Martyr of the Madura Missions*. Madurai: De Nobili Press, 1947.

Schrimpt, Robert. "Le diable et le goupillon." In *Goa 1510–1685: L'Inde portugaise, apostolique et commerciale*, edited by Michel Chaindeigne, 115–34. Paris: Ed. Autrement, 1996.

Schulman, David D. *Tamil Temple Myths*. Princeton: Princeton University Press, 1980.

Schurhammer, Georg, s.j. *Francis Xavier: His Life, His Times*. Translated by M. Joseph Costelloe, s.j. 4 Vols. Rome: Jesuit Historical Institute, 1977.

Schurhammer, Georg, s.j. "Jugendprobleme des hl. Franz Xaver." *Studia missionalia* 2 (1946): 83–86.

Schurhammer, Georg, s.j. *The Malabar Church and Rome during the Early Portuguese Period and Before*. Trichinopoly: St. Joseph Industrial School Press, 1934.

Schurhammer, Georg, s.j., and G.W. Cottrell Jr. "The First Printing in Indic Characters." *Orientalia* (Lisbon: BIHSI, 1963): 317–27.

Serão, Vítor. "Quadros da vida de São Francisco Xavier." *Oceanos* 12 (1992): 56–69.

Sievernich, Michaël. "Geographical Mapping of India in the 18th Century: The Contribution of the German Jesuit Joseph Tief[f]enthaler (1710–85)." In *Intercultural Encounter and Jesuit Mission in India (16th–18th Centuries)*, edited by Anand Amaladass and Ines G. Županov, 290–320. Bangalore: Asian Trading Corporation, 2014.

Silva, Chandra R. de. "The Portuguese and Pearl Fishing off South India and Sri Lanka." *South Asia* 1, no. 1 (March 1978): 18–20.

Snow, David A., and Richard Machalek. "The Sociology of Conversion." *Annual Review of Sociology* 10 (1984): 167–90.

Sorrentino, Antonio. *L'altra perla dell'India*. Bologne: Collana "studi e saggi," 1989.

Souza, George Bryan. "The French Connection: Indian Cottons, Their Early Modern Technology and Diffusion." In *How India Clothed the World: The World of South Asian Textiles, 1500–1850*, edited by Giorgio Riello and Tirthankar Roy, 347–63. Leiden: Brill, 2009.

Souza, Teotonio R. de. *Medieval Goa: A Socio-economic History*. New Delhi: Concept Publishing, 1979.

Srinivas, M.N. [Mysore Narasimhachar]. *Social Change in Modern India*. Berkeley: University of California Press, 1966.

Strasser, Ulrike. *Missionary Men in the Early Modern World: German Jesuits and Pacific Journeys*. Amsterdam: Amsterdam University Press, 2020.

Strathern, Alan. *Kingship and Conversion in Sixteenth-Century Sri Lanka: Portuguese Imperialism in a Buddhist Land*. Cambridge: Cambridge University Press, 2008.

Streit, Robert. *Bibliotheca missionum*. Vol. 4. Münster: Achener Missionsdrukerei A.-G., 1929.

Sweetman, Will. "Bartholomaus Ziegenbalg, the Tranquebar Mission, and 'The Roman Horror.'" In *Halle and the Beginning of Protestant Christianity in India: Christian Mission in the Indian Context*, edited by Andreas Gross, Y. Vincent Kumaradoss, and Heike Liebau, 2:797–811. Halle: Verlag der Franckeschen Stiftungen zu Halle, 2006.

Sweetman, Will. "The Cessation of the Oracles: Authenticity and Authority in Jesuit Reports of Possession in South India." In *Intercultural Encounter and Jesuit Mission in South Asia (16th–18th Centuries)*, edited by Anand Amaladass and Ines G. Županov, 156–78. Bangalore: Asian Trading Corporation, 2014.

Sweetman, Will. "Reading Jesuit Readings of Hinduism." *Jesuit Historiography Online*, edited by Robert A. Maryks. Leiden: Brill, October 2019. https://referenceworks.brill.com/display/entries/JHO/COM-217891.xml (accessed September 21, 2024).

Tambiah, Stanley J. *World Conqueror and World Renouncer: A Study of Buddhism and Polity in Thailand against a Historical Background*. Cambridge: Cambridge University Press, 1976.

Tavares, Célia Cristina da Silva. *Jesuítas e inquisidores em Goa: A Cristandade insular (1540–1682)*. Lisbon: Roma editora, 2004.

Tavim, José A.R. da Silva. "From Setúbal to the Sublime Porte: The Wandering of Jácome de Olivares, New Christian and Merchant of Cochin (1540–1571)." *Santa Barbara Portuguese Studies* 2 (1995): 94–134.

Thani Nayagam, Xavier S. "Antão de Proença's Tamil–Portuguese Dictionary, 1679." *Tamil Culture* 6 (1964): 117–32.

Thani Nayagam, Xavier S. "The First Books Printed in Tamil." *Tamil Culture* 7 (July 1958): 288–308.

Thani Nayagam, Xavier S. "Tamil Manuscripts in European Libraries." *Tamil Culture* 3 (July 1954): 219–30.

Thekkedath, Joseph. *History of Christianity in India: From the Middle of the Sixteenth Century to the End of the Seventeenth Century (1542–1700)*. Bangalore: Theological Publications in India, 1982.

Thomáz, Luís Filipe F.R. "Factions, Interests, and Messianism: The Politics of Portuguese Expansion in the East, 1500–1521." *Indian Economic and Social History Review* 28, no. 1 (1991): 97–109.

Thomáz, Luís Filipe F.R. "L'idée impériale manueline." In *La découverte, le Portugal et l'Europe*, edited by Jean Aubin, 35–103. Paris: Centre culturel Calouste Gulbenkian, 1990.

Thomáz, Luís Filipe F.R. "Le Portugal et l'Afrique au XVe siècle: Les débuts de l'expansion." *Arquivos do Centro Cultural Português* 26 (1989): 61–256.

Trento, Margherita. "Martyrdom, Witnessing, and Social Lineages in the Tamil Country (Seventeenth and Eighteenth Centuries)." *Annales HSS* (English ed.). DOI: 10.1017/ahsse.2022.26 (accessed September 22, 2024).

Trento, Margherita. "Śivadharma or Bonifacio? Behind the Scenes of the Madurai Mission Controversy (1608–1618)." In *The Rites Controversies in the Early Modern World*, edited by Ines G. Županov and Pierre-Antoine Fabre, 91–121. Leiden: Brill, 2018.

Trento, Margherita. *Writing Tamil Catholicism: Literature, Persuasion, and Devotion in the Eighteenth Century*. Leiden: Brill, 2022.

Varela, Consuelo, and Guy Martinière, eds. *L'état du monde en 1492*. Paris: La découverte, 1992.

Vaz, Francisco Xavier. "Primeiros clerigos indios." *O oriente portuguez* 6 (1909): 210–11.

Ventura, Ricardo Nuno de Jesus. "Conversão e conversabilidade Discursos da missão e do gentio na documentação do Padroado Português do Oriente (séculos XVI e XVII)." PhD diss., Lisbon University, 2011.

Viele, Christopher. "Devotional Christianity and Pre-Indology in Early Eighteenth-Century Kerala: Johann Ernst Hanxlee, S.J., Alias Arnos Padiri, Scholar and Poet." In *Transposition and Transformation, Controversy and Discovery: On the Christian Encounter with the Religions of Eighteenth and Nineteenth-Century India*, edited by Karin Preisendanz and Johanna Buss, 1–48. Vienna: Samlung De Nobili, 2021.

Visvanathan, Susan. *The Christians of Kerala*. Madras: Oxford University Press, 1993.

Vriddhagirisan, V. *The Nayaks of Tanjore*. Annamalinagar: Annamalai University, 1942.

Vu-Thanh, Hélène, and Ines G. Županov, eds. *Trade and Finance in Global Missions (16th–18th Centuries)*. Leiden: Brill, 2021.

Walker, Anthony R. *Between Tradition and Modernity and Other Essays on the Toda of South India*. New Delhi: B. R. Publishing Corporation, 1998.

Weintraub, Michael. "Translations: Words, Things, Going Native, and Staying True." *American Historical Review* 120, no. 4 (October 2015): 1195–217.

White, David Gordon. *Myths of the Dog-Man.* Chicago: University of Chicago Press, 1991.

Wicki, Josef, S.J. "The Confraternity of Charity of Henrique Henriques." *Indian Church History Review* 1, no. 1 (1967): 3–8.

Wicki, Josef, S.J. "Der einheimische Klerus in Indien." In *Der einheimische Klerus in Geschichte und Gegenwart*, edited by Johannes Beckmann, 17–72. Schöneck-Beckenried: Administration der Neuen Zeitschrift für Missionswissenschaft, 1950.

Wicki, Josef, S.J. "Jesuitenmaler und -bildhauer in Indien im 16. Jahrhundert." *Neue Zeitschrift für Missionswissenschaft* 38 (1982): 30–39.

Wicki, Josef, S.J. "Kanara und die dortige Jesuitenmission 1646, 1648 in der Darsterllung des P. Leonardo Cinnamo S.I. Honävar Anfang 1648, in addition to 'Istoria del Canara regno dell'India orientale nelle prov. Goana della Compagnia di Gesù,' scritta dal padre L. Cinnamo superiore di quella nuova missione (ms. A.R.S.I., Goa 34, II, ff. 308–372)." *Sonderbruck aus Portugiesiche Forschungen. Erste Reihe. Aufsätze zur Portugiesischen Kulturgeschichte* 16 (1980): 261–345.

Wicki, Josef, S.J. *Missionskirche im Orient.* Immensee: Neue Zeitschrift für Missionwissenschaft, 1976.

Wicki, Josef, S.J. "Pedro Luis, Brahmane und erster indischer Jesuit (ca. 1532–1596)." *Neue Zeitschrift für Missionswissenschaf* 6 (1950): 115–26.

Wright, Jessica, Leon Grek, and Wendy Laura Belcher, eds. and trans. *The Jesuits in Ethiopia (1609–1641): Latin Letters in Translation.* Introduced by Leonardo Cohen. Wiesbaden: Harrassowitz Verlag, 2017.

Xavier, Ângela Barreto. "*Conversos* and *Novamente convertidos*: Law, Religion, and Identity in the Portuguese Kingdom and Empire." *Journal of Early Modern History* 15 (2011): 255–87.

Xavier, Ângela Barreto. *A invenção de Goa.* Lisbon: Imprensa de Ciências Sociais, 2008.

Xavier, Ângela Barreto. "Languages of Difference in the Portuguese Empire: The Spread of 'Caste' in the Indian World." *Anuario colombiano de historia social y de la cultura* 43, no. 2 (2016): 89–119.

Xavier, Ângela Barreto. "Reducing Difference in the Portuguese Empire: A Case Study from Early Modern Goa." In *Changing Societies: Legacies and Challenges*, vol. 1, *Ambiguous Inclusions: Inside Out, Inside In*, edited by Sofia Aboim, Paulo Granjo, and Alice Ramos, 241–61. Lisbon: Imprensa de Ciências Sociais, 2016.

Xavier, Ângela Barreto. *Religion and Empire in Portuguese India: Conversion, Resistance, and the Making of Goa.* Albany, NY: SUNY Press, 2022.

Xavier, Ângela Barreto, and Ines G. Županov. "Ser brâmane na Goa da Época Moderna." *Revista de história* 172 (São Paulo) (January–June 2015): 15–41. http://dx.doi.org/10.11606/issn.2316-9141.rh.2015.98757 (accessed September 2, 2024).

Xavier, P.D. *Goa: A Social History*. Panaji: Rajhauns, 1993.

Zachariae, Theodor. "Über die 'Breve noticia dos erros que tem os Gentios do Concão da India.'" *Nachrichten von der Königlichen Gesellschaft der Wissenschaften zu Göttingen, Philologisch-historische Klasse aus dem Jahre 1918*, 1–34. Berlin: Weidmannsche Buchhandlung, 1918.

Zeron, Carlos. "Political Theory and Jesuit Politics." In *The Oxford Handbook of the Jesuits*, edited by Ines G. Županov, 193–215. New York: Oxford University Press, 2019.

Županov, Ines G. "Amateur Naturalist and 'Professional' Orienalist: Paulinus a S. Bartholomaeo in Kerala and Rome (18th–19th c.)." *Revista de cultura/Review of Culture* 20 (2006): 77–10.

Županov, Ines G. "*Antiquissima Christianità*: Indian Religion or Idolatry? (17th–18th c.)." *Journal of Early Modern History* 24 (2020): 471–98.

Županov, Ines G. "Aristocratic Analogies and Demotic Descriptions in the Seventeenth-Century Madurai Mission." *Representations* 41 (1991): 123–48.

Županov, Ines G. "Curar o corpo, sarar a alma: A missão médica jesuíta na Índia do século XVI (Curing the Body, Healing the Soul: The Jesuit Medical Mission in Sixteenth-Century India)." *Oriente* (Revista quadrimestral da Fundação Oriente) (2005): 3–19.

Županov, Ines G. *Disputed Mission: Jesuit Experiments and Brahmanical Knowledge in Seventeenth-Century India*. New Delhi: Oxford University Press, 1999.

Županov, Ines G. "Goan Brahmans in the Land of Promise: Missionaries, Spies, and Gentiles in 17th–18th-Century Sri Lanka." In *Re-exploring the Links: History and Constructed Histories between Portugal and Sri Lanka*, edited by Jorge Flores, 171–210. South China and Maritime Asia Series. Wiesbaden: Harrassowitz and the Calouste Gulbenkian Foundation, 2006.

Županov, Ines G. "'I am a great sinner': Missionary Dialogues in India (16th Century)." In *Cultural Dialogue in South Asia and Beyond: Narratives, Images, and Community (Sixteenth–Nineteenth Centuries)*, edited by Corinne Lefèvre and Ines G. Županov. Thematic issue of the *Journal of Economic and Social History of the Orient* 55, nos. 2–3 (June 2012): 415–46.

Županov, Ines G. "Jesuit Proselytism versus Resilient Religious Pluralism: Two South Indian Missions in the 16th and 17th Centuries." In *Intercultural Encounter and the Jesuit Mission in South Asia (16th to 18th Centuries)*, edited by Anand Amaladass and Ines G. Županov, 199–231. Bangalore: Asian Trading Corporation, 2014.

Županov, Ines G. "Lust, Marriage, and Free Will: Jesuit Critique of Paganism in South India (Seventeenth Century)." *Studies in History* 16, no. 2 (July–December 2000): 199–220.

Županov, Ines G. *Missionary Tropics: The Catholic Frontier in India (16th–17th Centuries)*. Ann Arbor: University of Michigan Press, 2005.

Županov, Ines G. "Orientalist Museum: Roman Missionary Collections and Prints (Eighteenth Century)." In *Ancient to Modern: Religion, Power, and Community*, edited by Ishita Banerjee-Dube and Saurabh Dube, 207–35. New Delhi: Oxford University Press, 2009.

Županov, Ines G. "Passage to India: Jesuit Spiritual Economy between Martyrdom and Profit in the Seventeenth Century." *Journal of Early Modern History* 16 (2012): 121–59.

Županov, Ines G. "Prosélytisme et pluralisme religieux: Deux expériences missionnaires en Inde aux XVIe et XVIIe siècles." *Archives de sciences sociales des religions* 87 (1994): 35–56.

Županov, Ines G., and Pierre Antoine Fabre, eds. *The Rites Controversies in the Early Modern World.* Leiden: Brill, 2018.

Zurara, Gomes Eanes de. *Crónica dos feitos notáveis que se passaram na conquista da Guiné por mandado do Infante d. Henrique.* Lisbon: Academia portuguesa da história, 1978.

Zwartjes, Otto. *Portuguese Missionary Grammars in Asia, Africa, and Brazil, 1550–1800.* Amsterdam: John Benjamins, 2011.

Index

Accommodation 1, 7, 26n74, 33, 35nn110, 37, 39, 39nn118, 42, 51, 53n165, 64, 66, 69, 70n211, 71–72, 74, 80–82, 89–90, 92
Afonso, Pedro 95
Aguilar, Gaspar de 83–84, 84n259
Albuquerque, Afonso de 14, 19–20
Ambalakkadavu 81–82
Angamaly 36, 38–39
Anquetil-Duperron, Abraham Hyacinth 87, 100, 100n327
Antonio, Gaspar 95
Augustinian 26, 33, 36, 40
Avūr 71, 85

Baldaeus, Philippus 83
Bardez 20, 26
Barradas, Manuel 91
Barros, João de 78, 78n237, 84
Bartoli, Daniello 7
Bassein 33
Basto, Pedro de 8, 8nn14–15
Belur 66
Benares 87, 98
Benedict XIV 75–76
Bernoulli, Johann 100, 100n327
Bertoldi, Carlo Michele 85
Bertrand, Joseph 103, 104nn333–334
Beschi, Costanzo Giuseppe 81, 83–85, 93
Besse Léon 59n179, 69
Bignon, Jean-Paul 87
Bijapur 20, 28, 66
Bouchet, Jean Venant 66, 69–71, 85, 92n294, 101, 101n329, 102
Boudier, Claude Stanislas 97, 99, 99n321, 101
Bourzés, Noël de 84, 101, 101n329
Bragança, Constantino de 24
Brahman 10, 20, 26, 32, 41n127, 42, 42n128, 50–54, 58, 64, 70–73, 80–81, 83, 83n261, 87, 90, 99–100, 102–103
Bramane, Pedro Luís 31, 104
Brandolini, Broglia Antonio 71, 72n218, 74n227, 75
Brazil 6, 84n258
British 7n12, 48, 52, 80n243, 83, 94n302, 99, 103

Brito, João de (or Jean de) 58–59, 58n180, 60–61, 61n184, 71, 76, 92
Cabral, Pedro Álvares 13, 37
Calmette, Jean 86, 86n270, 94, 96
Camões, Luís Vaz de 14
Canarim 24, 24n67, 79
Canonization 6, 29, 30n89
Capuchin 9, 26, 36, 69, 71n217, 76, 92, 102n332
Cassini, Gian-Domenico 97
Caste 32, 42n128, 44, 44n136, 47, 48, 48nn151, 153, 56–58, 58n178, 60n182, 61–62, 62n189–190, 70, 74–75, 81, 89, 89n280, 90, 102–103
Castro, Mattheus de 32
Certeau, Michel de 10, 11n25, 14n38, 25n69
Chandernagore, Chandannagar 69, 84, 97, 99
Cinami [or Cinnami, Cinammo], Leonardo 64, 64n196, 65, 65nn199–201, 66, 66n203
Clement XIV 102
Coeurdoux, Gaston-Laurent 10n23, 76, 83, 94, 94n302, 96–97, 99–101
Coimbra 34, 59n180
Colbert, Jean-Baptiste 97
Confession 27, 78–79
Confraternity 20–21, 47n149
Conversion 1, 17, 19–20, 24, 26–28, 31, 35, 37, 41–44, 48, 50–53, 57–58, 61–63, 67, 69–70, 73, 90, 102–104
Coromandel coast 2, 11, 19, 43, 48, 66, 68
Costa, Baltasar da 81, 82n249, 83
Costa, Manuel da 5
Cranganore (Kodungallur) 33n103, 38, 39n117, 41n127, 53n164
Cristãos novos, Jews 10, 14, 31, 34, 50, 73
Croze, Mathurin Veyssière de la 11, 11n27

Dellon, Charles Gabriel 35, 92
Desvaulx, Nicolas-Jacques 94
Dictionary 45, 65, 81, 84–85, 86n270
Discalced Carmelite 41, 68, 82, 85, 93
Divar 26

Dominican 19, 25, 38
Dubois, Abbé Jean-Antoine 94, 94*n*302
Ducros, Gilbert 86
Dumont, Louis 57, 57*n*177, 89
Dutch 41, 48, 68–69

Egypt 13, 73
Enlightenment 10, 92*n*294, 97, 100–101
Estado da Índia 8, 13, 17, 33, 37–38, 44, 64, 66, 78
Ethiopia 12, 13*n*31, 18, 18*n*49, 27

Fabroni, Carlo Agostino 71
Fenicio, Giacomo 90–91, 93*n*299
Fernandes Trancoso, Gonçalo 50–51, 53, 73, 89–91
Ferroli, Domenico 59*n*179, 74
Flos sanctorum 46*n*142, 83*n*253
Fontaine, Jean Baptiste de la 69
Franceschi, Angelo de 63, 64*n*195
Franciscan 14, 19, 21, 23, 26, 36, 38
François-Marie de Tours 69
French 1–2, 5–6, 8–11, 57*n*177, 65*n*199, 66, 68–69, 71, 74, 76, 84, 85*n*263, 86–88, 91*n*289, 92*n*294, 94, 96–97, 98*n*318, 99, 101, 102*nn*331–332, 103

Gabelsberger, Anthony 97
Gama, Vasco da 2, 13
Garcia (Mendes), Francisco 40, 92–93, 93*n*296
Gargam, Memmius René 86, 86*n*270
Garnier, Louis 103
Goa 1–3, 5, 8, 14, 17, 19–22, 22*n*61, 23–31, 33–34, 35*nn*107, 109, 36, 39, 40*n*124, 42, 51*nn*158–159, 53*nn*163–164, 54*n*166, 55*nn*169–170, 56*nn*171–172, 174, 175, 57*n*177, 59*n*180, 62, 64–66, 72–73, 78–79, 80*n*244, 90, 94*n*303, 95–96, 102*n*332
Gonçalves, Diogo 6, 90–91
Gonçalves, Sebastião 1–2, 2*n*1, 5, 27, 42, 44
Goubil, Antoine 97
Gregory XV 73
Guerreiro, Fernão 6, 7*n*12, 28*n*82

Hanxleden, Johann Ernst 84*n*258, 85–86, 86*n*269
Hariścandra 93, 93*n*296
Henriques, Henrique 45–46, 46*n*145, 47*n*149, 50, 78, 80, 84
Hospital 21–22, 25, 95

Idolatry 73, 100
Italian 5–7, 28, 35–36, 41, 50–51, 53*n*165, 55, 56*n*171, 65, 68*n*206, 83, 90

Jaipur 97–98, 98*n*319, 99–100
Jantar Mantar 99
Japan 6, 33, 36, 54*n*166, 64, 65*n*199, 79
Jarric, Pierre du 6–7, 7*n*12
Jesuit 1–3, 5, 5*nn*4–5, 6–12, 13*n*31, 18, 21, 23–32, 32*nn*98–99, 33, 35–36, 38*n*115, 39–42, 44–48, 48*n*153, 49–50, 53–54, 54*nn*165–166, 55–59, 59*n*180, 60–61, 61*nn*185–186, 62–64, 64*n*197, 65–66, 68, 68*n*208, 69–70, 70*nn*211–212, 71, 71*nn*216–217, 72–90, 91*n*288, 92–93, 93*n*299, 94, 94*nn*302–303, 95, 95*nn*305, 307, 96–97, 98*nn*318, 319, 99–102, 102*nn*329–330, 332, 103–104, 104*nn*333, 335–336
João da Cruz 44, 44*n*133

Kanara 33, 65*nn*199, 201–202, 68
Kangxi 96
Kaṉṉiyākumari 63, 91
Kannur 13, 19, 66
Karumattampaṭṭi 63
Kerala 6, 11, 18*n*51, 37–38, 42, 49, 62*n*189, 63, 67, 68*n*206, 85, 90, 92
Kilakkarai 43
Kirwitzer, Wenceslaus Pantaleon 96
Kochi (Cochin) 13, 19–20, 31, 32*n*94, 36, 41, 42*n*127, 44, 45*n*140, 51*nn*158–159, 53*nn*163, 165, 55*n*170, 56*nn*171, 174, 66, 68, 72, 73*n*221, 96
Kollam (Quilon) 13, 42*n*127, 44, 45*n*141
Konkani 64, 78–79, 80*n*242
Kōttār 91
Kozhikode (Calicut) 13, 44, 66

Laerzio (Laertio), Alberto 7
Laínez, Francisco 71
Laplace, Pierre Simon 97

Latin   5, 18n49, 37, 40n120, 41, 45, 50n156, 56n172, 78–80, 83–84, 86–89, 90n286
Letters, cartas, epistolae   9, 14n37, 23n64, 44n134, 46n144
Lettres édifiantes et curieuses   9
Lisbon   6nn10–11, 8nn13–14, 12nn29–30, 13n31, 14n37, 15n40, 16n46, 17n48, 19, 20n55, 21, 22n61, 23n62, 26, 28, 31n92, 32n96, 33n102, 34, 35n107, 36n112, 59, 73, 76, 78n237, 92nn292, 294, 93n296
Lockman, John   9
Louis XIV, King   97
Loyola, Ignatius of   25, 30, 32, 33n102, 45n140, 77
Lucena, João de   6
Lucino, Luigi Maria   74

Macau   36, 70, 70n211, 76n232, 95
Maffei, Giovanni Pietro   5
Malabar   6, 9, 10n23, 11n26, 18, 24, 36–39, 41n127, 44–45, 59n179, 64nn195, 197, 65n199, 66, 68–70, 71nn216–217, 73, 75n230, 76–78, 90n286, 91
Malabar Rites Controversy   9, 69–70, 71n217, 76n233
Malayalam   39, 41, 78, 85–86, 90, 93
Manucci, Niccolò   92
Manuel, Dom   13–15, 15n40, 16
Mar Abraham   38
Maracci, Giovanni   65, 65n199
Maratha   67
Marathi (Marasta)   79–80, 93n296
Marava   58–60, 64, 67–68, 79
Margão   21
Mar Jacob   38
Marthanda Varma   63
Mar Thoma I   41
Martin, Alexander   103
Martin, Pierre   68–69, 69n209, 71
Martins, Manuel   82
Martin V   15
Martyrdom   18n50, 30n90, 58, 60n180, 63–64, 76
Mascarenhas, Nuno   72
Mascarenhas, Pedro   26
Mastrilli, Marcello   30n90, 64
Mathura   98

Maudave, Louis-Laurent de Féderbe, Chevalier   94
Mauduit, Pierre   69
Melaka   36
Menezes, Aleixo de   33, 40
Misericórdia   20–21
Mission   1, 7n12, 8, 19, 22, 23n64, 33, 37, 41–42, 49–50, 50n157, 53n162, 54n165, 59n179, 63–64, 64n195, 66, 69, 72nn219–220, 73nn221, 223–225, 74n226, 77, 81, 81n247, 82n250, 84n260, 86n270, 87n273, 90n284, 95n305, 104nn333–334
Mission du Carnate (Carnatic mission)   8, 10, 68, 71, 74–76, 79, 87
Mission du Maduré (Madurai mission)   7–8, 10, 33, 42, 49–50, 53n165, 54, 60n180, 64, 68–69, 70n212, 75, 89, 103, 104nn333–334
Missions étrangères de Paris   2
Montserrat, Antoni de   100
Moriset, Claude   101, 101n329
Mosac, Antoine   94
Mughal   7n12, 31, 86, 87n273, 97, 100
Mumbai (Bombay)   3n3, 20n54, 35n107
Murr, Sylvia   10n23, 94n302
Muslim   1, 13–14, 20, 35, 43, 64, 67, 88, 98
Mylapore (São Tomé de Meliapor)   19, 36, 66, 68, 71, 102n332
Mysore   3, 57n176, 63–68, 71–72, 75

Narwar   100
Nayaka   49–50, 54, 57, 60, 67, 81
Nayar   42, 62–63
Nicholas V   15
Nobili, Roberto   1, 7, 42, 50–56, 58, 72–73, 80–81, 84n260, 85, 89–90, 94, 102–103
Norbert de Bar-Le-Duc   76

Padroado, Portuguese   2–3, 5, 8–9, 12, 15–17, 19, 32–33, 36, 38–39, 41, 53, 66, 68, 72, 74, 92n294
Palayakkayal   43
Palmeiro, André   72
Papin, Gervais   96
Paraiyar, untouchable   61, 70, 75–76
Parava   19, 40, 42–51, 60, 79–80, 103

Paris   1–2, 3n3, 9, 10n23, 13nn31, 33, 14, n36, n37, 38, 15n39, 25n69, 35n109, 37n113, 52n160, 57n177, 65n199, 67n205, 70n212, 85n263, 86n270, 87–88, 89n281, 91n289, 94n302, 96–97, 98nn318–319, 100nn324, 327, 102n329, 104n334
Paulinus a Sancto Bartholomaeo   85, 86nn267, 269
Pereira, Gaspar de Leão   28
Persia   12, 73
Pius IV   28
Pondicherry, Puducherry   1–2, 9, 67n205, 68–69, 71, 74n228, 76, 87, 92, 94, 97n314, 102n332, 103
Pons, Jean-François   86–87, 99
Prester John   12, 15, 78
Proença, Antão de   82, 83nn253–254
Propaganda Fide   9, 32, 37, 41, 65n199, 66, 68, 70n211, 72, 73n225
Protestant   9, 11, 59, 68n207, 82n250, 85
Pudukkottai   67
Pyrard de Laval, François   35

Quadros, António de   26
Queirós, Fernão de   8, 92n292

Rachol   21, 79, 93n296
Ramnad   48, 59–60
Ranquet, Louis du   103
Ricci, Matteo   72
Rodrigues, Francisco   35, 36n111, 94n303
Ros, Francesco   33, 39–42, 73, 90
Rossi, Giacomo Tommasso de'   85
Rubino, Antonio   96, 102

Sá e Lisboa, Cristóvão de   33, 72, 73n222
Salcete, Salsete   20–21, 26
Sanskrit   51, 53, 80, 84–88, 88nn275, 277, 89, 93–94, 96–97, 99
Sawai Jai Singh II, Maharaja   97
Schurhammer, Georg   2n2, 23n64, 39n116, 45n139, 93n299
Science   97, 97n317, 99, 99n320
Sebastião, the king of Portugal   1, 2n1, 25n67, 27, 42, 44, 50n156
Seringapatam, (Srirangapatna)   64
Sethupathi   60, 67

Society of Jesus   1–2, 5–6, 9–11, 15, 17, 25, 26n74, 32, 62, 66, 72, 76–77, 83, 95, 102–103
Spanish   5, 7, 24, 34–35
Sri Lanka, Ceylão   8, 31n92, 43
Stephens, Thomas   79–80, 80n244, 86
Strobl, Andreas   98
St. Thomas Christians, Syrian Christian   11, 18, 33, 37–42, 49n154, 73, 90, 92
Sylveira, Gonçalo de   18
Synod of Diamper (Udayamperur)   33, 40
Syriac   37n113, 39, 41, 90

Tachard, Guy   69, 71, 97
Tamil   8, 42, 45–49, 51–52, 54–55, 58, 60n180, 61–63, 64n195, 67–68, 70n212, 71, 78–82, 82nn250, 252, 83–85, 93, 102, 104n336
Telugu   49n155, 54–55, 60, 78, 81, 86n270, 87, 102
Tēvacakāyam Piḷḷai   62
Thanjavur   68
Tiefenthaler, Joseph   100
Tiruchirappalli   56, 67
Tiswadi,   26
Torsellini, Orazio (Horatius Tursellinus)   6, 110
Tournon, Charles-Thomas Maillard de   69–71, 71n217, 72, 74n228, 76
Tranquebar   11, 48, 68, 82n250, 83–84, 94
Translation   18n49, 79n242, 82n250, 90n286
Tuticorin   46n145, 47

Ujjain   98

Valignano, Alessandro   5, 35, 46, 62, 72, 79
Valle, Pietro della   28–29, 29nn84–85
Vaṭakkaṇkuḷam   61, 63
Vaz, José   14, 33, 44
Vedas   94
Vico, Antonio   53n165, 55
Vikramaditya   93
Vincenzo Maria di S. Caterina da Siena   93
Visdelou, Claude de   71n217, 76n232
Vitelleschi, Muzio   73n222
Vitoria, Francisco de   14n36
Voltaire   10n23, 25n69, 88n276, 94, 99, 100n323

Wicki, Joseph 2*n*1, 6, 21*nn*58–59, 23*nn*62, 64, 29*n*87, 32*nn*96, 98, 47*n*149, 65*nn*199, 201–202, 93*nn*296, 299

Xavier, Francis 1–3, 5–7, 17*n*48, 20*n*54, 22–23, 25, 29–30, 31*n*92, 33*n*101, 40, 42, 44–47, 50–51, 58, 60, 62*n*190, 64, 78, 82*n*252, 85, 89*n*279, 93*n*298, 95*n*304, 96*n*309

Ziegenbalg, Bartholomaeus 82
Zurara, Gomes Eanes de 12

Printed in the United States
by Baker & Taylor Publisher Services